DATE DUE

THE CONNOISSEUR'S GUIDE TO THE MIND

How We Think, How We Learn,
and What It Means to Be Intelligent

ROGER C. SCHANK

SUMMIT BOOKS

New York   London   Toronto   Sydney   Tokyo   Singapore

Summit Books
Simon & Schuster Building
Rockefeller Center
1230 Avenue of the Americas
New York, New York 10020

DESIGNED BY BARBARA MARKS
Manufactured in the United States of America

1   3   5   7   9   10   8   6   4   2

Library of Congress Cataloging in Publication Data

Schank, Roger C., date.
The connoisseur's guide to the mind : how we think, how we learn, and what it
means to be intelligent / Roger C. Schank.
p.   cm.
Includes bibliographical references and index.
1. Thought and thinking.   2. Learning, Psychology of.   3. Intellect.   4. Schank,
Roger C., date.   I. Title.
BF441.S24 1991   91-19430
153—dc20   CIP

ISBN 0-671-67855-8

The work described in this book was supported in part by the Defense Advanced Research Projects Agency,
monitored by the Air Force Office of Scientific Research and the Office of Naval Research.

The Institute for the Learning Sciences was established in 1989 with the support of Andersen Consulting,
part of The Arthur Andersen Worldwide Organization. The Institute receives additional funding from
Ameritech, an Institute Partner, and from IBM.

The author gratefully acknowledges the following publishers to reprint the material indicated.

Arco Publishing Company, Inc.: from *The Arco Self-Tutor for High Test Scores: Correction Officer*, 7th edition,
edited by Hy Hammer, copyright © 1983, 1978 by Arco Publishing Company, Inc. Reprinted by permission
of the publisher.

Free Press: from Thinking in Time by Richard Neustadt and Ernest R. May, © 1986 by Richard E. Neustadt
and Ernest R. May. Reprinted by permission of Free Press, a division of MacMillan, Inc.

Prentice Hall: from *Human Problem Solving* by Allen Newell and Herbert A. Simon, © 1972. Reprinted by
permission of Prentice Hall, Englewood Cliffs, New Jersey.

To my "eating friends":
Anatole, Arthur, Elliot, Jean-François,
Jerry, Jorge, and Maurice,
who are always ready for, and appreciate,
good food, good wine, and good ideas

Contents

CONTENTS

Preface

I love to eat and I love to think. But, I really don't want to spend too much time analyzing what I eat. I just want to eat good things. I don't want to prepare them, or even know that much about how they were prepared. I just want to order them and have them appear and taste good. To do this, I have to know enough to order intelligently. I must learn something about what is available to be ordered or who is good at preparing what.

It is possible to enjoy good thinking just as one enjoys good eating. One can appreciate the work of others, listening or reading, as the opportunity presents itself. This might mean knowing what courses to take and which teachers to listen to, or which authors have something important to say.

In this way, eating and thinking have an important similarity. One can appreciate the work of others, and feel quite knowledgeable, without becoming either a chef or an author. One only has to learn enough to appreciate what is being served.

Eating and thinking have another thing in common. Sometimes one cannot simply order, one has to produce. In the case of eating, many of us are happy to be bad cooks, or at least not as good as various experts we are aware of, knowing that we will not have to eat our own cooking forever.

We need not learn to understand what a great chef is doing when he cooks, because restaurants are available. But, in this regard, thinking is quite different from eating. We are almost constantly engaged in thinking. Though we could stand idly by while we think badly, knowing that libraries will always be available, it is important to understand enough about how our own minds work, so that we can make effective use of them.

This book is about eating and thinking. I have spent most of my adult life thinking about thinking. I have also thought a lot about eating. Unfortunately, no one pays me for this so I have spent more time on thinking. This is okay because thinking is great fun. Even more fun is thinking about thinking.

For many years, researchers in the field of Artificial Intelligence (AI) have been thinking about thinking. It might seem odd, at first glance, that such work be done with computers, rather than, for example, with psychology. Of course, work on thinking does take place in psychology laboratories. But, in AI we have the luxury of being able to build explicit models of the thinking process without having to worry about details such as, *can what we are saying be proved?* Instead we worry about whether what we propose as a model of how thinking works can actually be built. To put this another way, in AI we think about the process of thinking rather than what can be proven about thinking.

So my coworkers, students, and I have been thinking about thinking for many years. We watch real people think and try to build models of what it is we think they are doing so we can get computers to do the same thing. Of course, we also eat, and because professors spend a great deal of time talking about their work in odd corners of the globe, we get to eat odd cuisines in those odd places.

So, even more fun than thinking about thinking is thinking about thinking and eating. I hope that you agree because that is what this book is about.

Chicago, Illinois
January 1991

CHAPTER 1

Knowing in Japan

This book is about food. It is also about wine. It is also about the mind. What do these things have in common? I like food and wine. Probably you do too. It gives us some common ground upon which to start. Besides, minds are pretty difficult to discuss if they are empty of knowledge, and it is more fun to discuss a mind that contains knowledge about food and wine than one that contains knowledge about physics.

How do we find out about how minds work? We can observe the products of minds at work. We can see what people produce, listen to what they say, analyze how they behave, and so on. But, the only minds we have internal access to are our own. We can sometimes "hear" ourselves thinking, if we know what to pay attention to. Understanding how the mind works means, among other things, being able to notice consciously what we are doing quite naturally without thinking about it.

We all can be researchers into our own minds, and into intelligence in general, if we are first given some hints about where and how to look. While I am providing those hints, I will also be doing what any writer must do, namely tell a story (or, more accurately, a series of stories). The process of both telling stories and noticing the processes at work in the selection, formulation, and understanding of those stories can make for some convoluted reading. The mind naturally jumps around from place to place. Books usually don't. But, you cannot both understand a story and understand your understanding of that story without some effort. So, bear with me until you get used to it. It will seem quite natural after a while.

Let's start the process. People like to hear stories. And I like to tell stories. But before I tell a story, let's talk a bit about what it will involve. I will provide a running commentary on what you do with the information you are getting. This is tricky, as I don't know who you are, what you already know, or what you are likely to learn from what I say. But, this will not stop me from trying. Here's my story.

I have a pretty simple rule about traveling: Good food is worth the trip. Traveling can make you think about things you may not have considered previously. The same is true of eating. There is nothing like exquisitely cooked sweetbreads washed down with Haut-Brion to make you think about life. When good thinking can be combined with good eating, send me a ticket—I am ready to go.

This rule evolved because I am often invited to give lectures, and I have to decide whether to accept the invitation. Going around the world is exciting at first. But, after a while, when you've been on more planes than you care to count, you start to wonder if the trip is worth the trouble when a cheery voice asks you if you'd please come and talk to his eager audience of businessmen or computer programmers or graduate students. My rule for deciding used to be simple enough: If I'd never been to the place before, I'd go. Why not? I'd never have gone to Newfoundland any other way, and the place really was like no other I'd ever seen.

Time for some comments. I am an academic. You have stereotypes about academics, whether you admit that you do, or even realize that you do. You may have thought that a university professor teaches and therefore doesn't travel much. You may have thought that professors wouldn't know about either sweetbreads or Haut-Brion. You may have thought that anyone would take a free trip when offered, especially to an exotic place. I cannot know which of these things you thought, but I do know that you thought something about these subjects before you started reading this. I can also predict safely that you learned nothing from what you read if what I said was in no way surprising, if your memory structures were the same as before you started reading. But, if you were surprised, if you found yourself asking, what kind of guy is this who is writing this stuff, who sees the world this way, or who has had these kinds of experiences, that was the beginning of wondering. And, wondering starts the process of learning.

What sort of learning is this, you ask? If you are learning anything at all it is about me, a subject you probably weren't that interested in. Actually, I am trying to point out what you do when you learn in general. You were learning about me, but to do so, you had to start someplace. You start, therefore, with a stereotype, maybe more than one, about professors, writers, men with beards, whatever. From this stereotype you begin to construct a more realistic description. You do this by confirming the parts of the stereotype that turn out to be true, and abandoning those parts found to be in error. Those that were unused remain in place. So, for example, you still think I am about six feet tall, as opposed to about ten feet tall or two feet tall. No discussion of height took place (nor will it) and so you still rely upon your "default fillers," information about the usual height of men and the number of eyes they can be presumed to have. Default fillers are everywhere. They keep us from sweating the small stuff. Now back to my story.

I'd already visited a lot of places because of the rule of going where I hadn't yet been. The rule needed refining, however, or I'd have been permanently stuck at home, avoiding all the places I had already been, or only going to colleges in obscure sections of Alabama. So I added food. I used to watch a television program while I was growing up called "Have Gun Will Travel." I always loved the title, so it became my motto, slightly modified: "Have Good Restaurant? Will Travel." If the invitation includes the possibility of some really good food, or even just exotic food, I am ready to go. Good food is worth the trip.

And so, one day, I found myself in the first-class lounge of Air France in Paris, ready to board a flight to Tokyo.

Wait, what is going on? How do professors get to travel first-class? Is this guy very rich? These are the kinds of questions we ask ourselves all the time. They are an intrinsic part of the learning process. We ask questions and then look for answers, maybe later in the text. A good writer anticipates such questions and provides the answers. He does this because he knows implicitly what I am now making explicit: Namely, stereotypes can be violated, but when they are violated by a lot, an explanation is in order. So, now you want to know the answer? It's simple: I ask for first-class tickets. If I don't get them, I don't go. Why do I have that rule? I leave that as an exercise for the reader.

I had accepted an invitation to give the keynote address at a computer professionals' meeting in Tokyo. I was living in Paris at the time, so I worried for a while about whether my rule made any sense under the circumstances. I mean, the restaurants weren't going to be better in Tokyo than in Paris. But you can't eat in three-star restaurants every night, and I do like Japanese food a great deal. So even though I had been to Japan before, off I went. Besides, my hosts had sent a first-class ticket and that meant—at least on Air France—sevruga caviar and Dom Pérignon champagne, or at least it sometimes meant that. One doesn't usually think of flying to eat the food, but Air France first class has got its food act together, which is no big surprise when you think about it.

As I checked in, I looked around at who was going to be on the flight. This may not matter much on your usual New York–Chicago run, but we were talking eighteen hours here with a stop in, of all places, Anchorage, Alaska. It boggled my mind that to go east from Paris to Tokyo, we had to fly west to Alaska. Somehow I didn't think of the United States as being on the way.

The check-in area was full of old Japanese businessmen with an occasional European, but I was looking for someone to help kill the eighteen hours. English is the only language I can speak for more than fifteen minutes without getting a headache. Then I spotted an attractive woman about my age. She was with an older and, I might add, peculiarly dressed man, all in pink and white, but I wasn't looking for any more than friendly conversation. The woman looked vaguely familiar, and I assumed this meant she was an American. Most Americans look vaguely familiar when you have been living out of the country for a while. I looked at her, and she gave me a big smile, which immediately surprised me. Something was wrong here. Women are usually a little more guarded than that.

My seatmate was a German man who spoke good English and, more important, loved to drink champagne and wine. He insisted that one must consume equal amounts of water and alcohol, so he kept the stewardesses hopping and admonished me to drink more—something, I might note, that I rarely hear people urge me to do. We had a good time and both fell asleep. I forgot about the woman until we landed in Anchorage, when I decided to see whether she felt like chatting in the airport lounge.

She smiled another one of her big smiles as I approached, but she was arm in arm with her oddly dressed mate, so I wasn't encouraged to come near. I gave up, went back to sleep after we got on the plane, and forgot about the whole thing. I did walk by her seat once or twice, but she had the window seat and was doing no more than smiling.

When we landed, I noticed that she had changed her outfit and was now rather elaborately dressed. As the airplane door opened, she stepped out into an array of lights and cameras. Clearly, she was *somebody*. I trailed along, now really curious. I never got very close as she was whisked off to a waiting limousine, but she did have to go through customs, so I got to see the color and size of her passport—no doubt about it, she was an American. She must have been a movie star, but even though I *do* go to the movies, I couldn't figure out who she was. After eighteen hours, I had gotten a good look, but it hadn't helped.

Well, that's the first part of the story. Not too fascinating so far, I'll admit. But, I want you to think about what I was doing. I was trying to find the right stereotype for this lady. It is far from true that we are all nobly trying to abandon our stereotypes. Actually, we become panic-ridden when we don't have a useful stereotype ready. I was almost relieved to find out she was a movie star (well, I hadn't really found that out yet). I wouldn't have known what to do with her otherwise. I couldn't place her, couldn't find out what category she fit in that would allow me to comfortably predict her behavior. Prediction is the name of the game here. We each need to know what the rest of us are going to do next. This is important for survival. We want to recognize crazy people, sexy people, trustworthy people, interesting people, when we see them. We want to know what's coming next. Saying to ourselves, "Ah, I understand, she's an X," helps a lot if we know how to predict the behavior of Xs. We need stereotypes. To see what I mean here, fill in the blanks: *Hippies have _____ hair. Truck drivers have _____ on their chests. Republicans wear _____ to bed.* I am not interested in the answers here. The point is simply that we have answers, or can make up answers. This process is called "slot-filling," and it is critical to understanding. Understanding means being able to predict what will happen next, what word will come next, what idea will come next. We have, in effect, open slots for each of these things. The better we predict, the more we understand.

Back to Tokyo. The movie star was gone. To me Japan means sushi, so with nothing else to do anyway, off I went to the nearest sushi bar. Finding a sushi bar or anything else in Japan is either impossible or trivial. It depends upon whether you have ever been there before. I *had* been there before, but I forgot that Tokyo isn't New York. I wandered around the streets looking for a sushi bar, but none showed up. I tried to figure out why. I tried to remember any sushi bars I had been in before. Suddenly, I remembered the last time I was in Tokyo. I was thirsty. I had had enough beer so I decided to drink the tea. I don't really like tea, but sugaring it usually helps, so I asked for sugar. They had some trouble understanding me, but pointing and lots of funny motions got me the sugar, which I promptly put in the tea. Oh boy, was that a mistake. The waiter erupted in violent laughter. He announced loud and clear in Japanese (sometimes you needn't understand a language to know what they are saying) that this American moron had actually put sugar in his tea. The entire restaurant was on the floor, all holding their stomachs. Until I left, each and every person who entered the restaurant heard about my faux pas. For all I know, ten years later they are still hearing about it.

I thought I'd pass on trying to find that particular sushi bar, but in trying to think about where it was, now with the intention of avoiding it, I remembered that it was underground—that was where I would find sushi bars. Tokyo is half underground, and I tried to imagine why. Toronto and Montreal are underground, too, but obviously because of the cold. Is Tokyo as cold, or are they thinking about nuclear attack? Pondering this, I went downstairs the first time I could find some stairs that went down. Presto, I found a nice sushi bar.

I realized that I had never been in a sushi bar in Japan by myself and that I had really been in only one or two. I should have been nervous about knowing exactly how to behave, what to order, from whom, where to sit, and so on. But, I am willing to eat just about anything, so I didn't have any trouble in getting fed. The language problem was big, of course. I had some trouble remembering the word *toro*, which is the fatty tuna that makes the best sushi. But sushi bars are sushi bars the world over, and even though I know the names of only a few fish in Japanese, Japanese restaurants are always set up for pointing. Plastic models of all the food that is available are displayed in the windows of each restaurant. One cannot help wondering about plastic food. It always looks realistic and is an interesting though bizarre art form, but how did it develop? Why do the Japanese like to show what can be ordered rather than tell you? This custom is all very convenient for tourists, of course: Menus written in Japanese characters are not decipherable by the average American. But this practice must precede the advent of tourism. Perhaps the Japanese themselves have trouble reading their own language. Alphabets are a relatively recent phenomenon in Japan. A display may have been the best way to tell the folks what they could eat.

The quality of a sushi bar really depends on only two things. First, the fish must be fresh. The Japanese are fanatics about this and rightly so. Fish that isn't fresh stinks. Second is presentation. Talking about how food looks as a major issue may seem silly, but no one who is involved in preparing food regards it as foolish. After all, sushi is just raw fish and vinegared rice with a little green mustard thrown in. You could slice a hunk of tuna and put it on the plate with some rice on the side, and it might taste as good, but you can be sure no one would visit your restaurant.

I remember going to a Japanese restaurant in San Jose, California, that I used to frequent when I lived in California twenty years ago. I was a little earlier than usual, but I asked for sashimi to start, as I always did. The waitress told me that I would have to wait about half an hour for the chef to show up. Half an hour? Chef? "What chef?" I asked. "Who needs a chef to make raw fish? Give me the tuna, and I'll slice it."

The waitress declined this invitation and, smiling the kind of smile that only Japanese waitresses smile, she went away, and I waited the half hour. Years of eating and attempting to slice raw fish have taught me that waiting for the chef really is a good idea. The art of presentation is meant to convey that you are eating something other than a fish that has recently died and been thrown onto a plate untouched. Sushi chefs make a fish look like food.

I just did something that I'd like to point out. I got reminded. Reminding is a very important mental phenomenon. I was thinking that
making sushi shouldn't be so difficult and I remembered a story
from my own experience that referred to that point. Keeping data
around from prior experiences is valuable, so that old experiences
can be compared to new ones and a new generalization can be
formed. We need to be reminded in order to make sense of the world
around us. Reminding is the basis of learning because reminding
will happen when odd things occur that have caused wondering to
start.

Anyway, I had a fine meal in Tokyo and got to practice all the
Japanese I know, which consists entirely of the names of various
fish.

Off I went to sleep. I awoke to a phone call telling me where
to meet my hosts for lunch. I must confess that the part of visiting
Japan that I like the best is the absolute astonishment that Japanese
people have that an American is not only willing to eat their food
but actually likes it. They started this lunch as usual, informing
me that Japanese people like to eat raw fish, and would I like to
try some. They say this with wondrous excitement, hiding snickers
that barely conceal their glee at the expectation that I soon am
going to be nauseated beyond belief. As you might expect, their
smiles drop when I tell them that I actually like Japanese food and
am quite used to it. Of course, they don't quite believe it, so some
hope remains.

At this point, two challenges are thrown down. First, I must
explain how I can be used to Japanese food. Second, they begin
to plot how to really disgust me at the next meal, since obviously
plain old raw fish isn't going to do.

The answer to the first question is simple enough. I grew up
in New York in a kosher home. Our family, like many other Jewish
families, believed that the home should be kosher, but outside the
house, anything goes. This might seem odd, but kosher homes, at
least in the world in which I grew up, were for grandparents, who
could always eat with us (not that mine ever did) if they wanted
to. But, grandparents didn't have to eat out with you, did they?
So, all of Brooklyn lined up for Chinese food on Sunday afternoon,
assuming Grandma hadn't shown up.

My family ate Chinese food on alternate Sundays and occasional Wednesdays. The other Sundays we ate Italian food. Only
Jews and Italians lived in my neighborhood. I never figured out

where the Chinese food came from. As long as we remembered to eat in the Jewish shift at the Italian restaurant, we had a good time wolfing down pasta. The Jewish shift started four hours after Mass ended on Sunday. The Italians ate before us.

This scheme worked well enough. We had to hide it all from the grandparents, of course. I remember one day my mother got sick, and her mother asked what was wrong. My father said it must have been something she ate, and the ten-year-old me volunteered that it obviously was the shrimp. Of course, I knew that one didn't say this sort of thing to my grandmother, but it just came out, and now it looked as if my grandmother was sick, too. I felt really awful, but nothing was ever said again. Years later I learned that my grandfather had been wolfing down bacon, lettuce, and tomato sandwiches most of his life. I gather my grandmother had learned to live with this sort of thing.

Then there was the problem of what to do on special occasions. Chinese was too pedestrian and Italian was too . . . well, Italian. Jewish food was out. We knew all too well that Jews couldn't cook. Not that they could be blamed for this. Any culture that has a proverb like *when a Jew eats a chicken, one of them is sick* is not a culture that is banking on its gastronomic expertise to bail it out of a tight spot.

The answer to our celebration problem appeared in the form of Mr. Tanaka, who helped my grandfather import beads from Japan. He liked to eat in Japanese restaurants, which weren't all that plentiful in New York in those days. Since my grandfather couldn't take him out to eat without starting open warfare with my grandmother, it fell on my parents and me to go with him. We all liked sukiyaki and tempura a great deal, and so all birthdays and other family occasions that were not celebrated at Lou Siegel's (New York's only fancy kosher restaurant) with my grandparents were celebrated at Saito, our favorite Japanese restaurant.

So, I had been eating Japanese food all my life. But now my Japanese hosts became obsessed with trying to gross me out. I gave my lecture, and we took off for a special place (they told me, giggling) that I would really like.

We started with horsemeat sashimi. Now for a guy who has eaten goat testicles and been only slightly nauseated, this was easy stuff. I mean, why shouldn't one eat horse? Is eating cow somehow more noble? What makes one animal more edible than another? One answer is taste, although this doesn't seem to be the primary criterion of most people. We don't eat dogs because they are too close to us, and we don't eat elephants because they are too far away. Most people don't eat snakes and bugs because they seem yucky. But, we agree on eating animals that are domesticated but not pets, which would include horses, it seems. Anyway, I soon realized that we don't eat horse because it really isn't that tasty. I suppose it could be if it were bred for sitting around instead of for running, but as long as horses actually work for a living, they probably won't taste too good.

The next courses were all raw fish. No problem, you would think, and, in fact, they weren't a problem. I can't tell you any of their names, not simply because I heard only their Japanese names, but also because these fish were all completely unrecognizable shellfish. But, shellfish raw, especially the kind that lives in curly snail-like shells, isn't all that exciting, and rather than getting grossed out, I was getting a little bored. My boredom caused an end to my hosts' fun, and they just sighed and asked if I liked "club." I said okay, and they smiled and bowed and disappeared.

I was confused about why I never got to go to this club they had mentioned, but as clubs don't interest me in the least I was happy to be let out of it. The next evening, I discovered that "club" meant "crab" as I was being taken to a crab-only restaurant. You get crab sashimi and crab tempura and crab sukiyaki and even crab dessert. It was great fun, though a little tacky, decorated in Early Crab, with the whole place just reeking of it. One thing this restaurant lacked, and the one before it, too, I suddenly realized, was presentation. How food looks really does matter.

Old-style French cuisine was heavy on sauces and hearty food, but the new style of French food, the so-called nouvelle cuisine, is really much stronger on presentation. Sauces are done artfully. Portions are smaller and presented in a decorous way. Instead of a hunk of duck drowned in orange sauce, slices of duck, arranged in a circle, with circular patterns of sauces, are more likely to be served. The French have learned the importance of presentation from the Japanese.

Of course, they have not learned about cooking from the Japanese. In fact, the Japanese may not have learned about cooking yet. The food they do best is raw. Their next best creations are usually cooked at the table by the waitress or by the patron. Lots of dipping in and out of boiling pots but very little work by a chef. The art of being a Japanese chef is the art of cutting, while the art of being a French chef is the art of combination.

After all, when you think about it, food is food. Some parts and types of ducks and cows and carrots and peas are better than others, but the art of cooking is knowing how to combine ingredients with other ingredients in pleasing ways. The reason that French cooking is seen as being the best in the world by most people is that French chefs are encouraged by their clientele to be inventive, to try new ideas, which mostly means new combinations. Of course, cooking relies on other important factors, such as knowing how much to cook something and even how to slice something, but, by and large, these are not inventive processes. Cooking has its standard procedures quite apart from the creativity a chef imparts. This creativity is what makes going to a restaurant with a new and well-thought-of chef so exciting for food lovers.

The crab restaurant in Tokyo was an interesting touristic experience, but not an interesting culinary experience. How many ways you can prepare crab is not really a mark of inventiveness in food, although you could provide some interesting answers to the question. But expecting an interesting answer is unreasonable. People have a habit of avoiding thinking in even the most challenging and novel situations. They attempt, ordinarily, to reduce whatever problem they are working on to a previously solved problem, almost as if they were mathematicians who don't want to bother proving a new theorem from scratch if they can use an old proof and build on it.

So the owners of the all-crab restaurant basically copied all the ways anyone had ever thought of serving fish in Japan. I certainly like going to places I haven't been to and found the place interesting. But the place—the food especially—wasn't memorable. After all, if crab sushi were the best kind of sushi, you would see it in every sushi bar. In fact, you rarely see it, because raw crab isn't that tasty, and cooked crab can be served in better ways than on a bed of rice. The place was memorable in the sense that it was unique, but I didn't learn anything about food from the experience.

When I go to a restaurant, I have many goals. I certainly want to eat a nice meal, but I also want to remember the meal. Pleasurable experiences are fine, but if you don't remember them, you get that pleasure only once, and you can't even be sure of that. Memory has an important function for people besides enabling them to recognize their spouses each morning. We talk a great deal about learning from experience, but from which experiences?

We don't ordinarily think about learning from eating a meal, but learning from the meal is one reason we eat it. A more important reason, of course, is that we are hungry.

So what did I learn from the crab restaurant? Well, I learned that I am in no hurry to visit it again, but I need not protest too much if by chance I do—I won't be poisoned or underfed, just bored. And I also learned about the importance of presentation. Actually, I already knew about the importance of presentation— most of what we learn we already know. This is why we don't always realize that we are learning anything at the time. I knew about presentation because I had already observed that the Japanese cared a great deal about it and that the French had copied it. What I hadn't really thought about before was the extent to which even the Japanese, who care greatly about such matters, could screw up in certain instances. I realized that crab is probably not so easy to present neatly, a subject to which I shall refer later.

My Japanese hosts soon tired of the game of grossing me out and passed me on to the next set of hosts, who took me out to dinner and began to tell me how the Japanese people are very strange because they eat raw fish, and did I want to try some?

Around this time, I decided to go home. I headed for the airport after dinner in time for the Air France flight to Paris. As I checked in, I saw the woman from the flight to Tokyo in the line in front of me. It was certainly weird to see her again. I hadn't expected to see her, after all. Actually, I had long since forgotten about her. I had looked for her picture in the Japanese paper that was delivered to me in my room. I was hoping to learn her name if I found her picture, but I didn't find it.

In the airport, I had expected the usual things that happen in airports to happen—checking in, waiting, boarding, and so on— and I hadn't added her to my list of expectations. Nevertheless, I was able to cope, recognize her, and laugh. She saw me and laughed as well; I guess she had noticed me on the flight after all. I asked her who she was, and she replied that she was nobody special, which was obviously untrue. I told her that I had looked for her picture in the paper to find out who she was, but quickly added that I was really looking for my own picture because I had given an interview or two to papers while I was in Tokyo. She then asked me who I was, and I replied that I, too, was nobody special.

She took this as a cue for telling me about herself. She said that she was indeed a famous actress but that she doubted that I had heard of her since she made pictures only in Europe and hardly ever appeared in America even though she was an American. I said that she should try me anyway. I went to the movies in Europe, maybe I would know her name. She told me, and I laughed. I knew her name all right, but not from the movies. She had been the homecoming queen at my college and had dated a boy in my fraternity.

I said that I knew her from college, and she denied it, saying that she had been to college for only one year and that was to study acting. Nevertheless, she was the same person.

As soon as she realized that we actually had gone to school together and that I hadn't the slightest idea who she was professionally, we became friends. She changed her seat so that we could sit together, which we did for eighteen hours.

She had come to Tokyo as the headliner for an important fashion show. The man dressed in pink on whose arm she had been hanging was the designer Courrèges, and he was showing his line in Tokyo. He used her name and presence as an attraction. She assured me that she was known in Japan as well as Europe. He also had brought a large number of models with him for the show, and they were, she told me, in tourist class. I went to look. The place was wall-to-wall models, really kind of difficult for the mind to comprehend. My image of the passengers in the back of a 747 is a version of the tired huddled masses yearning to breathe free, so wall-to-wall models in their place makes me want to revise my view of the whole situation. I could picture a guy who got a middle seat, who might have been complaining bitterly prior to boarding, suddenly taking on a new perspective. Anyway, I went back to my seat.

The actress who had been so unapproachable on the earlier flight suddenly became a regular human being. We talked about our lives. We talked about college. She moaned about not having had children and not having a husband like every other successful, career-oriented woman of her age I have known. We exchanged telephone numbers, but she lived in Rome, and I never saw her again.

I told this story to a fraternity brother who would remember her, and he enjoyed it. We both tried to recall whom she had dated at our fraternity. She hadn't been able to remember him, but my friend and I were determined to figure it out. Eventually, we did. He was one of the nerdiest guys in the fraternity. No one had been able to figure out how he had managed to get a date with the homecoming queen. But this wasn't the only anomalous thing about him. He had also, two years later, managed to be elected president of the fraternity. We never figured out how he did that either.

The preceding story is about my experiences in Japan, certainly, but it is also about how thinking works. It is about expectations and anomalies, explanations and reminding, generalizations and memory search. It is about learning and the effective use and evolution of knowledge. This is a book about the mind. It is about how we think, what kinds of mental operations we perform, why we do what we do, how we learn, how our memories work, why they work in the way they do, and, in general, what it means to be intelligent. I am telling you this now because many times what I am writing about won't be obvious at all. This book is not intended to be a technical book on the mind, full of rules that the mind employs, algorithms for changing those rules, data structures that store the knowledge, and so on. This book uses none of such jargon, and talks about everyday matters, but is still intended to convey the same story.

As I talk about food and wine and travel and other subjects near and dear to my heart, I will also talk about the mind. A little fun and a little work. A little reliance on things we already know and understand in order to enhance and adapt that knowledge to explain things we less readily understand. Learning has to start someplace.

CHAPTER 2

Spanish Expectations

'm off to Spain. Jorge, a professor whom I met in Barcelona last year, has arranged for me to teach in a summer school in the hills outside of Madrid. Actually, I hadn't realized that Jorge had anything to do with this invitation. I accepted because I thought a week in Spain would be nice, and, anyway, they met my price.

Upon arrival, I am shuffled off to one of those institutional lunches. With twenty professors and one hundred students all eating at the same time, the food is terrible, even in France. This time, in Spain, the food is just boring. An overcooked steak, a hunk of salmon, maybe some spaghetti or potatoes. All okay if you didn't come for the food. But of course, I did come for the food. Now, any serious eater would tell you that Spain is not the place to eat. He would not be wrong. But, someone who prides himself on eating can usually find some redeeming features in any cuisine, so, as usual, I am optimistic.

I am even more optimistic after I spot Jorge. In Barcelona, Jorge went into raptures on the pleasures of jamón de Jabugo, a certain kind of raw ham made in Jabugo in Spain. Jorge speaks of ham the way wine connoisseurs speak of wine. He claims that jamón de Jabugo captures the smell of the barnyards in Jabugo, which, of course, would not be something that would be terribly exciting if it had been said about a wine. But he really is referring to the air in Jabugo and the special food that the pigs eat in Jabugo. Now the fact that Jorge is Jewish makes for some skepticism about his raptures over ham. But more important, perhaps, Jorge is decidedly overweight, a sign I find encouraging in anyone who professes to know food.

Anyway, I am happy to see Jorge and am wondering what good things his arrival portends. Jorge seats himself at my table at lunch and informs me that he is not eating. This is a good omen. Overweight people fail to eat at table for only two reasons, one horrible and one wonderful. I assume from the smile on Jorge's face that he is not about to inform me that he has started a diet. Instead, he is saving himself for something special.

He announces that tonight he is going to Segovia, forty miles away, for cochinillo asado.

Taking the bait, I ask, "What is cochinillo asado?"

"Cochinillo is the Peking duck of Spain," says Jorge.

"Have you ever eaten Peking duck?" I inquire, knowing full well that this is not your everyday Spanish offering.

"No," he says, but he has read about it. Again, I know this is a man after my own heart.

Cochinillo, it turns out, is the specialty of Segovia. As we are not far from Segovia, in culinary miles, it turns out we can get it where we are as well, though not in our cafeteria. But, Jorge says, as cochinillo was invented in Segovia, that is where we must eat it. So a few hours later, having taken Jorge's advice to lighten up on the spaghetti, I am off with a group of seven others to Segovia.

Segovia is a pretty town, dominated by a Roman aqueduct, but I am here to eat, not to see the sights. Spaniards may not take their food all that seriously, but they do take siestas seriously, especially in summertime, so they don't start dinner until ten o'clock or later. Of course, I have heard this, but I don't quite believe it. Even though I am jet-lagged, my stomach sees eight o'clock, and it is hungry. Regardless of my stomach, we first tour the town and don't settle in to eat until ten.

I have often wondered why some cultures are obsessed with pig meat. Unfortunately, after this meal, I don't know whether it was the Spanish or simply Jorge. The meal starts with jamón de someplace other than Jabugo, which Jorge assures me is good, but not great. He can't smell the right smells in this ham. For me it is simply nice. I don't have the pig vocabulary that Jorge has, but I do recall the Jabugo ham we ate in Barcelona was a lot better.

This is followed by a sausage that is indescribable, so I won't describe it. Suffice it to say that it is primarily made of blood, which is something I like, but is definitely an acquired taste.

Cochinillo, you might have suspected, is pig. More specifically, it is a baby pig that has been baked for a long time at a low temperature and then for a while at a very high temperature. The result is a juicy meat with a very crisp skin.

To determine if the cochinillo has been properly prepared, the waiter cuts it in front of the diners: The trick is that he cuts the pig, which is brought to the table head and all, with a plate. The idea is that the meat and bones ought to be soft enough, and the skin crisp enough, that any dull object will suffice to break the pig into the appropriate pieces without any effort at all.

The cochinillo does indeed remind me of Peking duck, although the Chinese, in paying proper homage to the skin that they have tried so hard to get right, serve the skin as a course in itself. The Spanish serve cochinillo simply as one might serve any kind of meat. I guess Spain isn't close enough to Japan.

The interesting thing about all this is not the cochinillo really, but the concept of regional cooking. Cochinillo is found only in this region of Spain. One is inclined to wonder why, if this stuff is so good, it hasn't spread elsewhere. Or, to put this question another way, if pig tastes better when prepared differently, why hasn't cochinillo disappeared?

To a lover of food, these are silly questions. A food lover relishes the notion of a regional cuisine. One loves to find the special food that is made in some obscure corner of the world. And, for an American food lover, one deplores the difficulty of finding real regional differences in the United States. One wishes that Ohio cuisine differed from New England cuisine. Some differences exist, of course. Texas has Mexican food; in California they have taken bean sprouts to new heights; and lobster is available in Maine. But these aren't exactly regional cuisines in the same sense as the cochinillo at Segovia. The difference is one of cultural imperative, and therein we have an entrée into the mind.

Let's go to Italy for a moment. Suppose you are eating in Italy and have decided, as any American might, to start with soup, followed by meat with pasta on the side. You order this, and the waiter begins to snicker. He points at you and talks about you to other waiters, just as the Japanese did when I sugared the tea. This fool has ordered two soups! Indeed, if you ordered two soups at home, you might expect people to talk about you there as well, although perhaps not with the same glee. But you didn't know you had ordered two soups. Why would you suspect that Italians consider pasta and soup to be the same sort of thing and therefore consider both to be the first course? They are wondering why this American wants two first courses and of exactly the same kind. But is soup pasta? Is pasta soup? In Italy, soup ordinarily has pasta in it, and, in effect, soup is simply another way of preparing (and serving) pasta.

The Italian waiter laughs at you for the same reasons that Segovians eat cochinillo. That is the way it is done. A meal in Italy is not considered to be complete without pasta. Similarly, a Japanese finds a meal without rice to be incomplete and will go out of the way to eat some rice, even if he has had pasta at the same meal—and even though, to an American, rice and pasta are the same thing. An American waiter would laugh at the Japanese who ordered pasta and rice in just the same way as the Italian waiter laughs at soup and pasta. Everyone is quite sure what elements a meal needs to be a meal and what events would violate the concept of "mealness." Obviously, no one is right about his concept of a meal. What everyone is right about is his notion of expectation and expectation violation. Or, to put this another way, regional cooking depends upon the inviolate nature of expectation. Expectations lend a kind of sameness to our lives that make our lives both more stable and more dull. Cultural stability depends upon the freezing of expectation. Food lovers depend upon the violation of expectation. Food lovers, in other words, feed upon the cultural stability, or frozen expectations, of other people's lives.

This might all seem a sad state of affairs except that there would be mental chaos without it. Mental life depends upon expectations. When we walk along the sidewalk and see a truck coming down the street towards us, we do not leap out of the way. We know that the truck is more than likely to continue going down the street and that it probably will not veer slightly and run into us as long as we stay on the sidewalk. But how can we be sure of this? Maybe the driver wants to kill us, or maybe he is drunk and has lost control of the truck, or maybe we only think that we are on the sidewalk but we are actually in the street. If one thought about all these possibilities each time one took a walk, walks would be rare indeed.

But we actually do think about all this, in a very passive, non-conscious kind of way. We don't make every inference that we possibly can when confronted with a new situation, but neither do we avoid making them. To see what I mean here, let's start with a simple sentence and list some of the inferences. The sentence is: *Jorge took Roger to Segovia to eat cochinillo asado.* Suppose you were trying to understand that sentence out of context. That is, you know nothing of the particular people or their goals. There are two actions, *going* and *eating*. Each has it own set of possible inferences. Here are some inferences that you could make:

possible reasons for actions
    going:
        Jorge wants to be in Segovia
        Jorge wants Roger to be in Segovia
        Jorge wants to do something that can be done only in Segovia
    eating:
        Jorge was hungry
        Jorge thought that Roger was hungry
        Jorge likes cochinillo
        Jorge thought that Roger liked cochinillo
enablement
        Jorge thought that eating cochinillo would enable Jorge to do something he wanted to do
        Jorge thought that going to Segovia would enable him to do something that he wanted to do
results
    going:
        Jorge was in Segovia
        Jorge was able to do something that he wanted to do in Segovia

eating:
    Jorge was happy
    Jorge was no longer hungry
    Roger was happy
    Roger got to learn something new about food
results of results
  eating:
    Jorge felt he had taught Roger something
    Roger had something new to write about
side conditions
  going:
    Jorge had to find a way to get to Segovia
    Jorge had to have the time available to get to Segovia
    Jorge had to know how to get to Segovia
    Roger had to be willing to go to Segovia
  eating:
    Jorge had to know where a restaurant was
    The restaurant had to serve cochinillo
    Jorge had to have money to pay the restaurant
    Roger had to trust Jorge's taste

These are actually only some of the inferences one could possibly have made from this sentence. After all, we know the facts here. In actuality, Jorge could have had the intention of killing Roger and using the cochinillo as a cover for getting Roger out of town to a place where the murder might easily take place. Paranoia is really no more than inferring gone awry. We must make assumptions about the goals and plans of the people with whom we are interacting, and we are never really certain that we have made the right ones.

In 1973, my students and I conceived of and wrote the first computer program that understood sentences well enough to make inferences from them. This program, MARGIE, would analyze a sentence into a representation like the one above and then begin to make inferences by following rules based upon the kinds of categories I listed above. To do this it needed all kinds of mundane knowledge. For example, it had a rule that said, when an object struck another object, the first object was probably undamaged, but the struck object was probably damaged. This worked fine for *John hit Mary with a rock,* but terribly for *John hit the rock with an egg.* Rules like this had to be entered and re-entered until we got all the mundane details right.

Here is some output from that computer program:

Inference Mode

Input:	John told Mary that Bill wants a book.
Output1:	A book about what?
Output2:	Mary knows that Bill wants a book.
Output3:	Bill wants to come to have a book.
Output4:	Bill wants someone to cease to have a book.
Output5:	Bill wants to read a book.

Input:	John gave Mary a beating with a stick.
Output1:	A stick touched Mary.
Output2:	Mary became hurt.
Output3:	John wanted Mary to become hurt.
Output4:	Why was John angry?

Input:	John gave Mary an aspirin.
Output1:	John believes that Mary wants an aspirin.
Output2:	Mary is sick.
Output3:	Mary wants to feel better.
Output4:	Mary will ingest the aspirin.

Input:	John is going to go to the store.
Output1:	John wants to be at the store.
Output2:	What does John want to buy?
Output3:	John will trade money to the store for something.

Paraphrase Mode

Input:	John advised Mary to drink the wine.
Output:	John told Mary that drinking the wine would benefit her.

Input:	John killed Mary by choking Mary.
Output1:	John strangled Mary.
Output2:	John choked Mary and she died because she could not breathe.
Output3:	Mary died because she was unable to inhale some air and she was unable to inhale some air because John grabbed her neck.

Input:	Reading a book reminded Rita to loan the book to Bill.
Output:	Rita remembered to give the book to Bill and she expects him to return it to her because someone read the book.
Input:	John prevented Bill from giving a banana to Mary by selling a banana to Rita.
Output1:	Bill was unable to give a banana to Mary because Rita traded John some money for a banana.
Output2:	Mary could not get a banana from Bill because Rita bought a banana from John.

There was one terrible problem with this program, which came to be known as "inference explosion." There was no way to turn the program off. Every time the program made an inference, it would, in essence, create a new fact. And each fact could itself be the source of important inferences. But where to stop? For example, when John punishes his son Fred by spanking him, it is reasonable to infer that Fred was unhappy, and in pain. It is reasonable to assume that, when someone is unhappy and can identify the source of that unhappiness, he might strike back. Is it therefore reasonable to assume that Fred hit John? And, if that is true, is it reasonable to assume that John hit Fred again? Or, to take the other path, if Fred was hurt, it is reasonable to assume that Fred might seek medical attention. If Fred were hurt badly, it is reasonable to assume that the doctor might call the police. If the police are called, it is reasonable to assume that they might arrest John. John might go to jail. Fred might grow up without a father. Fred might turn resentful towards the police. Fred might become a criminal.

Where do we stop? There is no obvious spot. Each of these inferences is a little less likely than the one before it. But when do we turn them off? This combinatorial explosion of inferences is a serious issue in building effective computer programs that exhibit intelligence. But people do not seem to have this problem. Why not?

People don't explode when they have to reason about possibility because people have found ways to limit their possible reasoning paths. Or, another way to put this is that when people expect to have pasta as part of their dinner, they don't wonder why they expect this, or why someone is serving it to them. They do have to wonder about why it isn't being served to them. They get concerned when their expectations fail, but with food, expectations rarely fail, unless one ventures out from one's safe little world. Regional cuisines keep inferences from exploding.

Where do these handy food expectations come from? This is a rather easy question to answer, at least from an individual perspective. They depend upon what you have already eaten. Certainly, an American child expects French fries and a Coke with his hamburger just as surely as a Japanese child expects rice with his fish. Expectations, especially food expectations, form the basis of our understanding of the world around us. We expect the sun to rise in the morning; we expect our mothers to be asleep or making breakfast or there when we cry. We expect "Sesame Street" to come on at four. We pattern our world on the basis of such expectations.

These expectations pervade every aspect of our lives. We expect the next word written here to be in English, to be a noun, and to be a word we will understand that will somehow elaborate upon the ideas I am expressing. When expectations fail we get confused. A child at four, for example, has expectations so rigid and so extreme that he is very content in his world, in the safeness of it, and he is very easily upset if something different happens from what he expects.

We need expectations to help us not have to work very hard at inferring. We don't think about why there is a fork on the table because we expect it to be there. But, if there were an ax on the table, we would have to figure out why. We don't ask why we have to pay for the meal in a restaurant, but we would have to work hard to understand why we were asked to pay the host if we were invited over to dinner at someone's house.

I recall one time being invited to someone's house at dinner time. The host, having made no preparations for dinner, ordered food to be delivered. This was fine, except that I was asked to pay. I was confused, but found out that the reason was the host was a woman so the men in general were supposed to pay. Obviously, I had "dinner at a home" expectations, whereas my host had "men pay for women" expectations.

Which expectations are operating under which circumstances is a big problem for an understander, as we shall see in the next chapter. The more one has a set of clear expectations, however, the easier life is. Expectations allow us to do less inferring, but this also means, in effect, that we do less thinking. Inferring is work, and people avoid work when possible in mental arenas. This is good, because we really don't want to have to rethink everything all the time. But, people who look to avoid inferring, who expect things to be the way they were, will come to demand that things be the way they were. They will expect and demand rice if they are Japanese, pasta if they are Italian, bread if they are French, and so on. None of these people are right or wrong. But, they are all victims of the need to limit having to make inferences.

Expectations are built gradually over time as a child witnesses sequencing, a very basic human capability. One way in which I like to interact with small children is to pick them up and jostle them around. Some children love this and others like it less, but any small child who sees me more than once quickly learns to expect to be thrown around when I appear. Some present themselves to me and ask to be thrown around, but gently. Some jump on me and demand it, and some hide behind their parents when I appear. In all these cases, they have learned the sequence: *Roger appears → get thrown around*. It takes no more than one try for them to learn this. If I fail to throw them around, they still do not fail to expect it. To unlearn an expectation is more difficult than to learn it in the first place. Expectations stay forever.

Once, when I was a small child, my mother made cookies for me, something she very rarely did, and placed them in an ice bucket. If she made cookies rarely, she placed them in an ice bucket even more rarely. Nevertheless, to this day, when I see an ice bucket placed on a table, I quickly check for cookies. I know that they won't be there, but I check anyway.

One could say that I associate ice bucket and cookies, and certainly, if I were given a typical word-association test, I might easily confound the tester with such an association. But, although expectations can take the form of associations between objects, they are much more important than that. Expectations are mental connections between events.

With all this in mind, let's take a look at an imaginary dinner in an imaginary restaurant. For simplicity's sake, let's imagine the restaurant to be a McDonald's in Ohio, and let's imagine the diner to be an eight-year-old boy. What expectations might be in his mind at the exact moment that he sets foot in the restaurant?

Certainly he is expecting to eat a hamburger. He is also expecting to stand on line, to have his parent produce some money after he orders, to have to carry his own tray or have it carried for him if he is not up to this task. He expects to play in the McDonald's playground that is attached to the restaurant. He is expecting to get a shake if he has been used to getting one. He expects some sort of paper gift to be available, like a cute bib or something to wear on his head. He may expect clown pictures or actual clowns. He may expect an argument to break out between his parents if he doesn't eat his French fries, if that sort of thing has happened before.

In short, he expects to see the world more or less the way it was last time, where last time can be defined in a variety of ways. Last time may mean the last time he was at this particular place, at any McDonald's, at any fast-food restaurant, or at any restaurant at all. When he asks where the crowns to wear are, he may be expecting Burger King, be told that this is not Burger King, and begin to cry that Burger King was where he really wanted to go. One never knows which expectations are most salient, nor which ones will be active in another person. It depends upon how he has characterized things. All we do know is that we have expectations in abundance.

If our eight-year-old Ohioan is such a bundle of expectations, imagine his grown-up counterpart in Segovia. He expects that certain foods will be cooked in certain ways, that they will be served at certain times, and even that the chairs will be a certain type. In Segovia, as in most of Spain, this means hard wood and high backs.

When you have been eating in this fashion all your life, unless you are especially curious or adventurous, you have no reason to change. And this is why Segovia has regional cooking and the rest of the world as well. Food is cooked the way it's supposed to be cooked, the way it has always been cooked.

Change comes slowly, proceeding almost exactly the way language change takes place. Most people don't think about their language changing. They see their language as immutable. They talk of saying things correctly. Of speaking proper English. When I was a kid, I was taught not to say the words "kid" and "ain't." Both requests seemed absurd. I had never heard anyone say "ain't." I found out later that people used to say "ain't" quite frequently, so "ain't" had made it into the textbooks as something not to say, and was now, in effect, being taught as a new word.

Everyone I knew said "kid." Attempts to prevent its use have clearly failed. One wonders why anyone tries to prevent this kind of change, but then, if you are my age, you hear your kids say, "It was so fun," or, "I asked her and she went 'okay' . . .." These are both new locutions that have arrived and taken over in the last ten years. They are incorrect today and people my age wince when we hear them. But, they will probably be perfect English in fifty years.

It is because of language change that different languages exist. French, Italian, Spanish, and Romanian were all once Latin. But, political changes occurred, keeping one group apart from another, and gradually each group of speakers adopted different conventions. Their language changed. People who are certain about how a language must be spoken are quite sure that they know how to speak proper Spanish or Italian although these are changing all the time. What exists at any given moment is seen by the participants as immutable. This is true of language, and it is equally true of food.

The differences between languages are actually not limited to countries, but to speaker communities, which tend to be much smaller. One town speaks somewhat differently from the next in Europe. And, just as differences in language occur from town to town in Europe, cooking differences exist as well. The language of Madrid is not that different from that of Segovia but is much different from that of Paris and even more different from that of Berlin, and foods differ in exactly the same way. Change occurs, in both cases, because of regional migration and integration, because cultures interact and affect each other gradually. These changes are, for the most part, hard to see, but they are becoming easier to spot in the age of airplane travel. When you fly from London to Rome, for example, it is obvious that the language the locals are speaking when you get off the plane is quite different from the one the locals were speaking when you boarded.

People are often quite sure, when they talk about language differences, that the language they speak is a language, while what others speak, which is different from their own speech, is somehow not as much of a language and is maybe a dialect. In food, as well as in language, people seem to imagine that they are the savants who really know. Most people feel that other people speak funny and eat weird stuff. Many people are revolted by the idea of eating raw fish, or squid, or brains, or other foods that other groups think of as perfectly normal. Many Americans think that New Yorkers speak funny, Southerners speak funny, and the British speak funny. Obviously, all these people speak correctly. And they all eat correctly. In each case, they satisfy their own expectations and violate those of others.

To an English speaker, Dutch and German are kind of similar.

An average Joe may not be sure whether these are two languages or one; an educated type is more certain that each is a distinct language. According to the standard definition of a language, Dutch and German are indeed two distinct languages because they are mutually unintelligible. When someone in Amsterdam goes to Berlin, unless he has studied German, he has as much difficulty understanding what is being said to him as does an average resident of Des Moines. But, as it happens, there is no natural barrier between Holland and Germany. So, while a Dutchman who speaks the local dialect of Dutch and lives right on the German border will claim that he speaks Dutch and not German, he is perfectly capable of understanding and communicating with his neighbor across the road who lives in Germany, is a German, and speaks the local dialect of German. In fact, that German is capable of this communication because he speaks exactly the same language as his Dutch friend, word for word, accent for accent, no different in their respective languages than two Americans from Dubuque would be. How can this be?

The solution to this puzzle is that both Holland and Germany have their official languages, as well as the dialects of those languages spoken in a particular village. No one walked into Germany one day and said, "Now everyone will speak German." A language evolves over time, and each community of speakers grows into larger communities. Each new community speaks a language that is nearly but not quite identical to the language of the community that it came from. Thus, the language spoken in one town in Germany is almost, but not exactly, identical to the one next to it.

This is not true of the United States because the country did not grow in the same way as Europe did. Still, the people in Brooklyn speak somewhat like their friends in New Jersey who speak somewhat like their friends in Philadelphia, but Philadelphia and Brooklyn accents are different enough from each other. Yet they sound quite a bit alike when compared to an Alabama accent.

Of course, accents and dialects are different things but not that different. The fact that NBC is equally available in Alabama and Brooklyn and the fact that people from these places travel quite a bit probably means that American English will never become a group of mutually unintelligible dialects. Yet, dialects would evolve if given enough time and if the contact between places were eliminated.

In Germany and Holland, more time, less travel, and no TV helped preserve dialects. As a result, one could walk across the two countries, starting at the westernmost town in Holland and ending at the easternmost town in Germany, and ask each person whether he can understand the language spoken in the town to the east. Each town understands the language on either side of it, but somewhere on this trek, people will begin to tell you that they speak a dialect of German rather than a dialect of Dutch.

What, you might ask, is the difference between a dialect and a language? The official German language must be taught to the members of each village so that Germans can have a language in common. This was not done until relatively recently, since Germany hasn't been a country for much more than one hundred years. What, then, is official German? Well, it is just one of the dialects of German, naturally the one the king spoke, the dialect of Berlin. Official Dutch is from Utrecht, which is nowhere near Berlin. So, these languages are mutually unintelligible. The old joke is that a language is simply a dialect with a good army.

Languages change imperceptibly, slowly. Yet, the English we speak isn't the same as that which our parents speak, nor is it the same as that which our children speak. Of course, we understand each other, but, going forward or back enough generations, we would not. The rules of which we are most certain, defining what constitutes an acceptable sentence in the language we speak, are, in fact, in a constant state of change.

We find this true, of course, of everything we have right and proper rules for. Rules for dress, for what constitutes polite and proper behavior, and for who can do what in society are all constantly changing. So, too, do ideas about food change.

Regional cooking depends upon rigid conceptions of what constitutes proper food. These vary from community to community only gradually, just as the language those communities speak varies. The key concept in all this is expectation. If we expect a meal or a sentence to have a certain structure, we will not tolerate very much difference from the norm before we claim the meal to be inedible and the sentence ungrammatical. We will tolerate slight differences, however, and this is where creativity, in both food and language, comes into play. Creativity means breaking the established expectations, the rigid rules, by a small amount—within the rules of slippage, so to speak.

But such changes must be gradual. We don't like having our expectations violated since expectation violations make us think hard, as we shall see. What never changes is the will to stay the same. Changes in expectation can be difficult to take, and chefs in regional restaurants make changes at their own risk.

Differences in regional cooking are affected mainly by two things. First, we have the problem of ingredients: The same things are not available everywhere. Second, as we have seen, we have the problem of tradition as embodied in the frozen expectations of a community. But, in America, to a large extent, the expectations are the same across the country, and with some notable exceptions, the ingredients are the same as well. The development of good food or good restaurants in America, once it gets started, should be rather easy. The expectations that need to be changed are not that deeply ingrained in the first place.

So, Ohio, for many reasons, will never have a town famous for its cochinillo. You need a certain rigidity of expectations built over generations to create cochinillo. Further, if cochinillo were that great, the restaurant in Ohio that invented it or imported it would be copied in minutes in Albuquerque and in Dubuque. Well, maybe not in Dubuque that fast; in New York first, then later in Dubuque.

The irony of all this is that people who relish good food have to go to far regions to find what are, in essence, the least creative people from a culinary point of view. Rigidity of expectations has caused these regional chefs to solidify their expectations in such a way that they never change what they cook. Each region gets narrower and narrower and thus more different from its neighbors. This rigidity of expectations and fear of deviation create tastes that are new for the food lover unfamiliar with that region of the world. Thus, we have the irony of having the most rigid of chefs producing for food lovers what they are always seeking, a new taste. The only other way for them to find such new tastes is to locate truly original and creative chefs who are willing to deviate entirely from the cuisine in which they were brought up. So each end of the creativity scale is responsible for gourmets' delights, for entirely different reasons.

In a melting pot of different peoples where rigid expectations are much harder to maintain and, therefore, much easier to change, regional cooking is much less likely to exist. No one would be concerned about introducing cochinillo in Ohio—if people were known to like it in Ohio. By the same token, if people were known to eat it only in Ohio, it would soon disappear. While people in Segovia can take pride in their regional dish, those in Ohio never do. Soul food, the sort of stuff that isn't that good but tends to create and to stabilize a cultural identity for those eating it, exists only where cultures are trying hard to hold on to something, some former time, that is escaping them. Black Americans don't eat pigs' feet because they like the taste. Polish-Americans may think they like kielbasa, but what they like is eating kielbasa, which is something else entirely.

Culture is no more and no less than shared expectations. These expectations can be about food and language, but they also can be about music, dancing, proper behavior when a female enters the room, and so on. In Japan, when someone pours beer in your glass, you are supposed to raise your glass up towards him; if you don't, he will feel insulted. He will infer that you don't respect him. However, in France, you are expected to keep your glass on the table. If you grabbed your glass and pushed it towards the pourer, it might appear boorish, as if you wanted the wine that he was going to serve himself. A Frenchman might infer that you were really thirsty and thus order another bottle. We guess about what others are thinking all the time. We make inferences to establish what might be true besides what we are explicitly told. It is important that we do this, or else we could not communicate without spelling everything out in detail. On the other hand, it is important that we not do too much of it, or else we will combinatorially explode.

The solution is to limit ourselves to situations within the bounds of our experience. We can do this by not venturing too far from home, both literally and figuratively. If we stay within our own culture, the inference problem is simpler. We need not be figuring out what other people mean all the time. As long as people do what is expected, we can do a lot less mental work.

The mind is so full of expectations that it is a kind of prediction machine, assuming what will happen next in every aspect of the world. When I arrived in Spain, I expected that there would be an airport; that there would be taxis at the airport; that there would be a place to change money; that the taxi driver would take me where I wanted to go; that we might have trouble communicating; that the taxi would have a seat in it; that the driver would expect money; and so on, ad nauseam. We don't think about expectations much of the time, but when they are violated, we are surprised. When a driver appeared at the airport with my name on a sign, I was surprised; when I found out he was waiting for more people than me, I was surprised. When I found Jorge, I was surprised. When Jorge didn't eat, I was surprised.

These surprises cause conscious thought to begin. We ask why these things have happened, we try to explain them to ourselves, and we try to understand if we should learn from these experiences in such a way as to prevent our being surprised again. Thinking, especially conscious thinking, means checking out why our expectations have failed. For the most part, we find ready answers. We can find other times in our memories when these expectations have failed, and we can compare the situations. We learn from experience by altering our expectations according to experience.

To put this another way, knowledge, what we know of the world, is no more than what we expect to happen. We really don't "know" anything, in the sense that what we know quite often turns out not to be the case. Of course, there are certain truths, certain definitions, that are not expectations at all. We don't expect that two plus two will turn out to be four, we define four that way. But knowledge of the human things, what will happen next in the social world we inhabit, is no more than expectations, and expectations can fail.

When we try to get a computer to understand English sentences, when we try to get a robot to drive a vehicle in the streets of Boston, when we try to get a machine to reason from experience about medicine or law, what we do is attempt to give that machine knowledge. We can't understand anything unless we know something else first. Then, understanding becomes a process of trying to relate what we are trying to understand to what we have already understood. Understanding is easy when what has happened conforms precisely to what we expected to happen. When things occur exactly the way they occurred last time, no expectations are violated. We understand.

But, when our expectations are violated, we have work to do. To know more, we must understand new experiences and relate what we have understood to what we have previously understood. In this way, we constantly revise our expectations. This is learning.

Some of us are more eager to learn than others. Some people hate to have their expectations violated. They avoid new situations, new experiences, and new foods. They insist that things not change, that everything be the way it was. To them, we owe regional cuisine and other good things that satisfy our expectations every time and thus fail to threaten us with having to think.

Other people are constantly seeking to learn, to grow, to know more. This means putting oneself on mentally shaky ground, where expectations fail constantly.

So some people go to Segovia and try to figure out what Segovians expect and what we should expect from them. In doing this they open themselves up to ridicule when they fail to know what others expect of them, and to a great deal of mental effort when their own expectations fail. The Segovians, on the other hand, not those Segovians who have opened up a nouvelle cuisine restaurant, but those who serve cochinillo, have no problem with this kind of risk.

And somewhere, descendants of Segovia, Segovian-Americans if they exist, might well be eating cochinillo. They would eat it because of the expectations they once had: People like to be reminded of the past, in order to formulate and solidify expectations. They would eat it because they want to stay in their own community, where expectations hardly ever fail. They would eat it because they expect to eat it on special occasions and therefore need not plan what to do on special occasions. But they would also eat it because it tastes good, which is true. It is worth the trip despite the extra inferring and despite the fact that it requires a new set of expectations. Jorge knows his pig.

CHAPTER 3

The Language of Korean

I rarely eat out alone, even when I am traveling, but if I do, I try to eat in a place that is quick rather than elegant. Since I like good food even if it must be quick, I try to choose places that can be both fast and good, which to my mind means something Oriental.

One day I had to fly into LaGuardia and then pick up my son at Kennedy an hour later, around dinner time, so I found myself, once again, at South River. Now, South River may seem like a strange name for a restaurant located between LaGuardia and Kennedy airports, but I have long since stopped trying to figure out how Korean restaurants get their names. In any case, finding a Korean restaurant in the Flushing section of Queens is not at all strange, since, to judge by the faces on the street and the sheer number of Oriental food shops and restaurants, Flushing must have more Chinese and other Orientals than Chinatown in Los Angeles. This is a relatively recent development, since Flushing was a Jewish section of New York when I was a kid. But things change and, from a food point of view, at least, they sometimes change for the better.

Unlike Chinatown, which is full of tourists as well as Chinese, Flushing has yet to be discovered by visitors from Dubuque, so, as is quite common, I was the only non-Oriental (and possibly the only non-Korean, but I couldn't tell for sure) in South River on this particular evening. The place was packed.

It occurred to me that I didn't notice my uniqueness for quite a while. I wondered whether the other patrons took note of the fact that I was the lone Caucasian sooner than I realized it, but mostly I was curious about why I was unaware of this fact. I concluded that I felt quite comfortable in this restaurant—I had been there many times before. But I usually feel comfortable in any Oriental restaurant.

Jews, for reasons best known to themselves, love to eat in Chinese restaurants. If you are new in town and want to eat in a Chinese restaurant, look for the Jewish section of town—you'll always find one. Perhaps this is how the Chinese got to Flushing in the first place. I don't know, but it is certainly how they stayed in business. Gradually Cantonese restaurants gave way to Szechuan restaurants and later Hunan. The Jews in New York still eat in all of them, but I am not sure they have begun to try Korean ones yet since most eaters are not all that adventurous. They are afraid of ordering things they might not like. And, ordering in a restaurant that you have never been to before is not easy.

Learning about Chinese food was easy for me because my first job was in California. I naturally looked for the Chinese restaurants, and found plenty, but discovered that all the dishes I was used to eating were either Cantonese dishes or ones invented for Brooklyn Jews. In California, the Chinese food was different. It was spicy, with interesting sauces and a wide spectrum of ingredients. I liked it.

Someone told me about moo shu pork with pancakes. I tried it and thought it was great. I heard that dumplings were a good thing to try, so I did and became a dumpling fan. They have a fish in the Pacific that I had never heard of called abalone (always cooked with oyster sauce, apparently), which appeared on all the Chinese menus, so I tried that and thought it was terrific. I mentioned this to people in Palo Alto where I was living, and they told me that, if I liked abalone with oyster sauce, I really ought to try it at a place called North China in San Francisco. I did and found it much better than the abalone I had had before; soon I began to appreciate the difference between fresh and canned.

That was twenty years ago and far from Flushing. Now I don't have to worry about what to order, although it took me three or four visits to a Korean restaurant to find out.

At first, I ordered dumplings and squid and other things that I might try in a Chinese restaurant. But, Korea, while near China, is not China. So the Chinese-like items they had on the menu were exactly that, copies of Chinese food, not what Koreans actually have concocted for themselves. What is unique about Korean food is obvious if one only looks at the tables at South River. But on this particular evening, while I was by myself, I also realized for the first time why I had never noticed before.

At nearly every table in South River, save a few in the center of the restaurant, is an electric barbecue. When you walk in and seat yourself and you know nothing about Korean food, you are likely to go for the empty tables in the middle, which are the first ones you see and are also the least crowded. Of course, they are the least crowded because no one goes to a Korean restaurant without barbecuing—well, no one except a first-timer.

If you give them a chance to seat you, the first thing they ask, of course, is "barbecue?" But, they ask it, naturally with a Korean accent, and, as this is not exactly the first sentence one expects to hear from a hostess, one is most likely to answer "no smoking"—if one answers anything at all—and find oneself at the non-barbecuing tables, where the question of barbecuing never comes up. In fact, if you happen to order meat intended for the barbecue, you are likely to hear vague discontented noises coming from the waitress that make you think you had better order something else.

But I had been through all these trials, had ordered everything but barbecued meat, liked it all and kept coming back, until one day I was randomly seated at a barbecuing table, and I failed to order barbecued meat. After all, I never had ordered it before, and the waitress stared at me in serious disbelief. She insisted I order barbecue, which I did, since I never fight with waitresses when they tell me what to order, unless they are warning me off something that is "not for American tastes"—in which case I fight tooth and nail.

So when barbecue came to the table, I became a lover rather than a liker of Korean restaurants. I don't actually like meat very much, which is one of the reasons that I hadn't found out about barbecue before. I find meat too dry and too heavy, and so I avoid it unless I know that I can get it properly cooked, which for me means hardly cooked at all. Americans tend to cook meat to death no matter how much you insist, unless you are at a restaurant that really cares about meat, like a serious steak house or a restaurant run by French people.

But at the barbecue in a Korean restaurant, all they do is slice the meat into wafers and marinate it in a spicy sauce. So, if you like spicy and you like undercooked, you can barbecue your own meat, slice by slice, at your own table. Eating like this is wonderful, and I recommend it. Just make sure that your table has a barbecue.

This was the lesson I learned while waiting for my son's plane to arrive at Kennedy. I came in alone and immediately headed for the barbecue tables. I was asked by the hostess whether I wanted to eat at the barbecue tables, and I, of course, said that I did. She then asked if I wanted to order two portions; when I said that I was alone, she said I'd have to sit at a non-barbecue table. It seems that the minimum order is two portions before they will turn on the barbecue; otherwise they offer to cook one portion in the kitchen and bring it to you. I had little choice, so I asked for that and in so doing learned why you want to do it yourself.

Cooking it piece by piece, you control the amount of cooking, the temperature when you eat it, and thus the crispness and life of the food. When someone has done that for you, the food will have had time to dry out. When it is all piled back on top of itself, it creates a giant lump of lukewarm meat that is not as appetizing or as tasty as it once was.

Little by little, with experiences such as these, I am learning about Korean food. So if you should happen to go to a Korean restaurant with me, you might want me to order for you. After all, I most likely know more about Korean food than you do.

In general, of course, I know more about many different kinds of food than most people, largely because I like to eat and am adventurous about eating. On occasion, those with an independent spirit object to my ordering for them. It is my habit, for example, to order for graduate students who find themselves eating dinner with me. Being graduate students, they have little ability (and, I might add, little cause) to object to this. Ordering for other people is especially important when you are going to share what they eat, as is true, for example, in Chinese restaurants where the diners traditionally all share. Calvin Trillin, the well-known writer, once wrote that his nightmare was eating at a Chinese restaurant with a group of meat-and-potato types, all of whom ordered the Oriental equivalent of meat and potatoes. He concluded that there should be no democracy in Chinese restaurants, a dictum with which I heartily concur.

I might add that people with whom you have a dominant relationship—children, students, and such—shouldn't get to order for themselves, even if you don't have to share what they order. It is outrageous to take someone to a great Chinese restaurant and have him order the hamburger that is listed under "American food" at the end of the menu. Well, to be honest, not too many great Chinese restaurants offer hamburgers anymore, but some did years ago. Anyway, you get the idea.

One of my graduate students, finding himself with me in an Indian restaurant in Washington, D.C., asked me whether, since he had finished his Ph.D., he might be allowed to order for himself just this once, since only he and I were present. I agreed with some trepidation. I had taken him to a tandoori restaurant with a tandoori oven, which was hard to find in this country at that time. My former student promptly ordered the only dish the restaurant prepared that did not require the tandoor. He had managed to find the hamburger of the tandoori restaurant. I resolved not to let this happen again.

Because of my generally haughty attitude about food and because of my actual experience in the subject of ordering in restaurants, my friends really do let me order for them when we are in a restaurant whose cuisine is unfamiliar to them. But, perhaps more surprisingly, they also let me order in a restaurant that neither they nor I have ever been to before. What do I know that would make me any better than you at ordering in a place I have never been to before? The answer to this question is really very simple—knowledge. The real question is: knowledge of what sort?

Usually when we think of knowledge, we think of encyclopedic knowledge, the kind of information that one might find in the *Encyclopaedia Britannica* on the breeding habits of dinosaurs. When we say that someone is very knowledgeable, we mean that if we ask him why the sky is blue, he might actually know, and that he very likely also knows the year George Washington was born, how to put the decimal point in the right place, and what the square root of two is.

Of course, this kind of thing is very nice to know and is basically the kind of knowledge that we go to school to acquire. But it is not the kind of knowledge that we use on a daily basis, nor is it the kind of knowledge that allows us to function in the world. Understanding the nature of that kind of knowledge, the kind that we do not by and large acquire in school, is central to understanding how the mind works.

As I mentioned in the previous chapter, all important knowledge is in the form of expectations. We cannot really know anything for sure. Certainly, we claim to know our own names, or that George Washington was the first president, or that the Mets won the 1986 World Series. But this kind of factual knowledge is the least interesting type of knowledge that there is. True, schools are obsessed with teaching factual knowledge. This is one reason why schools have become more and more irrelevant in today's world. There are just too many facts to know and not enough reasons to know them.

This is one reason why this book is about food and wine and not about baseball. In baseball there are statistics to memorize. There are facts to learn. Learning, in the context of baseball, means, for the most part, learning who had the highest batting average in 1927. Unfortunately, this is the type of learning that schools usually emphasize: memorization, followed by testing. In real life, on the other hand, learning means the acquisition of new types of slots and new rules on what will fill those slots.

Earlier I mentioned the concept of slots and slot fillers. Understanding how we understand means, among other things, understanding how many different kinds of slots there are. We have slots for everything. What is the next word in this _____1_____? Or the next word in this _____2_____? Why am I writing in this _____3_____? Do I have a _____4_____? It is possible to leave out the _____5_____ in this fashion and still be _____6_____. Right? How come?

The first thing to understand here is that driving the whole slot-filling business must be various mental structures that are being activated by certain mental events and are demanding to have their various slots filled. Marvin Minsky has called these structures "frames." A key question is what kinds of frames might exist. Looking at the examples above, it is clear that there must be sentence frames, structures for sentences that demand certain types of words to come next and fill them. There also must be conceptual frames, structures of well-formed thoughts that have conceptual slots and demand certain kinds of concepts to fill them.

Missing word number 1 is probably *sentence*. But, in number

2, the word could be *sentence* again, or it could be *one*, which is the pronoun that stands for *sentence*. It actually doesn't much matter which it is from the point of view of the understander. Understanding depends upon the meaning of the words, not the words themselves. The important point here is that we have these kinds of slots. A reader knows what's coming. How can this be? How can a reader or a listener know what someone else is about to say? Because an understander's knowledge is bound up in the slots and the frames that contain those slots. Knowledge means, among other things, having information about which frames should be called into play at any given moment that would cause certain slots to be filled in those frames and would cause us to begin searching to fill the remaining empty slots. Context helps to provide such frames. For example, in number 4, the sentence would be impossible to figure out if the preceding three sentences had not been there: *Do I have a _____?* could be just about anything. But, in context, the missing word is probably *point*, or something quite like it.

In numbers 5 and 6, the words that are missing are not at all obvious. Number 6, for example, could be *understandable, comprehensible, clear, readable,* and so on. Nevertheless, the idea behind the words is quite clear. The idea behind 6 is about understandability in the absence of words. So we see that we have sentence frames that cause us to look for words that will fill those frames, and we also have conceptual frames with slots tied to the meanings that underlie those words.

Such frames, or knowledge structures, contain the essence of what we know. We have knowledge structures about kinds of sentences, kinds of conceptual structures, groupings of events, reasons for groupings of events, and so on. For each of these knowledge structure types, we have to know the various different knowledge structures that there are, the conditions under which each might become active, the types of slots each contains, and the kinds of concepts that will fill those slots. Understanding means being able to predict not only what word will come next, but what event will come next, what plan will come next, what goal will come next, and so on.

These structures are bundles of predictions, each containing slots and slot fillers. Knowledge structures get built over time when we compare each experience we have to each seemingly related experience we have had. We understand the things that people are likely to say and the things that people are likely to mean. We also understand events that are likely to occur and thus can anticipate what people might be saying about events that they are relating to us because we know a great deal about what they could be saying based on what we know about what could be happening.

But notice that this is all guesswork. We don't really know anything. Learning occurs when we cannot fill a slot with what has usually filled that slot, or when we cannot even determine what slots need to be filled, or when we cannot determine what mental structure should have been available to provide slots to fill. This latter happens rarely, however. Even when we do not know what knowledge structure ought to be operating, we are happy to assume that we do know. One important way we learn is by realizing that we had the wrong frame in mind. We very rarely have no frame at all in mind; we are used to being wrong.

So now, with a belief in your own frames, some information about Korean food, and the further desire to watch the mind in action, let's go to a new Korean restaurant. Let's return to Main Street in Flushing, look around for a place that looks nice, and settle on Ko-Hyang, which bills itself as a Korean and Japanese restaurant. I don't find this too troubling, as South River bills itself the same way. The Koreans were occupied by the Japanese for many years, so I guess this is some kind of obeisance to their former rulers, or perhaps Koreans learned to like Japanese food because of the occupation. I say this with only a mild likelihood that it is true, since I have never seen anyone order sushi or sashimi in a Korean restaurant. Since raw fish needs to be especially fresh, I am somewhat concerned that anyone ever would order it, but it is available. I notice that Ko-Hyang even has a sushi chef sitting behind the sushi bar, bored out of his mind. This noted, I turn my attention to the menu.

As I said earlier, when entering a Korean restaurant, the first thing you want to do is check out the tables for the barbecue. None has one, it turns out, which means they are likely to bring one to you, so I look for a gas or electric hook-up. I discover none at my table, so I ask the waitress whether one person can order barbecue, and she sadly says no, only two people. Oh well. You might wonder why I keep coming to these places alone. I am wondering this, too.

I scan the menu looking for my favorite things or new variations on my favorite things. Koreans make many nice dumpling dishes, so I look for one I haven't seen before. They have something called fried dumplings which doesn't sound so good since I am not a big fan of fried things, but I decide to try it anyhow. They don't have one of my favorite dishes, which goes by the name of scallion pancakes. Actually they may very well have it; the problem is that the English name is rather unrelated to what it is, and it may have been well hidden under some other name. I look for something called pizza or weird dumplings but, finding nothing, I give up. I am searching for a main dish. Koreans like squid, and so do I, so I am searching for a squid dish that looks good when I discover "barbecue-at-your-own-table squid." It says nothing about two people, so I order it somewhat sheepishly, afraid of being turned down, but I am not. The next moment a wok-shaped barbecue appears and is miraculously plugged in.

Moments later, the appetizers arrive. In every Korean restaurant I have ever been to, exactly the same appetizers come at the beginning of the meal, regardless of what you have actually ordered. Mostly these are vegetables like spiced cabbage or bean sprouts and also some little tiny fish to be eaten whole. Suddenly, I realize why I like to eat at Korean restaurants when I am alone. You have so much to do. You don't have to bring a newspaper to read while they cook your meal. From the moment you order, you have so much to choose from and are never bored. This is especially true if you have something to barbecue, as I do now.

A lump of raw squid arrives, and I do nothing. Will the waitress cook it for me, or am I supposed to? I wait. She arrives and places some of the squid on the barbecue. Am I expected to take it off myself? When do I do that, and how do I eat it? Immediately, lettuce arrives. This is an answer to the second question, I realize, and probably to the first, as well. Korean barbecue is often placed in a large lettuce leaf with some sauces and other goodies, wrapped up, and eaten like a taco. As this is a messy process, it is something one does for oneself. I am probably on my own from here on in. I realize that, of course, I am being watched by various workers in this establishment, who are testing to see whether I know what to do. I begin the process, and everyone goes away.

I usually have Korean beer with Korean food, but this day I am especially thirsty and ask for some water too. An entire pitcher arrives. I am being told that this stuff will be too spicy for me. Koreans don't much approve of water drinking. I resolve not to touch the pitcher.

I am enjoying the barbecued squid, though not as much as I

like the meat barbecues. So I decide to experiment to see whether undercooking the squid will improve it: I place a new batch of squid on the barbecue only to discover that squid is really not for eating undercooked, at least not in chunks this size. Not surprisingly, given that one never sees squid sashimi or squid sushi that is sliced thick, my new lettuce taco is very tough and difficult to chew. I resolve to cook the next batch quite well.

Just out of curiosity at whether I really am being observed, I place the next batch of squid in a big lump in the center of the barbecue, instead of spreading it about. Minutes later someone appears to spread it out for me. I smirk to myself. Minutes later, someone new appears to put it all back in one big lump. I wonder whether people are just looking around for something to do or whether I am the highlight of the evening in this place.

When I finish, each waitress worries about whether it was too spicy. Since I have eaten it all and not touched the water pitcher, you might find this a superfluous question, but I think that Korean waitresses just have to ask this question of non-Koreans. They secretly hope that it was too spicy, I suspect, but who knows?

So I successfully ordered at a Korean restaurant that I had never been to before. What did I have to know in order to do this? I had a number of knowledge structures available to help me. I had knowledge about restaurants for sure, but also about restaurants that serve Asian as opposed to European cuisine, and some new knowledge structures that I was testing from my limited experience with Korean restaurants. I had all kinds of slots to fill: slots for the main dish, slots for foods I like and know to look for, slots for foods I expect might be done properly in a Korean restaurant, as well as "things that can be put on a barbecue by one person," a new slot I was hoping to fill. Knowledge comes in this way. We don't really know a set of facts, loose and unrelated. Rather, we structure our knowledge like a *paint-by-numbers* painting, filling in the empty slots with information when we can, hoping to create to a unified whole. The key to knowing anything, therefore, is to know what you don't know. This last remark will take some explaining.

If I tell you that a mutual friend, let's call him Joe, had a great meal at Lutèce, you might have a number of questions that you want to ask, if you know that Lutèce is a very fancy restaurant in New York. For example, if you know that Joe usually eats at McDonald's and likes it, you might wonder what the occasion was that caused him to eat in such a fancy place. If you know that Joe couldn't possibly afford to eat at Lutèce, you might wonder who took him there. If you know that Joe goes to fancy restaurants only in order to impress women, you might ask who the new woman was. If you knew that Joe was a famous gourmet who ate only at restaurants that prepared something special for him, you might ask about the dish that induced him to eat at Lutèce this time. And, if you knew that Joe ate only duck and that Lutèce does not prepare duck well, you might wonder about why Joe chose Lutèce.

Obviously, I could go on and on about the possible questions that might come to mind if the world were in some state or other. The point is that such questions *do* come to mind. When we know that certain things are true, we know enough to wonder about new information that conflicts in some way with the facts that we know. You cannot wonder whether they will let you order the squid barbecue when you are alone if you have never had the experience of being denied the meat barbecue for that reason. You cannot wonder about Joe if the things you know about Joe don't come to mind or if you don't know anything about Joe at all.

To put this another way, understanding of the world comes from ignorance of the world. But, if you are massively ignorant, you can't understand anything. If you don't know Joe at all, and you don't know any more about Lutèce than the fact that it is a restaurant, then when you hear that Joe ate at Lutèce, your mind doesn't react much. You can't wonder about how it all came about that Joe ate at Lutèce because you have too much to wonder about. How tall is Joe? Is he married? What does he do for a living? Is he rich? Does he eat at Lutèce often? The list is endless and entirely idiosyncratic.

So with too much to think about, too many blanks to fill in, thinking about nothing is easiest. But if you are Joe's girlfriend, and you know Joe goes to fancy restaurants to impress women— or if you are Joe's wife, and you know that Joe goes to fancy restaurants with friends and always picks up the check, and you can't afford it—then your mind knows exactly in which direction to go. Intelligent thought, true understanding of a situation, depends upon a great deal of knowledge, enough knowledge to generate some good questions that will start the thinking process going.

Thinking depends upon having a line of thought to follow. A

line of thought means having things to wonder about and a plan of attack about how to wonder about them. This means knowing what you don't know but would like to find out about.

All of this process is not quite conscious, of course. We know what we are wondering about but not how we happened to begin to wonder about something as opposed to wondering about something else. What we wonder about depends upon our own goals. The particular questions we generate for ourselves and attempt to answer on our own or ask someone else about depend upon finding out what we don't know that, if we did, would bring us closer to our goals.

The problem here is with the idea of goals. We all know that we have goals like wanting to be rich or to meet a nice girl or to go to college. Such goals are very high-level goals, which we don't work on directly very much of the time. We have other goals, however, daily goals, that we work on all the time. For example, the goal to taste something good, which comes from a high-level goal that is even higher than getting rich or going to college. It comes from the goal of survival, which triggers the goal of satisfying hunger. But checking to see whether the squid tastes better when it is cooked less comes from the daily goal of tasting something good, coupled with another daily goal of learning something new. Now, not everyone has either of these daily goals, but I do, and so do the readers of this book, I would assume.

When new information appears on the scene, an intelligent processor checks to see whether that information in any way relates to his daily goals. In the broadest sense, if one has a daily goal of learning something new, then any new information will suffice. But in reality, learning something new isn't really a daily goal. We have daily learning goals only with respect to particular topics. We always want to know something new about things we care about, our friends and family, work, hobbies and recreational pursuits, and so on.

Goals to acquire more knowledge about something get generated on the fly. I didn't walk into Ko-Hyang wondering about whether squid tasted better when it was undercooked. In order to wonder about that, I had to order the squid, taste it, remember why I like meat barbecues, and want to taste something better than I was tasting. Only then could I ask myself the question about undercooking the squid.

Being curious about what you don't know depends upon being aware in the first place that there is something to know that you don't now know. This phenomenon of "filling in the blanks" in your knowledge pervades every aspect of your thinking. For example, if we are in a restaurant together with our friend Joe, and I tell you that Joe likes squid, you assume that I mean that Joe likes to eat squid and that I am proposing that we order some squid and perhaps share it. You understand me when I say Joe likes squid, and you don't think for a moment about what you had to do in order to understand. But assume I had said, instead, that Joe likes Mary. Would you assume that I was talking about ordering some Mary and sharing it? Of course not. But why not?

When we hear that someone likes something, the understanding process immediately attempts to fill an obvious blank. This process is not necessarily conscious. The blank here is an action that we might expect Joe to do in the presence of squid. We ask ourselves, in effect, *what would I imagine Joe to do with a squid that would make him happy?* Or we ask ourselves, *what would Joe do with Mary that would make him happy?* The answers to such questions are obvious in some cases and less obvious in others. In the case of the squid, we could easily imagine that Joe likes squid to be in his fish tank at home. If the context were "gifts for Joe's birthday," then maybe Joe's liking squid might refer to porcelain objects that he collects. The possibilities are endless. What is the mind to do?

The mind is unhappy with blanks. It wants to fill in all the blanks it can find. So it guesses. It tries to guess intelligently, but sometimes it just has to make assumptions. Some guesses are easy. Contexts determine clever guessing, so in a restaurant, we assume that *Joe likes squid* means he likes eating squid. With Mary, the situation is not so simple. When we say that a person likes a person, we are also talking about actions that are to be performed with that person. But you can do far more activities with a person than with a squid. So we have some serious guessing to do when we are told that John likes Mary. Here again, context will help. If we are talking about the upcoming prom, maybe we are referring to whom John wants to ask out. If we are referring to employment possibilities, maybe John wants to hire Mary. In fact, the list is too long to guess about. We are in the same situation we were in before. The more we know we don't know, the harder finding out is.

In a real-life conversation, fortunately, we can ask. If we can't guess, asking someone a question is a good way to fill in a blank. Often, we feel stupid asking a question, because a question indicates that we have not been able to figure something out for ourselves. When we cannot guess properly, we are sometimes ashamed, especially when we know that we had been expected to guess properly. If we hear that Joe likes squid, and we say, *so, what's your point?* we force the speaker to spell out for us what he meant—that he was talking about what we should order.

On the other hand, we don't always want to be guessing. We can make mistakes in trying to figure out what others are saying. We prefer to be accurate, but we also prefer not to appear stupid. Often these goals are in conflict.

When the Korean waitress brought me a strange brown mixture at the same time that she brought me the appetizers, I could have just eaten it. But I had never seen it before. I knew enough about the situation to know that it was something odd. I had a set of expectations about what would be brought as appetizers, and I could fit this brown glop in anywhere. What were my choices? I could have just eaten it, but it didn't look edible by itself. I could have ignored it because I didn't know what it was, but that isn't like me. I could have attempted to figure out what it was by thinking about what it could possibly be. Or, I could have asked what it was, as I actually did.

All this thinking about the possibilities for this sauce is exactly the kind of thinking that you must do in order to understand anything that anyone says to you. Understanding language and understanding the world are really pretty much the same thing. In each case, we must try to fit in whatever new information we have just encountered with what we already knew. So if the waitress had asked me whether I would like something-or-other glop, instead of bringing the sauce to me, I would have had to go through more or less the same thinking process. First, I would have had to figure out whether I knew what she was talking about. One really does not want to say to the waitress in the diner when she offers ketchup for your hamburger, *what's ketchup?* Once I realized that I didn't know enough to answer the question sensibly, I would have had to decide whether I wanted to experiment or ignore the new input or ask about what it was for. In either case, language or action, one has to take new inputs and figure out what to do with them. In this case, the problem with the glop was that I didn't know what it was for, but I was willing to find out and try it. It turned out that it was a spicy sauce to be placed on the lettuce leaf in which the squid was wrapped. The waitress just said that it was for the squid. The rest I figured out for myself since I had seen lettuce-leaf-wrapping sauces before.

The entire understanding process depends upon inference. Inference means attempting to add information to what you have just seen or heard that will help you understand what is going on. Language is telegraphic. People say as little as possible, as if they are sending a telegram and paying by the word. Your job as an understander is to figure out what else they would tell you if they had the time and the inclination. The menu at Ko-Hyang doesn't say that the items that they list are foods and that they cook them for you and that you may ask for them and they will be brought to you on the assumption that you will pay them when you are finished. It doesn't say that anywhere because they expect you to infer all that. That is what is to be understood by the word *restaurant*, after all, and they have told you that they are a restaurant.

But this kind of inference is no different in principle from the inference required when the menu lists *squid in spicy sauce: barbecue at your own table*. You either know all the details of what this means, or you don't. If you know what it means, you pay no more attention to what you know than you did to the knowledge you have that restaurants will cook food for you and expect you to pay later. But if you don't know what the barbecuing entails or what this dish will look like or taste like, then you must ignore this dish or experiment or guess or ask.

The understanding process always gives you these four options. You may ignore information that you didn't know enough about to figure out what to do with it. Or you may assume that something new is like something old and try to treat it as if it were something you already knew about. Or you may pursue a line of reasoning based upon some intelligent guessing that relies upon knowledge of what you know about what you don't know. Or, knowing what you don't know, you may ask.

The middle two of these processes are both inference processes. Inference is a highly risky process, one that is wrong as often as it is right. But despite its inherent risks, it is the basic process upon which we all rely to make sense of the world around us.

Inference depends upon having particular expectations about particular events. When you hear, *Joe likes fish,* the inference process begins. It begins because an understander must determine what is known and then fill in what is unknown from whatever outside sources he can muster. At the root of what is known, before anything is said at all, is the basic structure of events. Any event has an actor, an action that the actor performed, an object of that action, and, as actions are in the real world, a direction or path of that action.

To put this another way, all events will fit into the following format:

actor:
action:
object:
path:

Now, having said this, we must be certain that we don't get confused between words and the concepts behind those words. So, while *like* is a verb, it is definitely not an action. An action is something someone does to something, and someone who likes something doesn't do anything at all. *Liking something* is, instead, a mental state. Further, it is a mental state that arises as a result of some action. Also, in this sentence, we have been told what this action is. Well, not really. We have actually just been told enough information that will enable us to make a good guess about Joe and fish such that we can infer what else was going on.

To see what I mean here, let's ask the question, *what action would Joe do with a fish that would produce some sort of pleasure for Joe?* To understand this simple sentence, we must ask ourselves this question. The answer is obvious, because we expect that people eat fish rather than have emotional relationships with fish. If the sentence had been *Joe likes Mary,* the opposite answer would have been equally obvious. Language understanding depends upon having specific knowledge about the world available to us in the form of expectations about what is normal. We can revise these expectations when we discover that Joe has a very weird sex life, but without such specific expectations about Joe, we assume Joe to be a normal man and ask ourselves the question: What action can I put in the slot for actions in the event I am trying to understand?

So we assume that the action is *eat.* But, it is important to emphasize, this is just an assumption. We could be wrong. There are some further inferences to make. We know why people eat, and we know the results of eating. In general, two inferences that we always try to make are those having to do with the reasons for actions and the results of actions. We make these inferences because we need to. We need to know why people do what they do and if the results of what they did accomplished the intended goal. Whether or not people tell us explicitly about these things, we work hard to figure them out. When you hear that I went to a Korean restaurant, knowing nothing about me, you assume that I must like Korean food, perhaps that I am Korean. If you knew that Korean restaurants are usually cheap, or that they are frequently open all night, then you might assume that I went there for those reasons. You always assume that I went there to eat, not to deliver barbecue sets, and you also assume that I eat because, being human, I need to, from time to time.

I mention these things because, if you want to understand the mind, one way to do it is to attempt to build one. Since that it precisely what I do when I am not eating, I have wondered about the question of what I will need to tell a computer if I want the computer to understand what I tell it. In other words, how can I get a computer to understand *Joe likes fish*, or *Roger likes Korean restaurants*? In order to do this, it is absolutely necessary to tell the computer every gory detail about the world that you and I naturally assume without thinking about it. We must make sure that the computer knows that Korean restaurants are often open twenty-four hours, that the best thing to eat there is barbecue, that to do so one must sit at the barbecue table and bring a friend, that these restaurants are cheap and usually populated by Koreans, and that eating is fun as well as necessary, that people sit down when eating, that they use forks except in most Oriental restaurants, and so on and so on and so on. Unless we do all this, no computer would ever understand the following simple story:

Roger went to South River but he forgot to bring a friend and got seated at the regular tables. He ate quickly and left quite unsatisfied.

Notice that, prior to reading this chapter, you wouldn't have understood this story either.

But what does it mean to understand a story? This is a very complicated question that we will delve into as we go on. For now let's give a simple answer. You can demonstrate how well you understand a story by answering a question such as, *what did Roger eat at South River?* with the answer: *He probably wanted to eat barbecued beef, but I would guess that he ate scallion pancake and squid instead.* Clearly, you could not have given such an answer unless you had read this chapter and gathered sufficient knowledge to fill in all the open slots. Equally as clearly, no computer could provide such an answer without doing precisely the same thing. How do we get computers to create such an answer? Let's go back to *Joe likes fish*.

The first thing we must do is represent the meaning of the sentence. To do this we use the format given above, together with a causal connection to the inference about results and the inference about reasons that we asserted were an integral part of the understanding process. The overall structure for this kind of information looks like this:

Reason in actor's mind

causes

Event (consisting of: actor action object path)

which in turn causes

Resulting state

The representation of the sentence in question, that is, what it means in enough detail so that we can input that meaning to a computer, is as follows:

humans get hungry from time to time
when humans get hungry this is a reason to eat
humans choose what to eat on the basis of taste
Joe is a human

causes

actor: Joe
action: ingest
object: fish
path: from plate to hand to mouth to stomach

which in turn causes

Joe's hunger is satisfied
Joe is pleased by the taste

This kind of representation must exist in the heads of humans and in the memories of computers for either to answer any questions at all about Joe and fish. Even this isn't quite enough, as many more details about time and place and other circumstances must be added. The particular way in which this mental representation is instantiated in either the human brain or the memory of the computer is of no particular interest as far as the mind is concerned. We are talking here about the kinds of things that one must know in order to understand. Whether this knowledge is encoded in meat and chemicals and neurons or in on-off switches, electricity, and silicon matters little here. Either requires having something to encode. For those interested in the mind, the question is: *What gets encoded?*

In any case, it seems clear that the answer is: *an awful lot.* In order to answer the question about what Roger ate in South River, we must encode not only one sentence but all the sentences from this chapter and relate the information that was derived directly from what was said explicitly to information that we know in general that would help us make inferences about all the things that were left out.

We can do this by filling slots. If we know there was an action, and we weren't told it explicitly (as with eating, above), then we infer it. We know there was an action because we have a slot for that action in our event representation structure. Similarly, we have slots for reasons, results, and a range of other things. We fill these in as best we can, guessing all the time on the basis of expectations that we have about how life normally proceeds. Thus, language understanding is a rather imperfect process. To understand, we must fill in slots, and to fill in slots, we must guess about what might fill them on the basis of knowledge we happen to have about such situations in general or by using specific information we have recently acquired.

To build a computer program to do this kind of thing, one needs to write rules about what words relate to what slots. So we write that *likes* is a word that relates to unknown actions that cause pleasure and that one way to figure out what action might be intended is to assume the normal action associated with an object that is liked. So, when we like a dress, it means that we like wearing it, or giving it to someone, or seeing it on someone. When we like a car we mean that we like driving it, or riding in it, or seeing it, or we appreciate its value or engineering. Language understanding is not all that easy, for humans or computers. But, in either case, it depends upon complex knowledge about the most mundane details.

Language understanding relies entirely on knowing what knowledge structure is active, knowing what slots it has in it, knowing what can fill them, and knowing the rules of a language that tell you where to find what. Let's consider what is entailed in understanding a sentence like:

Roger paid the check at South River.

There are many frames active here. There is the basic conceptual frame that looks for actor-action-object. There is the TRANS frame, which refers to the transfer of possession of an object. The word pay *is written in our mental dictionary as follows:*

Pay

when an actor has filled the actor slot and an action is needed, if the next word is some form of money, then fill the action slot with TRANS and the object slot with some form of money; the path slot gets filled with whatever institution or person is found next; if the next word after *pay* is a human, then fill the path with that human and look for a money word next; if no money word is found, default on some unknown amount and look for it in future or previous sentences

This is actually only a small part of what would be a much larger definition that we might give to a computer in order to understand the word *pay*. Notice that this is not a definition in the ordinary sense. It is really a set of instructions about how to set up and fill slots when a given word appears, by determining the context in which that word has appeared. People need rules like these to determine which knowledge structures are active and which frames are opened by those knowledge structures. Notice that if *pay* had had *for this in blood* following it, a whole different frame, not TRANS, would have had to have been activated.

Using a dictionary with a listing like the one above, then, would cause us to fill in the conceptual frame as follows:

actor: Roger
action: TRANS
object: money
path: South River

The remainder of the understanding task is to determine what other structures need to be opened and what slots need to be filled. One that would need to be opened and filled here is the *reason structure*. Why did I pay the check? You know why.

How do you know why? You know because people pay checks at restaurants when they have eaten in those restaurants. Thus, we can infer that structures for eating must be opened as well, enabling us to understand sentences such as *he liked the squid* that might follow, by telling us to put the squid in the *ingest* slot. Further, there is an *implicit contract* knowledge structure to be opened as well. Understanders know that people pay checks at restaurants because they have implicitly agreed to do so by ordering food at the restaurant. This information will fill the "reasons" structure that is always present and asking to be filled when any action is taken.

Language understanding is a process of gathering information about the world around us that enables us to determine which knowledge structures will activate which frames that will open slots so that we can fill in the slots that need filling in. The more we use a given piece of knowledge, the more we rely upon it and treat it as fact. So you may not assume, when you hear that a friend went to a Korean restaurant, that he had the barbecue, because you have no reason to make that assumption. But you do have reason to assume that he ate something, and if he tells you about his trip to this restaurant, you have reason to assume that he will tell you what he ate, and you will want to be ready to understand him by making some expectations here and there. So even if he never mentions that he sat down, you can assume it. And if he never mentions that he ate with a fork, you can assume chopsticks. And if he never mentions what he ate, you can chime in: *I assume you had the barbecue.*

CHAPTER 4

Searching Memory in Minnesota

Minnesota isn't exactly associated with great food in most people's minds, and it certainly isn't in my mind. And, I can tell you, after a visit to Minnesota, nothing in my mind has changed. No matter how hard I try, I can't remember what I ate or drank. Now for most people, forgetting a meal isn't exactly horrifying—in fact, it's the norm. But normality is hard to remember. How do you remember a meal? In the first place, you need something to be special to remember it. Not just anything will do. One hamburger begins to look like another in memory. Why should we store away each particular hamburger we have ever eaten? The hamburger with the worm in it—now that's memorable. If we want to find something in our memory store, we must have a unique handle. To find what I ate in Minnesota, I need a way of accessing that information by whatever stood out about it. Now that I put it this way, I still can't find a thing.

With the idea of novelty in mind, one question to ask myself is what I was doing in Minnesota. Suddenly, I have an image in my mind. It is 7:30 in the morning. I am walking in a procession, the one and only time I ever wore a cap and gown when it wasn't my own graduation. I am walking into a hockey rink, which is part of the campus of Gustavus Adolphus College. Now, Gustavus Adolphus College is not the everyday place for me to go, and you and I are both wondering why I am there. I am trying to remember. I am trying to reconstruct why I would have been there. I'll bet they paid me a lot of money. I wasn't going for the food. I mean, this place isn't even in Minneapolis; it's in someplace I never heard of, which isn't surprising since all I've heard of in Minnesota is Minneapolis. So the food wasn't why I came.

No, it had to be the money. But since when do colleges like this have the money to pay for outside speakers? Aha, the right question. Now I remember that Gustavus Adolphus was a Swedish king, that Minnesota is a Swedish kind of place, that the Nobel foundation gives money to places it likes to help, and what place better than a nice Swedish college? I am at a Nobel symposium. Of the five speakers, two have Nobel prizes. Well, I don't feel too bad about not having one since Nobel didn't think to invent a computer science prize, much less one in artificial intelligence.

I am still trying to remember what I ate, but instead I find myself wondering why three thousand people have arrived at 7:30 for a day of lectures in a hockey rink. Now this is the kind of thing I would always wonder, so it occurs to me that I have wondered it before. In fact, I asked this very question of the guy who was marching next to me, who happened to be the dean of the college. I remember asking it because I realized that, since we were in the middle of nowhere, finding three thousand people to attend these lectures wasn't going to be easy. Most of the attendees had to drive hours to get here. God knows what hour in the morning they had to get up at—and for what could easily have been a rather dull experience. Having a Nobel prize doesn't guarantee the ability to speak clearly and cleverly.

I remember asking because I remember the dean's answer. He said, *"You have to remember that most Minnesotans are of Swedish extraction, and Swedes love to suffer. If it doesn't cause pain, Swedish people don't want to do it."*

Can you imagine what the food was like? Okay, you may not

want to know, but let's try anyway. One way to recall something is to find some other aspects of the situation that might have made it distinctive. One question to ask myself is, who was there to talk to and to eat with? Aha. Good question. Now I remember one of the other speakers. I remember talking with him at a bar late at night and having a generally good time of the kind that intellectuals will allow themselves, namely we were having an argument. And we were eating. But what? I can remember saying that I had to have these somethings because I had never had them before. I will eat anything that is on a menu that I have never had before. Why? Because I am likely to remember it. Why eat it if you are going to forget it?

What could they have been? Fried something, no doubt. In the shape of a ball, I remember. Cheese balls, probably. It doesn't matter really, because now I am trying to remember the meal, and I can't, and that's the point. Now that I think about it, we had three meals—two dinners and a lunch, and I can't remember any of them. But wait. Maybe you can help. Can you remember them for me?

What, you say? What kind of crazy question is this? You weren't there. Just try, I say. Okay, you say: roast beef (overcooked); chicken (baked probably); cold cuts for lunch. Great. Probably right. The script wins again. When memory fails, we reconstruct from the script. Your guess really is as good as mine. And why don't we remember the details of these meals? People are really quite cautious about wasting resources. We never remember anything that we could easily reconstruct. Why waste precious storage space on roast beef? We have to save space for galette de truffes aux oignons. What is this? Something worth saving memory space for, as we shall see in Chapter 11.

We rely upon our ability to reconstruct rather than retrieve most of the experiences we have. Did you use a fork the last time you ate in a restaurant? Of course you did. How do you know? Do you really remember it? What did the fork look like? Actually, we remember very little of what we think we remember. We can figure out what we should remember and add in the details. You can make up what the fork looked like, too, if you need to. You know what forks look like in general. You can't remember anything too bizarre about this one, so it was probably your average default fork. If the restaurant were a fancy restaurant, we could jack it up a bit with higher-quality silver and some curlicues, and voilà, a memory! Only what we now have in our minds isn't a memory at all. We reconstructed the fork, which is a nice way of saying that we invented it out of whole cloth.

What's the difference between memories that we have to reconstruct and those that really are there in some storage place in the brain, waiting to be found? By and large, the idea that particular memories are in particular places in the brain is a comforting illusion. It seems simple, but the facts speak against it. Finding a particular memory in a particular place would actually be very difficult. It is also very nice that we can't do this. Imagine bumping your head and forever knocking George Washington out of your mind. We all know that brain cells are dying all the time. Why don't we lose George or Martha every now and then? To answer this, let's return to Minnesota.

It's my first night at this college, and we are being welcomed at a dinner. Let's try to reconstruct this dinner, to see whether we can find what I drank. Now, it's possible that one might find this information by saying to one's memory, *"Memory, find me a night some years back in Minnesota and find the dinner and give me back whatever drink is in the drink slot of the list of what was ingested."* This sounds like how a computer works, but it really isn't. It is a parody of how we imagine computers work. It certainly isn't the way the mind works.

Actually, some primitive artificial intelligence programs work this way. One of the reasons we can create programs that do some smart things is that we can create memories by making them collections of lists with elements on those lists filled in. So we can record whole meals by creating a kind of form to be filled out that has a place for the drink, the desserts, the color of the tablecloth, and so on. Then, if we need to know what we drank on November 11 at dinner, all we need do is find the meal list for that date and look in the drink slot. Simple. Computers could work this way. People could work this way. But people don't work this way, and computers shouldn't work this way if they are going to have any kind of intelligence at all.

meal of November 11

table settings:
silverware: very fancy real silver with curlicues on handle
tablecloth: red with white polka dots
number of people: 4

table shape: round
lighting: candles

meal:
appetizer: clams oreganata
salad: tossed with oil and vinegar
main dish: chicken in a white wine sauce
drink: Château Lascombes 1978
side dishes: scalloped potatoes, green beans
dessert: apple pie

A look at the above list shows why neither computers nor people are likely to work this way. Even though the details of that list are too boring to care about, a great deal is still missing. How did the food taste? How did it feel to be there? What were the people at the next table eating? What additional items need to be on the list in order to describe the evening completely? The total amount of information necessary to even come close to enumerating everything one can potentially remember about a meal is enormous.

And what if such elaborate descriptions really were in the mind? Of what use would such a detailed list be? It might be nice, in principle, to remember every detail, but why exactly? One reason that our memories don't work this way is that we really don't want to remember everything. With a memory full of lists like this, we would never forget anything. But forgetting is very important.

Wait. Hold on. The very advantage that computers have over people is that their memories are indestructible. All our popular images of computers are of giant brains that hold reams of information and are more reliable than elephants in the memory department. Now I am telling you that the one advantage that computers might have over people is no advantage at all. Why not? Isn't forgetting a bad thing?

Actually, forgetting is a very good thing. Why should I remember what I ate one night in Minnesota four years ago? In order for someone to remember an experience, some unconscious process in the mind has to decide that that experience might somehow be useful to recall later on. In some sense, the mind asks: *What would be the point of remembering this meal?*

But, what is the point of remembering anything at all? Why does the mind need to retain any information? For one thing, it is worthwhile to remember an event so that one is able to reason from it later on. So, quite unconscious to us, our memories are retaining information that might be something to learn something from. Memory is a learning process. The reason we remember things is so we can recall them later when we need them.

Because we know we will need to rely on prior experience, regardless of how neatly that experience fits, we try to remember. So, should I have remembered this now forgotten meal on a cold October night? There really are no *shoulds* about it. We don't remember things because we think that we ought to. We really aren't in that much control of our own memories. We remember what we need to remember, but our minds are not actually aware of what they need to remember. Nevertheless, we can watch ourselves and see what we are doing, at least to some extent.

Now, I have subtly shifted ground on you here but will come directly to the point. We don't choose to forget things; we choose to remember them. Forgetting is not a memory process. Remembering is the memory process. That is, you can choose to remember things or not. You cannot choose to forget things. Forgetting isn't something you do; it is something you don't do.

I didn't eat my meal in Minnesota and then say, *now this was a forgettable meal in a forgettable restaurant, so I think I will forget it,* and then proceed to purge each memory location that might have mistakenly stored some overcooked roast beef or non-curlicued fork in its October 13 meal list. I didn't bother to remember these things in the first place. If we remembered everything we did or saw or said in one evening, our memories would be like an overstuffed chair with no room for any more stuffing. How would we find anything? Imagine spending the whole day reading the Sunday *New York Times* from cover to cover and then actually recalling every word. What a frightening thought. On the other hand, we didn't read it all in order to forget it either. But what do we do? We certainly don't ignore everything we see and hear.

Actually, I probably could have told you a great deal about that particular evening in Minnesota at the end of the evening, or even at the end of the week. I would have thought that I remembered it, for a while at least, and then I would have believed that I had forgotten some of it when you asked me about it a week later. And I might have been embarrassed if I had met the dean of the college a year later and failed to recognize him or to remember the evening at all. People feel that they forget things, and they often feel that they would, on occasion, prefer to have remembered them.

Psychologists have postulated two kinds of memory, short-term memory (STM) and long-term memory (LTM). They have been able to show that we can remember certain things for very short periods of time (try to repeat this last sentence to a friend—it is possible). But STM fades fast. Try and repeat this chapter to a friend—the best you can do is to give the gist of the chapter, restating it in your own words.

Psychologists loved the idea of short-term memory when it was first proposed during the early days of cognitive psychology, when experiments were performed on subjects who were asked to learn lists of nonsense syllables. The idea was to see how well people remembered JUV, TIR, KAG, and so on. People can learn such lists well enough, but their memory doesn't last long, especially when they are asked to do something else in the meantime. Subjects who memorized such a list were asked to do something else, like some math, for example, and then were asked to repeat the list they had previously committed to memory. Not surprisingly, the subjects forgot most of the nonsense syllables that they had previously memorized. This caused the experimenters to postulate a short-term memory store where the nonsense syllables were held, which then had to be erased in order to do the math.

Some years later, a new breed of psychologists (for example, Don Norman) began to question whether such experiments showed any more than the obvious fact that remembering something meaningless is hard. We need to understand the content of what we are trying to remember in order to remember effectively. Nevertheless, there do seem to be some short-term memory effects. The immediacy of what we are doing at any moment is quickly forgotten.

Obviously, we must have another type of memory store, a more intermediate one (ITM), that allows you to talk about what you have read here to a friend but does not necessarily enable you to recall it for a very long period of time. Now, in talking about memory for what we read, I have crossed an important line. We would all like to recall what we read, but it isn't all that easy. We feel the effects of forgetting most severely when we fail to recall something for an exam, for instance.

The problem in remembering things is transferring between memory stores. Quite unconsciously, we are deciding not to transfer everything that winds up in STM into ITM. In fact, we transfer next to none of it. We take each input visual image or sound or taste or feel and determine whether it is worth putting into ITM. When we look at the face of a friend, for example, we do not transfer into ITM every single visual image that we receive. If we did, in the course of a ten-minute conversation, our mind would have had to store thousands of pictures of our friend. We are smart enough to know that we already have an image of our friend stored away and that one is enough, unless some new update is warranted. So we bring our old image up from memory, check to see whether anything is new, and—finding nothing—don't bother to transfer any information into ITM.

But what about the transfer into LTM? If we want to transfer an episode in our lives into LTM, it must also relate to what we already know. An event can be understood only in terms of what we already know. Imagine if the meal in Minnesota had been the first restaurant I had ever been to or the first dinner I had ever attended at a conference or the first time I had ever eaten antelope, or if the organizer of the conference had popped naked out of a cake. Any of these things would have caused me to remember the meal.

When we transfer an episode from ITM, where it sits for a few days so that we can tell our wives about our trip to Minnesota, into LTM, where it might be found years later if needed, we do so because goal-based processes in our mind are finding parts of the episode to be of enough relevance to retain it in order to learn something from it that relates to things that these processes are seeking to find out. We are deciding rather unconsciously, of course, that something in this experience was worth remembering so that when it comes up again, we can use that experience to guide our future behavior. Our interests, which translate into little knowledge-acquisition goals, are pursuing information that might alter our memories for the purpose of changing our data base of knowledge to cause us to learn.

Some interesting examples of people whose minds don't remember in this way can show us something about why memory works the way it does. In a very famous case, the Russian psychologist Luria described a man who was a mnemonist. This man could remember anything that was said to him in exact detail. When Dante was read to him carefully, each word pronounced distinctly, he could repeat it exactly, with perfect pronunciation, fifteen years later, even though he didn't speak a word of Italian. But this seemingly perfect memory had a serious side effect. As

Luria stated: "Trying to understand a passage, to grasp the information it contains, became a tortuous procedure for S. . . . As he
put it: Other people think as they read, but I see it all."

Normal people extract content from what they read and place
the content together in their memories with other episodes that
have the same content. Luria's subject kept getting distracted by
images that would cause a bench in one story to take him to a
bench in another, but he had trouble getting back to the content
of the original story. The images were more important to his memory than the content, so he could image a page of text, but not
the actions in the text. We learn from the content, however. We
must evaluate our experiences in terms of what we can learn from
them in order to learn from them. Remembering everything actually prevents you from concentrating on what can be learned,
allowing the rest to be forgotten.

We have a major problem, therefore, when we begin to learn
something new. We must alter our knowledge base by adding
what we are now processing to what we already know. But where
exactly do we add the new information? Where does a new episode
belong?

This question is not frivolous, although it is not one that any
of us is prepared to answer consciously. To give you a sense of
the problem, imagine that I have been presented with a menu from
this long-forgotten Minnesota establishment as a remembrance of
the evening, and that, it so happened, I have a copy of the menu
of every meal I have ever eaten. Imagine that I live in a house full
of menus. Where should I put the Minnesota menu?

I could choose to file all my menus by date. In that case, the
filing would be easy, but the retrieval would be difficult. I would
never be able to find this meal unless I knew the date, but I might
want to remember a meal by some other more significant aspect
associated with it. The food, for example. Suppose that I meet
Jean-François, and he happens to mention the dessert we ate at
Jamin. I immediately rush home to my file of menus to find the
one from the particular night at Jamin to which he is referring.
But, where do I look? If I have filed all the menus by their dates,
I will need to recall the date of the meal in question in order to
retrieve the right menu. Well, it was in March of last year; perhaps
I can find it this way. But, then he mentions that he thought that
the dessert at Zur Traube was better. Oh my, when was that? A
couple of years ago, but I don't even know what time of year. It
was on a business trip, and that could have taken place at any

time. I remember the weather was cool, but that just means it wasn't the dead of winter or the middle of summer. No, this cannot be a good filing system, but what would a better one be?

How about if I put all the menus from great meals in one cabinet, filed alphabetically by restaurant name? And how about if I put all the pretty good meals in another cabinet, but this time filed by location? This way, if someone asked me the name of a great restaurant in Florida, I could look it up in the great meal file—otherwise I could look for it in the Florida file. But if these files were very big, I'd still have trouble finding anything. Having copies of menus would be better so that I could put the one from Bern's Steak House in the Florida file and in the great wine list file, while hedging on whether it belonged in the great meal file.

The problem here is that this model isn't of much use. We cannot be filing memories by date or by alphabet or by the greatness of the dessert. Particular episodes have to be torn apart and labeled in many different ways. One particular dessert at Jamin is wonderful, and I have had it three times. I remember each meal because they were all special. I remember who was there and what else we ate. And, if you mention the names of certain people whom I ate with there and nowhere else, or you mention great restaurants or you mention the best lamb you ever ate, these items will cause Jamin to come to mind, too. Episodes in memory are not menus looking for filing cabinets. We remember something in many different ways by ripping an episode to shreds, putting it in a Xerox machine, and distributing the many copies of the many pieces to many different filing cabinets.

In order to transfer an episode from ITM to LTM, then, we must understand what that episode relates to, with respect to what we already know. Where do we put our record of a meal that we loved? Any place it might relate to. It alters our prototypical great meal; it alters our conception of a restaurant or a pleasurable experience, of great service, of creativity, of novelty, of romance, of ambiance, and so on. How can one experience do so much?

Actually, doing all this is quite difficult. It requires effort. It requires actually thinking about what has happened to us. Or, to put this another way, we cannot alter our memories without noticing the new items that will now take their place in memory. Jamin's dessert doesn't get labeled in the mind as the best dessert one has ever eaten without one's thinking first how great a dessert it was. This conscious thinking process serves to label and ship the new experience over to one of its natural resting places in LTM.

Now, let's go back to Minnesota for a minute. Why can't I remember what I ate? Well, where would I find it? Where should I look? In some sense, these are the wrong questions to ask. A better question would be: *What might I have thought about the experience at the time that would have caused the experience to be labeled and shipped over to LTM?* The answer to that question is much easier when we consider the actual situation. In order for me to remember the Minnesota meal, there would have to have been something noteworthy about it. Earlier, I mentioned some possible noteworthy events. If dining in Minnesota were my first meal in a restaurant or the first time I ate antelope, then I might have labeled and shipped the experience to *weird foods* or *new bizarre experiences.* Had something new and interesting happened in the restaurant, then I might have wanted to remember the setting of that experience, and some record of the episode might have survived as a kind of scene in which the other experience was wrapped.

For example, one meal I will never forget occurred in Florida when I was six years old. I was out to dinner with my parents and some friends of theirs. We waited a long time for our meal to arrive, and the wait seemed interminable. Finally, one of my parents' friends, someone I remember as a jolly round man, began to bang on the table with his silverware, hollering in a kind of sing-song, *''We want ser-vice.''* This was, of course, irresistible to a six-year-old boy, and when he encouraged me to join in, I was only too happy to oblige. Soon the others had joined in as well. My parents were mortified. The restaurant staff was running around trying to figure out what to do. In general, I had a wonderful time, and I never forgot it. Of course, I never did anything like it again, and I don't think my parents ever saw those people again. Too bad. My six-year-old self loved them. Memorable though that experience was, I don't remember what I ate then either.

Such an experience is memorable as long as it happens only once or twice. If something like that had occurred in Minnesota, I'd have remembered it, but, as it happened, nothing of interest occurred. The Minnesota restaurant was like any other, and the experience was like most *eating-in-large-groups-in-which-you-know-few-people* experiences. The food was not notable, and nothing notable occurred. It was not painful or horrible, surprising or upsetting in any way, so I could learn nothing to help prevent my being surprised again. In short, there was nothing to remember because there was nothing to learn from any of it. Even the people who were there were easy to forget in that context because they reappeared in other more salient contexts later on in the week. Those who didn't reappear forever vanished. At that time, they were new names and faces without significant experience attached to them. So I remember nothing.

But I want to remember. I need to know what I ate. If I can recall this meal, I win a big prize, I pass the memory exam. What do I do? Unfortunately, I can do only one thing, but before I do it, I want to go off on a small tangent. What about exams? Why is attempting to remember something so difficult when that thing is not an episode but a series of facts that we know we will be tested on?

We were built, after all, to be able to reason from experience. We needed to recall where water was located, who our enemies were, what methods of fighting them had worked in the past, and so on. Memory was set up as a case-based experiential system because all we had were cases of particular experiences, which were useful to generalize from. Any animal that was continually surprised to find an enemy in a given cave or failed to recall where to go for water would not remain an animal for long. Now when we want to remember the date of a battle or a principle of physics, we must adapt the nature of our memories in some way to make them useful for this purpose. Teaching is a difficult process precisely because the things being taught are so abstract. Where do we put the date of the Battle of Hastings in our memories? We can, of course, learn words and names, but these are arbitrary labels. We easily forget the name of someone we are introduced to because, unless it is the name of our mother or our favorite pet or something else of significance to us, names have no meaning. They do not relate to any actual experience. Popular advice on this subject is to repeat the name as soon as you hear it, *"Oh, Joe, nice to meet you, Joe."* This is not bad advice at all. The closer something arbitrary comes to something that is an actual experience, the easier for us to remember.

In teaching and learning, the more rules or dates and such are placed in a real context, the more they will be remembered. Of course, teachers know this to some extent and try to give a real feeling for what they are teaching by using pictures or good explanations or fun demonstrations when they can. What is harder to do but, nevertheless, very important is to make the experience your own. As I have said, remembering is an active process. In order to remember, one must do something that causes the experience to be memorable. It is one thing to hear someone talk about a physical law. It is better to see a demonstration of that law. But even better is to do something that exemplifies that law yourself and to have the action that you perform be a new one for you. Throwing an egg against a wall makes the memory more vivid than imagining throwing the egg or hearing about the principle behind throwing the egg or watching someone else throw the egg. Forgetting Jamin's dessert is hard only after you have actually tasted it. You can put this book down and then find yourself in Paris and ask yourself, *what was the name of the restaurant that Roger kept talking about?* You can forget the name Jamin, no matter how many times I mention it. But, if I took you to Jamin, you would not forget it, I guarantee. Memory requires experience. Trying to trick your memory into storing an experience it did not actually have is often a futile practice.

To see what I mean, try taking the following two U.S. history exams:

Exam 1:
1. Who was president during the Mexican-American War?
2. What year was President Garfield assassinated?
3. Whom did President Cleveland defeat in his first run for the presidency?
4. In what year did the draft riots take place?

Exam 2:
1. Who was president during the Vietnam War?
2. What year was President Kennedy assassinated?
3. Whom did President Carter defeat in his first run for the presidency?
4. In what year did the riots at the Democratic convention take place?

Most people who are over the age of thirty will find Exam 2 easier than Exam 1. But most teenagers would find the exams nearly equal in difficulty. The reason for this is simple. Both exams are just history to a teenager. For someone over thirty, Exam 2 is about experiences he either heard about or lived through. Remembering what you haven't actually experienced is very difficult. But if you have experienced something, it should remain in memory, right?

This having been said, we return to Minnesota again. What method of memory retrieval can I use to find this experience? It must be in memory somewhere, if only I knew how to look. Well, no. The memory really isn't there at all. We can answer many questions about the experience, but I really didn't choose to store much about this restaurant. I didn't think much about the experience because I didn't find much to think about, certainly not much about the food. You can't find what you didn't leave. No record exists (oh, maybe a little tiny one exists), so how can I find it? Easy. Reconstruct it.

We retrieve much of what we "remember" by reconstruction. Reconstruction is a fancy word for "we made most of it up." Of course, we often don't feel as if we made it up. We imagine the room where we ate and decide that the walls were red, but when we go back, we discover that they were blue. We are sure we sat next to an old man, but we see a picture, and he was actually quite young. We reconstruct memories by using what other things we remember that meet two criteria. First, we construct towards normality. That is, we try to make the scene conform to the normal, because if it were abnormal, we would have remembered it. We don't assume that the walls were polka-dotted, because we would have remembered that. We don't imagine that we ate something fantastic because we would have remembered that for sure. The second criterion is that we reconstruct by copying real memories. When we need a color for the walls, we don't make one up. We simply imagine another restaurant that we have seen and copy the color of its walls. Of course, the fact that we are not entirely aware that we are making things up can make us believe that we actually have remembered the wall color correctly.

The most famous work on reconstructive memory was done by Sir Frederick Bartlett in the thirties. He read a story to a group of subjects, and over a period of many years, he asked them to recall the story. They remembered less and less of the story, as one might imagine. But, far more interesting than that, the story itself was rather bizarre. It was an Eskimo folktale that included a great deal of information that made no sense at all to someone who was not conversant with Eskimo culture. When subjects were asked to recall the story, they made sense out of the pieces that made no sense originally. They added pieces to the story that were not there and tended to forget the parts of the story that made no sense. In other words, they reconstructed the story from a skeleton that they recalled. People are only too happy to add what they feel must have happened to their actual remembrances and then swear that they remember accurately. Here is a piece of the Eskimo folktale. See if you can repeat it accurately after you finish this chapter:

...So the canoes went back to Egulac, and the young man went ashore to his house, and made a fire. And he told everybody and said: "Behold, I accompanied the ghosts, and we went to fight. Many of our fellows were killed, and many of those who attacked us were killed. They said I was hit, and I did not feel sick."

He told it all, and then he became quiet. When the sun rose he fell down. Something black came out of his mouth. His face became contorted. The people jumped up and cried.

He was dead.

I now remember what we ate. It was steak. I remember it as if it were yesterday. A dark room. Steak that was overcooked that I tried to send back. It all comes back to me now. Yes, I am certain of it, but I know that I am not certain at all. We were at a fancy restaurant, and the college was trying to impress its guests. What do you serve as a meal for twenty people at a fancy restaurant in a small town in Minnesota? How could it have been anything else but steak? A nice, overcooked, reconstructed steak. Copied no doubt from other steaks I have eaten under similar circumstances. How do I remember sending it back? Easy, I almost always have to do that, since I detest steak that isn't very rare. The only time I don't is when I am concerned about being too much of a pain in the neck. Would this have been one of those times? Nah.

I started this chapter with a question about what I drank. Now, even colleges that are splurging don't serve Mouton-Rothschild. Obviously, I would have remembered it if they had. I always make a fuss if I can't have wine, especially if I am eating red meat. So I asked for wine, no doubt. Or maybe they were serving it anyway. Suddenly a memory comes back to me. I remember them asking if I wanted red or white and then seeing a carafe of each appear. It tasted as you would expect, like Gallo Hearty Burgundy or some such jug wine. I drank it and was reminded of drinking a wine labeled "French wine" on a boat in Sweden with my friend Maurice, but that's another story.

Well, actually, I am only now reminded of that night in Sweden; maybe I was reminded then, too. How can I know? I certainly might have been. And the memory of the wine I drank in Minnesota—is that a real memory? I have no way to tell, at least not by introspection. I could call and check with some of the others who were there that night. If I called five people, I'd probably get five different answers. We all reconstruct differently.

Now that I think about it, I could find out by calling Colleen, the graduate student who was most responsible for my going to Minnesota. That particular night was a big night in her life because she arranged for her new advisor to visit her old college, and she probably remembers it much better than I do. Remembering depends upon interest. Finding things in memory depends upon having been interested in them at the time that they occurred. Maybe Colleen remembers what we ate.

CHAPTER 5

Finding and Following Scripts in Atlanta

ecause my complaints about eating in places like Minnesota are never quietly voiced, whenever I go to a meeting or give a lecture out of town, my hosts are invariably thrown into paroxysms of concern about how to feed me. Businessmen have their feeding scripts, which include expense-account dinners at the finest restaurants in town; but academics usually go out in groups of ten, including impoverished graduate students eager to hear the words of wisdom dripping out of the side of the visiting eminence's mouth as he eats. When I arrive, full of disdain for the impossibility of eating a decent meal in Champaign-Urbana, Illinois, or Ithaca, New York, my hosts scheme for weeks about how to feed Roger so that he won't make jokes about their town in his next lecture. (My hosts do gain a side benefit from this routine— they always eat well with me, and they have come to anticipate this as one of the main reasons for inviting me. "We had to eat at Chez Expensif, Mr. Dean, Schank just wouldn't come otherwise.")

One cold night in Atlanta found ten of us eating at a Jewish-style French restaurant, which my hosts assured me would be just the thing for me. Needless to say, I was skeptical, but, with chin up and eyes on the lookout for a conspiracy to attract customers without feeding them well, I went in. Usually at a restaurant that claims to know what it is doing, I enlist the waitress in one of my favorite scripts, the *make-sure-the-food-isn't-frozen* script. A script is a kind of play that we can engage in where our lines are prepared by a kind of general societal agreement, where we anticipate the lines of our partner in their likely place in the play and react accordingly. We play our role the same way each time and hope that our partners do their bit. The more they do what we expect, the less we have to think up what to do. We can keep reading our lines and expect that our partners will do the same. Knowledge of a situation means knowing the script.

One problem here is that the script we have may not be the one that our newly chosen partner has. Usually, for the most common scripts, we see the world identically and we have no problem playing along. Otherwise, if the waitress didn't have the same ordering script in the restaurant that we expected, we might find ourselves saying, "I'd like the filet mignon," and hearing, *Who gives a damn? Get it yourself, Buster*—instead of the actual next line, which you and she both know is: "How would you like that prepared, sir?"

Actually, even an obnoxious line like the one above gives lip service to agreeing upon exactly what script is supposed to be in operation. The waitress at least recognized that you asked for something, and that implicit in the request was that she should get it for you. She could equally well have said, *Yes, and I'd like Robert Redford if he were available*, which would not even acknowledge that she agreed what play we were reading from.

In any case, to get back to my story, there I was running my *make-sure-it-isn't-frozen* script, which goes like this most of the time:

Me: Could you tell me which of the things on the menu are frozen?
Her: Everything is fresh, sir.
Me: I doubt that. Are you sure?

Her: Quite sure, I've worked here for ten years, and everything
is always fresh.

Me: Well, how about the shrimp? I'll bet that's not fresh.

Her: Oh no, that's fresh frozen, so is the swordfish, and the lamb
is from New Zealand.

Me: And the duck?

Her: The duck is local, sir, right from nearby Duckville.

Me: Good, I'll have the duck.

This particular night, the waitress assured me that the shrimp was
fresh—she had been watching when it was shipped in. This forced
me to go down one of my favorite paths in the frozen script, which
includes a discussion of which ports in the United States actually
have fresh shrimp—New Orleans and New York being the most
likely places to find fresh shrimp, and you can't even be sure there.
Atlanta isn't on the list. Shrimp deteriorates quite quickly, and one
just isn't going to find shrimp that tastes like shrimp in this country
unless the restaurant is rather fanatic about fresh, and that is exactly the kind of thing I am trying to find out. For these reasons,
I almost never order shrimp and certainly wouldn't in Atlanta no
matter what they said, much less in a Jewish-style restaurant. The
shrimp question is just the particular line in my script that I use
to test the credibility of the waitress.

But this particular waitress was feisty and insisted I didn't
know what I was talking about. I suggested that she ask the chef.
I was improvising now, having to think on my feet without my
script. Who knew what was going to come out of my mouth?
Even so, she objected. I had clearly fallen into a script of her own.
For her this was the *deal-with-obnoxious-customer-without-losing-the-
tip* script, and it included, among other things, a suggestion of a
trip to the chef by me, rather than by her.

So off we went. She suggested haughtily that this customer
needed to be informed about how a great restaurant serves only
fresh food and would he please tell me that the shrimp was fresh.
Of course, I wouldn't tell this story if the chef hadn't sheepishly
admitted that, of course, the shrimp was frozen. "It isn't possible
to get fresh shrimp except in New Orleans and maybe New York,"
said he.

What happened here was that our scripts had clashed. They
frequently do. The problem is that we have to make up so many
of them, and we have to learn to abandon them nearly as quickly.
Acquiring and abandoning scripts is one way that people get

through the thinking process without having to work too hard. Let me show you what I mean.

Imagine entering a restaurant without your trusty restaurant script. Say you forgot to take it along. What would happen? The first problem would be knowing why everyone was doing what he was doing. When a man in a tuxedo comes up to you and says "Yes?" his intentions are not clear if you have no script to make them clear.

Imagine walking down a street on a sunny day and meeting a man in a tuxedo who says, smiling, "Yes?" You would quickly take off in another direction. But being in a restaurant changes everything. You know, and he knows that you know, that he is asking for your name and whether you have a reservation, and so on. You both know this because being in a restaurant makes it so. You have agreed upon the game you are playing. You are in the same script.

The same is true when a smiling young lady comes over to your table and says, "Hi, my name is Milly, and I'll be your waitress this evening. I hope you had a nice day." But actually, sentences such as these can be interpreted as not only confirming that we are in the same script but also indicating that subtle turns in the script are about to unfold. We don't always know what kind of restaurant we have entered when we sit down. That is, we may not know exactly which variation of the restaurant script is being followed. But Milly, friendly girl that she is, has just told us. This is the *emphasis-on-friendly-and-cheery-rather-than-high-quality-food-and-service* path of the restaurant script. At this point, I would walk out, but let's stay anyway.

Milly hands us a large piece of paper and moments later comes back to ask us whether we are ready. Ready for what? Why doesn't this question come to mind? How is it that you know exactly what she is referring to? When you ask, because you forgot to take along your restaurant script, she leers at you angrily. Why?

For one thing, she has not forgotten her restaurant script, nor is she used to dealing with customers who have forgotten theirs. But she is quite used to dealing with customers who make suggestive remarks to her. This is another script entirely, and she naturally assumes that you, the innocent restaurant-scriptless customer, have gone into the *pick-up-waitress* script. She intends to let you know that she's not playing along.

The advantage of having a script available is that you can do a lot less work when you are attempting to understand the world around you. If I say that John recommended a particular restaurant, and you ask me what he had there, I do not respond *a good time*. And, when I respond *the lobster*, you do not assume that I mean that he had a lobster with him, as if it were a pet and I had said *the dog*, nor do you assume that a lobster was the vehicle that got him there, as if I had said *the Porsche*. The reason we don't make these errors is that the restaurant script does more than tell us what role to play and what lines to say when we are in a restaurant. It also helps us to understand what people mean when they talk about things that go on in restaurants. When we hear mention of food in a discussion of restaurants, we assume that the food is for eating. Scripts are an important part of language understanding. They tell us what is coming next.

Imagine that you have just entered a restaurant where you do not speak the language at all. In Japan, we find items to point to, as I have mentioned. But what happens when you cannot even guess at what to order or communicate in any way? This once happened to me in a small town in Israel. I know no Hebrew, and the owner of the only restaurant in town spoke no language that I knew. I walked in, looked at the owner inquiringly, established that we had no language in common, and then we stared at each other for a while. He began to motion towards his mouth. I took this as a question about whether I had come into this establishment to eat, so I nodded, and he showed me a table. The menus were in Hebrew, so I was lost. The owner asked me some questions and, upon realizing that this method was not going to work, went into the kitchen. He came back holding a dead chicken by the neck. He showed it to me. I took this to be a question about whether I wanted chicken. I knew no way to ask how he was planning on preparing this chicken. I didn't feel the need to ask whether the chicken had been frozen; I just hoped it hadn't rotted without proper refrigeration. I nodded okay. Sometime later, I was served broiled chicken, and I paid the check and left.

How difficult is it to operate without language? It depends upon the situation. The more stereotyped the situation, the easier it is to function. One can manage in airports and restaurants around the world simply by knowing the relevant scripts. On the other hand, to have an intellectual exchange about the nature of the mind is very difficult without language. Scripts make clear the intentions of all the actors in the script. As soon as the Israeli chef/owner established that I was indeed in his establishment because I wanted to play restaurant and not because I wanted to know how to get to Tel Aviv, he was willing and ready to play restaurant, too. Once we agreed upon the script, we could communicate without language.

When people do share the same language, their mutual reliance upon scripts is less obvious—but, nevertheless, present. When I tell you that our friend Jean-François went to Petrossian, and he had the caviar, you make certain assumptions. The primary assumption is that Jean-François ate caviar at Petrossian. If we know that Petrossian is a restaurant, then, when we hear that someone "had" something at a restaurant, we assume that he ate that something. But suppose I had said that Jean-François went to Petrossian, and he had the suitcase. You would not assume that he ate the suitcase. You would instead assume that you were missing some piece of knowledge. You would find the sentence somewhat incomprehensible, although you could make up some stuff that would make it all sensible, maybe we were trying to locate a lost suitcase and now know where the suitcase was at dinner time last night.

The primary problem in communication is that people don't say everything they mean. It is just too costly to do so. Imagine, for example, if I had given a more complete description of what I said earlier: *Jean-François walked from his hotel to Petrossian, opened the door, waited to be seated, was seated, asked for a menu while ordering a drink, read the menu, decided upon some caviar, waited for it to be served to him, ate it with a fork and knife and some bread and onions and egg, paid the check, and got up and walked down the stairs, out the door, and back to his hotel.*

This story has more information than its earlier version. But if you meet someone who talks like this, you quickly learn to avoid him. Most of the story you could figure out for yourself. Of course, you didn't know for sure that Jean-François was seated or that he paid or that Petrossian had steps, but, for the most part, people are willing to figure these things out for themselves. How do they do it? And why do they do it? And when do they do it? Why isn't getting all the details exactly as they happened simpler than doing all that work?

Basically, we have two answers to these questions: time and attention. No one wants to listen to information that he could figure out for himself, because figuring things out for yourself is much faster than listening to what someone else is saying and decoding that into what he means and then making reasonable inferences from what he means. We are limited when we speak to a certain rate of sounds per second. But we can think much more quickly than this. Ideas come at a significantly faster rate than sounds do.

Compounding this is the problem of focus of attention. When you hear a sentence such as the one italicized three paragraphs ago, you can reasonably ask, "What is your point?" It is difficult to figure out why anyone would be telling you all this. The less someone says, the easier it is to figure out the most significant aspects of what he has said.

As pointed out by Grice and illustrated by experimental results of Bransford and his colleagues, saying as little as possible and letting the listener figure out the rest is usually preferable to spelling out every detail. We don't usually need to figure out the rest, if it is standard, mundane, boring, and of no particular value. Yes, Jean-François used a knife and fork, but who cares? Commenting on his use of utensils is worthwhile only if that use is somehow surprising. When we speak, we do so, at least in theory, to tell about events not altogether predictable. We leave out what is easily predictable and of no import. The easiest way to do this is to rely upon our hearer's knowledge of the standard script when we are speaking and to use a script to help us when we are understanding.

Scripts are, at their heart, the solution to the problem of the combinatorial explosion of inferences referred to in Chapter 2. You will recall that our computer programs were exploding on us, raining inferences from every direction. Every time that John in any way interacted with Mary, our programs went wild trying to find out what else might be true about them, the actions they were performing, and the intentions that they had. The programs quickly ran out of memory, and so would any humans who were not capable of limiting their inference processes.

Giving scripts to the programs solved these problems rather easily. Without scripts, we might tell a story to the computer such as, *Jean-François asked the waitress for the caviar. He got champagne, too. It came to two hundred dollars.* And we would have a great many problems. We would know, for example, that Jean-François now had caviar and that the waitress used to have it but now didn't. We would know that Jean-François intended to eat the caviar and drink the champagne. We would know this because we would know the meanings of the words and can make inferences about why people do various things. But simple questions such as, *why did the waitress give Jean-François the caviar?* would be unanswerable except by a reply like, *because he asked her for it.* And, we would have no way at all to understand that he drank the champagne with the caviar and certainly no way to begin to figure out what came to two hundred dollars.

But these problems disappear if you give the machine a restaurant script with slots for ordering food and drink, and slots for receiving and paying the bill. Now stories like this are easy to understand. The script serves to connect discrete events and to make them into a coherent causal chain of events. Jean-François had to pay money because he ate caviar at a restaurant. The restaurant script tells us this. Without the script, we could not get computers to answer simple questions such as those given in the preceding paragraph because it would simply have no way to know that *the waitress gave Jean-François the caviar because that was her job.* Nor would it know that Jean-François must have eaten the caviar there before paying the bill, rather than taking it with him. To know this, you must know that he got the caviar in a restaurant where one eats rather than takes out. Now, it happens that Petrossian does allow you to pay for caviar and not eat it there. But Petrossian has no take-out liquor license, so Jean-François could not have gotten champagne there. Of course, he could have bought it elsewhere.

The critical thing here is background knowledge. The more you know about a situation, the more you can assume about events that occur within that situation. Scripts represent the default background knowledge that we have without ever having experienced something directly. If I know Petrossian, then I don't need to have a script to help me. But if I have never been to Petrossian and I hear that it is a restaurant, I can at least cope, or understand some things by default, as it were.

We don't, in general, realize how much we do this kind of default understanding. When I say—*Jean-François ordered lobster. He paid the waitress and left*—you don't think much about it. But if I tell you—*Jean-François ordered lobster. He paid the midget and left*—you wonder what I am talking about. You understand easily enough—*Jean-François went to Central Park. He opened the caviar and put it on the crackers. He was happy*—although you might wonder where the crackers came from. But if I tell you—*Jean-François went to Central Park. He opened the present and put it on the hat. He was happy*—you have difficulty figuring out what is going on. If a script is obvious, it is easier to understand.

We were able to use scripts in our programs to help the computer answer questions about what Jean-François ate, even when eating never appeared in the story it was reading. Later, we began to build programs that could read newspaper stories. By "read," I mean that the program could answer questions about what it had read, if what it had read conformed to a script that it knew. The program would fit the events that it was explicitly told about, something rather stereotypical—such as a plane crash or a diplomatic visit— into a structure that would allow the machine to fill in events that it was not explicitly told about. If an important person arrived at the airport in Washington and was met by the president, the program could figure out that this person had boarded a plane in his home country, that he had sat awhile, that he had walked down stairs to where the president was waiting, and so on. This is all rather simple and obvious when you have the script, but not when you don't.

But what of more complex actions? Are diplomatic discussions, for example, also script based? The answer to this is yes and no. They can be, of course. We can assume toasts to each other's countries, expressions of the positive feelings of the peoples involved, and so on. But presumably, what the diplomats talk about is not a script. Programs need more than scripts to help them understand what is going on. So do people.

Or, to put this another way, you must have background knowledge to see you through, but you also must be able to understand things that you were not prepared to hear and be able to change your scripts as new events appear. No knowledge structure is very valuable if it is too static. You must be able to cope with change in order to be intelligent.

Various psychologists, especially Ed Smith and Gordon Bower at Stanford, have run experiments to test the concept of a script. These experiments indicated that people could remember groups of sentences more easily if a script that was implicitly referenced by the first sentence in the story tied the sentences together. If the sentences did not invoke a script, people's ability to recall them was much worse.

One set of experiments showed that people tended to confuse stories with similar scripts, misremembering an event that took place in one script and imagining that it might have taken place in another similar script that they had also heard a story about. Their data started us wondering about how scripts evolve over time, how some are more related than others. This question is critical to understanding how we learn.

Jean-François, it turns out, loves to eat at Petrossian when he visits New York. In Paris, he likes to eat at Kaspia, Petrossian's rival. Jean-François is something of a caviar freak: He knows more about caviar than I could imagine could be known. Once, when we were eating in L'Espérance, a three-star restaurant that I really like about one hundred miles south of Paris, Jean-François got into an argument with the chef-owner about caviar—the American equivalent of which would be getting into a fight with Dustin Hoffman about acting. Nevertheless, Jean-François lectured poor Monsieur Meneau on the right place to purchase caviar in Paris and how it was obvious that he had been trying to save money, which was unworthy of a three-star restaurant. Meneau defended his turf in a fight that got too heated for my meager French to follow.

As a result of this fight and others that Jean-François has had, including those that he had at Petrossian about where they purchase their smoked salmon, my restaurant script has been modified slightly. When I hear that Jean-François has had caviar at Petrossian, I think about these things, too. I wonder whether he had a fight. I wonder why he didn't take me along.

So scripts are not immutable, or to put this another way, knowledge is not immutable. To understand anything, we must be able to fill in the blanks, to understand all the details that weren't said, so that we can create a coherent picture of what is going on. Understanding involves accessing this information. One important class of information of this type is the script. Certain situations have a rather rigid flow to them. One event follows another for well-known reasons. In order for a machine to understand events, it must be given scripts that explain the connectivity of events and allow it to fill in the blanks. In order for a person to understand events, he must develop scripts on his own. He does this by observing and generalizing, as we shall see. Understanding depends upon packaging up bundles of expectations about stereotypical events. The more expectations a script packages, the more we can know about a situation as it begins to unfold in front of us.

Scripts at once provide the power and the problems of human memory. Their power is that they tell us what is likely to come next. They help us make inferences without doing too much work. They package our expectations about restaurants, and airplanes, and department stores, and allow us to operate effectively in new situations by drawing upon generalizations made from similar situations. Much of our ability to understand depends upon scripts.

But there is a price we pay for this "inference made easy"

approach to thinking. When we come to rely upon knowing how things are supposed to be, which event is supposed to follow which event, how people are supposed to act in certain situations, we have little ability to cope when things don't turn out as expected. People in different cultures have different expectations about what is proper behavior, about which event naturally ought to follow which event. Often, they simply consider others to be wrong when they don't know the "right script." People find themselves ostracized for not following the rules that everybody plays by. But these rules are quite culture-specific. Scripts represent a kind of miniculture. If you know the Burger King script, then you are comfortable in that setting. You are comfortable precisely because you can predict the effects of the actions that you and others perform in that situation.

People come to rely upon situations where they know the scripts. Often they are afraid to venture into new arenas because they do not know the script and are afraid of looking foolish. The ability to learn depends upon the ability to abandon scripts that are failing and to acquire new scripts. This becomes more and more difficult to do as one gets older.

When we were writing computer programs to understand natural language, the introduction of scripts into those programs allowed us to make giant strides. Our first program that used scripts was called SAM (for Script Applier Mechanism). SAM read newspaper stories. It could answer questions, paraphrase, and even translate into other languages the stories that it read. Here is an example of SAM in action:

Input:
Friday evening a car swerved off Route 69. The vehicle struck a tree. The passenger, a New Jersey man, was killed. David Hall, 27, was pronounced dead at the scene by Dr. Dana Blanchard, medical examiner. Frank Miller, 32, of 593 Foxon Rd., the driver, was taken to Milford Hospital by Flanagan Ambulance. He was treated and released. No charges were made. Patrolman Robert Onofrio investigated the accident.

English Summary:
An automobile hit a tree near Highway 69 four days ago. David Hall, age 27, residence in New Jersey, the passenger, died. Frank Miller, age 32, residence at 593 Foxon Road in New Haven, Con-

necticut, the driver, was slightly injured. The Police Department did not file charges.

Spanish Summary:

Un auto choco contra un arbol cerca de la Carretera 69 el viernes al anochecer. David Hall, de 27 anos, que vivia en New Jersey, el pasagero, se murio. Frank Miller, de 32 anos, que vivia en 593 Calle Foxon en New Haven, Connecticut, el chofer, quedo un poco herido. El Departamento de Policia no acuso a nadie.

Question-Answering Output:

Q1: Was anyone killed?
A1: Yes, David Hall died.

Q2: Was anyone hurt?
A2: Yes, Frank Miller was slightly injured.

Q3: Why was Miller hurt?
A3: Because the automobile hit the tree.

Q4: Did Miller go to the hospital?
A4: Yes, he was in the Milford Hospital.

Q5: How did Miller get to the hospital?
A5: The Flanagan Ambulance Company took him to the Milford Hospital.

How did SAM do this kind of thing? It had a car accident script, a police investigation script, and so on. It had the ability to recognize when a given script was active, and from that point it filled in the blanks, so to speak. Once it knew that there had been an accident, for example, it looked for the names of the victims, their injuries, the type of vehicle, and so on.

Expectations were at the heart of SAM. It had expectations about which words would come next in a sentence, which actions would follow other actions, and which scripts would follow other scripts. SAM was a bundle of expectations, each from different sources. The key element in understanding how SAM worked, and in understanding how people work too, is to understand the source of expectations.

SAM had expectations such as:

if you see the word *swerve* then expect to see the word *off*
and
if you see the phrase *swerve off* then expect to see the phrase *the*

road, but if you don't see the word *road* and if the next word is
unknown then check to see if the word following the unknown word
is a verb or a time word, then if it is assume the meaning of the
unknown word to be the same as *road*
and
if you see the phrase *swerve off* that denotes a physical transfer of
location (called PTRANS) of a vehicle that would be found as the
subject of the sentence to a new location that may not be mentioned
explicitly but is probably someplace that the operator of the vehicle
did not intend for that vehicle to go
and
to find the operator of a vehicle in a news story if he is not mentioned
as the actor of a motion verb, look for a name followed by *the driver*
and assume that name to be the actor of the PTRANS
and
when a PTRANS is operating, if it was an unintentional PTRANS
assume damage to the object PTRANSed and in the case of a vehicle
to passengers in the vehicle
and
if a vehicle is damaged call up the *vehicle accident* script
and
if a person is damaged in a vehicle accident call up the *ambulance*
script
and
if the vehicle accident script is active be prepared to call up the *police
investigation* script
and
if the ambulance script is active expect:
sentences about possible transfer of injured people to the hospital
sentences about arrival at the hospital
sentences about the health of people in the vehicle
sentences about the eventual outcome of the health of those people
sentences about the health of people who did not go to the hospital

These are only the barest bones of the information that had to be
in a computer program in order for it to understand a story such
as the accident on Route 69. The real issue for a theory of mind,
as well as for a theory of computer understanding, is the organization of the information that needs to be present. We cannot
expect that a reader is prepared to see exactly the story that he
does see. In other words, all the information he brings to bear

must be encoded at a level of generality that would allow for its use in any situation.

So the mind is a bundle of expectations of the kind listed. But where are they to be found? The answer is that expectations are everywhere and are called up by everything. Words can call up expectations of other words. *Caviar* calls up expectations of eating, for example. *Jean-François got some caviar and ate it* seems normal, while *Jean-François got some caviar and wrote with it* requires further explanation.

Concepts can call up expectations of other related concepts. For example, good eating, a concept to which caviar relates, calls up the idea of dressing up, being served well, drinking champagne perhaps. The story *Jean-François ordered caviar but he spilled it on his tux* does not seem at all odd, while *Fred ordered caviar but it fell in the hay* does. The reason is simply one of what was expected and what wasn't.

Syntactic structures call up expectations of other syntactic structures. When we see a noun phrase following a verb, we expect the sentence to end, or a new verb in gerund form, or a time word, for example.

Central concepts (such as PTRANS) call up expectations about what can be legitimately inferred. When PTRANS is active we can assume that the actor wanted to go where he went and had something to do there when he got there. We can also assume that if he wound up somewhere else, he would be unhappy. This is true of PTRANS, regardless of the word that might have called up PTRANS in the first place. In other words, this is true of *go, travel, run, fly, drive,* as well as *took a trip, went for a vacation,* and *paid a visit to.* When PTRANS has been referred to, we must be ready to understand stories such as: Jean-François went to Petrossian; he returned happy. Understanding such stories means having a rule that says:

When PTRANS occurs intentionally on the part of an actor, it is usually executed with the intention of performing an action normally done at the location to which the actor has PTRANSed himself. If there is a characteristic action performed at the location in question, assume it has been performed.

Using this rule, if one knows that one eats caviar at Petrossian, one can answer the question, *why is Jean-François happy?* with ease. Otherwise, it is quite difficult to do so. Comprehension requires tacit knowledge of this type of information.

As bundles of expectations, scripts allow us to understand what *He was treated and released, no charges were made,* could possibly refer to. These sentences refer to specific expectations inside the vehicle accident script pertaining to subparts of that script, which are themselves scripts, namely police investigation and ambulance.

The answer to where expectations can be found is therefore of great importance in building a computer program that is intended to understand stories. To understand stories, one must understand almost every aspect of human existence. Our understanding of these aspects of life must be expressed in some form and put someplace. It cannot be a mystical process. The form is expectations. The place is in knowledge structures. A knowledge structure is an organization of knowledge in some general form that makes the information useful. One such knowledge structure is a script. But words can also be knowledge structures, although the knowledge they organize is of a different sort. Words tell us about the concepts they relate to and where other words fit in. Concepts tell us about the concepts they relate to and which inferences fire off from them. Scripts tell us other scripts that they relate to, which words normally relate to which concepts the scripts contain, and which inference paths should be naturally assumed. Scripts tell us what to assume happened, so that when we see sentences in a text referring to those events, we know where they fit.

A great deal of knowledge is required to do even the simplest kind of understanding. That knowledge has to be organized reasonably. Alphabetically won't do. Organizing knowledge is what intelligence and the modeling of intelligence is all about.

SAM was the first computer program that read newspaper stories, but it was rather slow. It did a great deal of work on computers rather slow by today's standards. A couple of years later we created FRUMP (Fast Reading and Understanding Memory Program). FRUMP whizzed through the UPI news wire, armed with fifty scripts. It could read and summarize news stories in seconds. Here is an example of FRUMP in action:

Input:
Washington, March 15—The State Department announced today the suspension of diplomatic relations with Equatorial Guinea. The announcement came five days after the department received a

message from the foreign minister of the West African country saying that his government had declared two United States diplomats persona non grata.

The two are Ambassador Herbert J. Spiro and Consul William C. Mithoefer Jr., both stationed in neighboring Cameroon but also accredited to Equatorial Guinea.

Robert L. Funseth, State Department spokesman, said Mr. Spiro and Mr. Mithoefer spent five days in Equatorial Guinea earlier this month and were given "a warm reception."

But at the conclusion of their visit, Mr. Funseth said Equatorial Guinea's acting chief of protocol handed them a five-page letter that cast "unwarranted and insulting slurs" on both diplomats.

Selected Sketchy Script $Break-Relations

CPU Time for Understanding—2515 milliseconds

English Summary:
The U.S. State Department and Guinea have broken diplomatic relations.

French Summary:
Le Departement d'État des États-Unis et la Guinée ont coupé leurs relations diplomatiques.

Chinese Summary:
meeigwo gwowhyuann gen jinnahyah duannjyele wayjiau guashih.

Spanish Summary:
El Departamento de Relaciones Exteriores de los EE UU y Guinea cortaton sus relaciones diplomaticas.

Input:
Mount Vernon, Ill. (UPI)—A small earthquake shook several southern Illinois counties Monday night, the National Earthquake Information Service in Golden, Colo., reported.

Spokesman Don Finley said the quake measured 3.2 on the Richter scale, "probably not enough to do any damage or cause any injuries." The quake occurred about 7:48 P.M. CST and was centered about 30 miles east of Mount Vernon, Finley said. It was felt in Richland, Clay, Jasper, Effington, and Marion counties.

Small earthquakes are common in the area, Finley said.

Selected Sketchy Script $Earthquake

CPU Time for Understanding—3040 milliseconds

English Summary:
    There was an earthquake in Illinois with a 3.2 Richter scale reading.

Input:
    The Chilean government has seized operation and financial control of the U.S. interest in the El Tentente Mining Company, one of the three big copper enterprises here. When the Kennecott Copper Company, the owners, sold a 51 per cent interest in the company to the Chilean State Copper Corporation in 1967, it retained a contract to manage the mine. Robert Haldeman, executive vice president of El Tentente, said the contract had been "impaired" by the latest government action. After a meeting with company officials at the mine site nearby, however, he said that he had instructed them to cooperate with eight administrators that the Chilean government had appointed to control all aspects of the company's operations.

Selected Sketchy Script $Nationalize

CPU Time for Understanding—3457 milliseconds

English Summary:
    Chile has nationalized an American mine.

FRUMP did not understand as deeply as SAM. It filled in only a little bit of what might be in a script. Its goal was speed and accuracy rather than thorough understanding. It operated by having very simple scripts (called sketchy scripts) that had only a few slots to fill and a few ways to fill them. So, when it recognized that a nationalization had taken place, it looked for the country that did the nationalizing, the industry that was nationalized, and the original owner. When it found those things, it quit. All it knew to do was to fill those slots.

Much understanding is like this, incidentally. Often we want to know only a little bit. If you are looking for a good restaurant and I tell you a long story about how Jean-François ate at Josephine's, all you might listen to is the name of the eater, the name of the restaurant, and the eater's general happiness about the whole affair. It would be enough to give you a good place to try.

The hard part in FRUMP, and indeed in any program invested with many knowledge structures, was what is called the script instantiation problem. How do we know that *nationalize* is the script we want to use to understand the above story? The answer is again a set of rules, which included things like:

If *seized* is seen then if the actor is a human or political entity and the object is a physical object, the central concept is ATRANS (abstract transfer of possession).

If ATRANS is present, then if the actor is a country and the object is a company, then check to see if the owner of that company is another country. If it is, and if the actor intends to operate that company, the sketchy script is *nationalize*.

Knowing what script is active is complex indeed. People aren't always so good at it. In fact, being bad at it is the basis of a great deal of humor. For example, some Groucho Marx jokes:

We went on a hunting expedition, we shot two bucks. That was all the money we had.
I shot an elephant in my pajamas. How he got into my pajamas I'll never know.
We also shot pictures of the native girls, but they weren't developed. We are going back next year.

Jokes often depend upon script instantiation problems, which fire off the wrong expectations about the right sense of an ambiguous word. Groucho set up expectations about which meaning of *developed* was meant, for example, by instantiating the *take-pictures* script. He then used the developmental sense of *developed*. People are easily fooled when it comes to expectations, but they rely upon them nonetheless.

CHAPTER 6

Altering Scripts: Bowing and Scraping at Taillevent

One of the advantages of being a professor is sabbaticals. Every three years, you get a semester off with pay. I am not sure why. The reason is somewhat clear for high school teachers. They can go to Italy and return with slides of Rome, which have educational value for them and therefore for their classes. As a student, I remember wondering who had managed to sell this bill of goods to the school system: Those slide shows were an incredible drag.

For university professors the concept is, I suppose, that you should have the time off to write a book, a concept I have never understood, since being a professor gives you endless time to write books on the job. Another possibility is that you might not know everything that is going on in your field, so you might move to a hot laboratory and become up to date, or learn some field that you don't already know about.

This is the concept anyhow, but I never quite thought it ought to apply to me. I always thought that sabbaticals were for living someplace you had always wanted to live, and well, yes, I could write a book there, but I could write a book anywhere. As it happened, one year I was able to string two semesters off in a row, so I packed up and went to Paris. I had always liked Paris and, of course, I had always liked French food, not to mention French wine. So the laboratory I chose to study at was the three-star restaurant circuit, interrupted by occasional side trips to taste wine. I had a more official designation than that of course: I was a visiting professor of something or other at a university that had nice bright professors and no offices to put them in and toilets that didn't work. Much conversation had to take place in restaurants—well, you get the idea.

Actually, these nice conversations didn't take place in three-star restaurants. In fact, I was astounded to discover that most French professors had never, or almost never, eaten in a restaurant rated three stars by the *Guide Michelin*.

A word is in order here about the *Guide Michelin*, I suppose. The Michelin Tire Company decided, at the beginning of the century, to get people to use their tires more by encouraging them to actually go places. So they wrote two guides, one to tourist attractions, and one to restaurants and hotels. Because it has been around for so long, the Michelin restaurant guide is kind of a bible for food lovers. But, like *the* Bible, it is slow to change. When Michelin gives a restaurant a three-star rating, which it does only rarely (the total number of three-stars in the world is only about thirty, most of which are in France), it tends to stay forever. One well-known case was a restaurant where the chef-owner died, but his wife kept running the restaurant. Michelin didn't take away the third star of this restaurant until the wife died, so as not to hurt her feelings, and she didn't die until many years later.

Actually, the three-star rating is not really an issue of feelings but of economics. A three-star rating ensures a restaurant of continual clients who are willing to pay very high prices. The chefs at these restaurants are the baseball stars of France. Everyone in France knows some of their names, reads cookbooks by them, buys food products that have their names on them, sees them on television in the French version of "Hollywood Squares," and so on. Three stars means money.

But does it also mean good food? By and large, it does. Of course, not all three-star restaurants are great and eventually they will be downgraded. But any restaurant that is superb has three stars, even if not every restaurant that has three stars is superb. Of course, there are up-and-comers and guide books that rate new ones as being superb more quickly than Michelin does. One such book is *Gault Millau*, which rates restaurants on a twenty-point scale. The French love twenty-point scales for some reason. When Gault Millau gives a 19.5 rating, its highest, it is as reliable as Michelin's three-star, more so because it is usually more up to date and without sentiment. Nevertheless, the cachet of Michelin is such that people talk about the three-star business as if God himself were giving out the ratings. Every year the *New York Times* faithfully reports the changes, who has lost and who has gained a star.

Most of all, what three stars means is ambiance. And this is the reason that most of my French professor friends have not eaten in three-star restaurants. My friends are willing to pay for food but not ambiance. They don't have too much money anyway—French professors are not paid much better than any other civil service workers in France. So they go for quality, trying to find the place that is as good as a three-star restaurant but one-fifth the price. This is not all that hard to do in Paris.

So one reason to live in Paris was to eat in the three-star restaurants. I was going to be in France for only a year, and I wanted to eat in all of them. And, like most Americans, I didn't care whether better restaurants existed that had yet to be discovered. I wanted to worship at the proper altars of great food, pay homage to the great chefs. Actually, this attitude makes three-star restaurants three-star restaurants. They can count on people like me to fill them up. But, as it turned out, at the moment I arrived in France, something horrible happened. The franc-dollar ratio hit 9–1.

"Horrible?" you say. Not for an American. Americans were ecstatic. Their dollars bought things that only yesterday they couldn't afford. And I was living on dollars from my friendly American university. Why was I unhappy?

Very simply, now that every American could afford to eat in a three-star restaurant, every American wanted to. The restaurants were overwhelmed. They were booked months in advance. Moreover, they were filled with Americans. The French hated this and didn't want to go to three-star restaurants anymore. Moreover, the Americans hated this; they didn't want to go to restaurants filled with Americans any more than the French did. Moreover, the restaurants themselves hated this. They would surely be filled as long as the franc-dollar ratio was so lopsided, but how many of their steady customers would they have alienated during that time? So the three-star restaurants in Paris decided to bar Americans from their restaurants. If an American-accented person called up to make a reservation, even if he spoke perfect French, he was denied a table, told that no reservations were available for three months and the restaurants hadn't started booking any further in the future than three months. But when a French person called, a reservation could be had, sometimes the same day.

Immediately, Americans began to scheme to get around this. They had the concierge at the hotel call. Soon, the three-stars were refusing reservations to people who were staying at hotels that Americans frequented or to people with names like Johnson and Edwards. This new form of discrimination was horrifying to most Americans, myself included—but it made me want to go all the more.

Some weeks after my arrival in Paris, my parents showed up for a visit. Surely this was the time to try out one of the three-stars, especially since my parents could be counted upon to pay for the meal. I called Laurance.

Laurance is one of my French professor friends who had never been to a three-star restaurant, so I figured she would be happy to be treated to a fancy meal in return for making the reservation for our group. She was more than happy to do this and so, on the very day when we had been refused a reservation at Taillevent for having an American accent, she called and got us a reservation.

One goes to any restaurant armed with one's restaurant script, as I have said, but we were going to have our script rewritten. We knew that this was going to happen; that was why we were going in the first place. Sometimes expectations are violated, and we become disoriented, wondering what to do. Other times, we go around looking to have our expectations willfully violated. We seek the thrill of confusion.

The first confusion was the number of tuxedoed personnel. I mean, you go into a fancy restaurant, and you expect a tuxedoed maitre d' and maybe a tuxedoed waiter, if they are really into that sort of thing. At Taillevent, we were greeted by seven people in tuxedos, all bowing in front of us. What these people did for a living besides bow, I didn't know, but it made for a nice entrance. As with any learning system, however, I had a problem. To what extent do I change my restaurant script at this point? I didn't expect seven bowing tuxedos upon entering. Is this a change in the script? Did I somehow fail to notice this scene every other time I entered a restaurant before? No, that seems unlikely. Well then, have I misunderstood where I am? Am I perhaps not really in a restaurant? This also seems unlikely. So I am left with the only other option available. I must consider this a bizarre exception to the restaurant script. But, what if I encounter it again? I don't want to be surprised by it when I eat again at Taillevent. In fact, I want to expect it. I will come to demand it. I demand seven bowing tuxedos. Where are they? They were here last time.

"Oh, monsieur," I might hear, "those bowing tuxedos weren't for you that last time; they were for the king of France, who was entering behind you. You just failed to notice him, and we wanted to be polite." Okay, that's an explanation I would understand.

What if I encounter this on my next trip to a three-star restaurant? I want to be able to remark to my dinner companion that, of course, one expects this at a three-star restaurant, or if I am being a little less pompous, I might want to exclaim, "Boy, this place reminds me of Taillevent."

When this kind of confusion happens, when expectations are violated, you need to remember the confusion. But how do I remember this episode? Am I to create a special new script for three-star restaurants? This might seem to be the right thing to do, but it might well be wrong. While I am fixated on the idea that I am eating at a three-star restaurant, the restaurant itself may be fixated on the idea that they want somehow to differentiate themselves from other three-star restaurants. So the very characteristic that I choose to generalize about may be the wrong one.

One thing that I certainly do want to do is to remember that this scene occurred at Taillevent, and as it turns out, this is exactly what Taillevent wants me to do as well. They know a very important principle of learning, namely that we focus upon unique events and try to explain them so that they do not seem odd. But if we cannot explain them except to say, well, that's what happens at Taillevent, then Taillevent gets remembered for its unique, and now defining, characteristic. Taillevent wants us to create a Taillevent script in terms of which others will be judged, and this is precisely what I do in order to recognize the place next time. So

I hypothesize a new script, one with a bowing tuxedo scene in it that occurs after I enter but before I am seated, that I label tentatively "Taillevent." This new script will also get the label "three-star restaurant" and maybe a few others such as "fancy places I have been." And I will wait. I will wait until one of these labels appears again. At that point, I will consider whether to abandon this multiple labeling scheme in favor of a better one, such as, *when entering before the king, expect bowing tuxedos.*

Having considered all these possibilities, I am seated in the twinkling of an eye. It turns out that these seven tuxedos all belong to me; in any case, they don't seem to go away. We seem to be surrounded by them but not in an obtrusive way. One of them is in charge of water and one of wine; one of ordering food and one of bringing food not ordered; and one of just standing around and smiling.

The wine list is excellent, and the menu is full of exciting things to try. My father orders filet of sole because he is part of a scientific experiment to see whether you can eat filet of sole at every meal that you eat in a restaurant for eighty years and live to tell the tale. So far, the experiment is a success. I try the venison, as does Laurance, naturally.

Well, I guess that the "naturally" needs some explaining for an American audience. The French have, as part of their eating script, the rule that they always order the same thing as everybody else. I think this comes from two things, a sense of sharing the experience with all the diners, and a realization that the chef probably can't make five different dishes equally well, all appearing at the same time at your table. It's a lot easier on him and better for the food if you order the same thing. Americans have exactly the opposite rule, of course. They want to taste everything, and so everyone orders something different and shares tastes. This is done in blatant disregard for the chef, who in most cases in America is justly disregarded.

The rules for who copies whom when Frenchmen dine together is complex, but someone is generally regarded as the expert, because he knows cooking better than his companions, an honor not lightly bestowed in France, or because he knows this restaurant or this region better than his compatriots, a much easier thing to grant, or because he is simply more powerful than the others and not to be offended. Of course, no one actually acknowledges any of these rules, and most Frenchmen would probably say I am wrong about all this, but they do it anyway.

In any case, all this left Laurance, as the guest, and as one unfamiliar with three-star restaurants, having to decide whom to copy. My father might have been a possibility until he ordered the filet of sole while exclaiming, "I can't see why we didn't go to McDonald's"—something he didn't really mean but in some deep sense loved saying. So both Laurance and I ordered the venison. I remember this because I remember what happened next.

The venison came with a side dish of pureed chestnuts. The taste was superb, and as Laurance and I both commented on this, my wife, who had ordered something else, did what was quite natural for an American and began to place her fork into Laurance's pureed chestunts.

Fortunately for all concerned, a tuxedoed hand appeared from out of nowhere, deftly grabbing the fork out of her hand and replacing it with another, so quickly that one might almost not have noticed if the man attached to the hand hadn't exclaimed, "Madame does not want to mix the taste of [whatever it was she was eating in a previous mouthful] with the taste of the chestnuts." Well, I don't know how much had survived from her last forkful of her previous dish on the tine of the fork, but it sure wasn't apparent to me, nor to the tuxedo, I suspect. He asked whether she liked it, and when she said that she did, a dish of her own appeared almost instantaneously, almost as if they had been waiting for all this to happen.

Well, that was Taillevent. The food was good, if not great, but the service was indescribable, which, of course, has not prevented me from attempting to describe it.

Now let me ask you a funny question. Is Taillevent a restaurant? To make this question even more absurd, let's imagine a trip to another, less distinguished, but considerably more famous, restaurant. Imagine that one day we meet, and you have read and appreciated my book on food and the mind, and you realize that I am knowledgeable about restaurants and what to order there. So, naturally, you ask me to take you to a special place. Off we go.

We enter this place, and you look for the maitre d' to come up and offer to seat us. But I say, "No, in this restaurant, you first stand in line," and I take you to the end of the line. You ask what this line is for, and I inform you that this is a line for ordering. You ask for the menu, and I say that there is no menu in the ordinary sense; if you simply look up, you will notice a brightly colored lighted plastic board that has printed on it the possible choices. You order, and the person behind the counter asks you to pay. You mumble something about not even having been served yet and that usually one pays after eating, but nevertheless, you pay up. You then wait around for a while until you are handed a tray with your food on it. We look around for tables and seat ourselves.

You complain that this restaurant doesn't seem like what you had expected. It screwed up the restaurant script entirely, you remark. Ordinarily, one sits, reads the menu, orders, is served, eats, and pays, but here one stands in line, looks at a lighted board, orders, pays, serves oneself, sits, and then eats. You complain that this restaurant, which you have since noticed is called McDonald's, doesn't really seem like a restaurant at all. The food wasn't too great either, you note in passing. I apologize for all this and promise to take you somewhere else tomorrow.

The next day, we go to Burger King. At Burger King, I hear you remark that the place reminds you of McDonald's. "Why?" I ask. You note that it has failed to adhere to the restaurant script in exactly the same way. You stood in line to order, were asked to pay before eating, had to seat yourself and to carry your own food, just as in McDonald's. Moreover, the food wasn't much different either.

What has happened here apart from my losing credibility for-ever as a restaurant connoisseur? Learning has taken place. The method of learning was reminding, and the effect of the learning was script alteration and reorganization. Let me explain. Are McDonald's and Burger King restaurants? Well, yes and no.

Most people don't really worry about this question in their daily lives, or so they think. In the ordinary scheme of things, it would appear to be an issue of what is crudely called *semantics*, another way of saying, *it all doesn't matter—it's just so many words*. But the truth is that this question matters a great deal to an un-derstander, because the word *restaurant* is, as we have said, a bundle of expectations. If those expectations are consistently in error, an understander will make a great many mistakes.

Saying that something is a restaurant implies that it will follow the restaurant script, that it will ask you to pay after you eat and not before, for example. Arguing whether Burger King or a caf-eteria is a restaurant or not is not interesting. What is important is that the script that you select when entering one of these es-tablishments be correct. You cannot continually be surprised by the lack of a maitre d' at McDonald's. Nor is it reasonable to be surprised by the bowing and scraping at Taillevent after the first time. We are supposed to learn from our experiences.

The way we learn from our experiences is by altering existing scripts when they prove to be inadequate. Eating at Taillevent forces you to modify your restaurant script so that when the word *Taillevent* appears, you can cleverly decide to expect tuxedos and miraculous fork switching when you taste pureed chestnuts. But, of course, people aren't so stupid. They expect fork switching not only when they eat pureed chestnuts but also when they use any fork for two different things. They might assume that tuxedos will bow and scrape at any three-star restaurant in Paris, or at any great restaurant in the world. The fact is that when a script fails, figuring out the generalizations that follow from the failure is quite tricky. To have more than one failure of the same kind helps. Then the two failures can be compared. It takes an experience at Burger King to really understand McDonald's.

At the point when two experiences seem to match on so many grounds, when they fail your expectations in the same way, when the explanation for that failure is the same, you can and must construct a new script. To do this, you must eliminate the differences and concentrate on the similarities. You must forget that one place has a salad bar and the other does not, that one gives out funny hats and the other does not. You need to forget this stuff so that these features don't become the criteria for what makes up the basis of the new script.

Once the similarities are gathered together, a new script is created, by copying parts of the old script, noting where and when it differs from the old script, and creating expectations from the conjunction of Burger King and McDonald's that you now expect will be valid in Wendy's. This new script, the fast-food hamburger place script, now exists as a kind of codicil to the restaurant script. Naturally, it is not immutable. We can expect that it will constantly be altered as new versions of fast-food restaurants are encountered that don't quite conform to the expectations brought on by Burger King and McDonald's.

Learning, then, can take two rather different but related forms. When an expectation fails in a script, we can attempt to remember that expectation failure, so that we record the exceptions. This exception-based learning works well enough. We can recall that Taillevent has bowing and scraping tuxedos, for example. But recalling all the exceptions we encounter can be tedious and quite difficult. We long to do a more generalization-based learning, the type of learning in which we can combine exceptions.

Ordinarily, combinations of exceptions can be quite useful, since usually exceptions are not unique. If we encounter one bowing and scraping tuxedo, we might encounter another. So we are not surprised when we do see such a place. We are ready to create a new script.

But what are the entry conditions for this new script? How do we know that we are in one script and not another? This is the script instantiation problem that we saw when we discussed FRUMP. FRUMP solved it by paying careful attention to the central actions and their slots and fillers. But more often we rely upon ready-to-wear category names for help. We expect the word *restaurant* to tell us which script is operating. Sometimes the culture we live in is helpful. Italy has at least four different types of places to eat—bars, osterias, trattorias, and restaurants. These names tell us what expectations to gather prior to entering, what script to be prepared to follow, in other words. The phrase *three-star restaurant* denotes something to those who know the items that, for Michelin, earn a restaurant the three-star designation. But what if we are novices? We must determine for ourselves what expectations make up any new script that we create. We could assume that tuxedoed waiters are part of any three-star restaurant, if Taillevent is the first three-star restaurant we have eaten in. But after a few visits, we would find that bowing waiters are a special feature of Taillevent, an exception, not a reliable generalization.

Most people tend to think of stereotypes as bad habits, generalizations to be avoided. But, as we have seen with scripts, such generalizations can be quite useful. Stereotypes allow us not to think. This can be very important if we want to avoid combinatorial explosion.

My friend Arthur keeps kosher, for example. My grandparents also kept kosher. This means that they follow the rules for eating prescribed by Jewish law. To understand what they will and will not eat, all we have to do is to look at the rules. But this, it turns out, is not so easy to do. The rules are written, often in a metaphorical form, in a variety of ways and in a variety of places. So different sets of rules have evolved for different sets of people. My grandmother ate only in places approved by certain orthodox rabbis. She would not eat in your house. In fact, she would not eat in her own house. She had no kitchen, since she had no rabbi who would approve it for her on a regular basis. This was great for my grandmother since it meant that she had to eat out every day. Of course, her choice of restaurants was somewhat limited, but it was probably worth it to her.

My grandfather went along with all this but sneaked in a bacon, lettuce, and tomato sandwich for lunch from time to time, as I said. My friend Arthur, unlike my grandmother, likes to cook and would prefer to go to more than only two restaurants in his lifetime. In fact, Arthur likes to go to three-star restaurants in France. My grandmother wouldn't eat in such places, my grandfather wouldn't eat in such places, but Arthur does. Why?

Arthur eats only fish and vegetables when he eats out. These items are kosher without much ado, unless they are served on plates or with utensils that were used for non-kosher foods. This latter problem is not a problem if you ignore it, however. Arthur chooses to ignore it.

I asked Arthur about this one day when we were having dinner together at a pleasant Italian restaurant we both like in downtown Manhattan. He ordered a pasta dish made with cream sauce and mushrooms on the grounds that even though he was not in a kosher restaurant, the ingredients were all kosher, so it would be all right to eat it. When the dish arrived, it had small red bits of things in it that looked suspiciously like meat. Since he could not eat it if it were meat, I asked him if he wanted me to taste the red things to see what they were. He laughed, said no, and then told me a story that he had just been reminded of. He said he had a cousin who decided to become more orthodox in his religious practices. The more he studied, the more he found out about orthodox Jewish rules. These included the fact that it was all right for a man to have sex with his wife during only two weeks out of every month. At this point he stopped studying. He told my friend that he just didn't want to know some things. My friend said that this attitude applied exactly to the current case. He just didn't want to find out that he couldn't eat the dish. He decided not to eat the red things, but to eat the rest.

So is Arthur kosher? He certainly is according to him but wouldn't be according to my grandmother. We want to make predictions about people based upon the stereotypes they say apply to them or that we have reason to believe apply to them. That having been said, I introduce you to Janet, a former Ph.D. student of mine. Janet is kosher. It is also Janet who took me to the first three-star restaurant I ever ate at while we were attending a conference in France. Janet reminded me of Arthur. In fact, the expectations I have of what Arthur will eat cause me to make assumptions about what Janet will eat, and vice versa. These assumptions are not scripts, in the sense that they are not a sequence of events; they are nevertheless bundles of expectations. And these bundles are in a constant state of flux. The ability to learn means the ability to modify expectations, creating new ones out of the ashes of the old that one hopes have more generality in their application than just being useful in the specific situation that failed.

Some psychological experiments that were of great importance in showing some of the difficulty with the immutability of scripts were done by Gordon Bower and his students at Stanford. They discovered that subjects who were read stories about various events in the life of a main character were unable to recall whether an event in question had taken place while the main character was in the doctor's office or the lawyer's office. Subjects exhibited what were called "recognition confusions" between events in one situation and another. It doesn't seem surprising on the face of it that someone would, when read a story about the doings of a character, be unable to recall whether that character was in one office or another, unless, of course, that distinction had been critical in the story. But science proceeds in strange ways. One of those ways is by testing the assumptions of theories that might have ramifications on the obvious.

In this case, the theory of scripts was being taken as a theory of memory by Bower and his students. Script theory says that there are specific situations that all people know about because they have experienced them so frequently. In each of these situations, expectations are made about what will happen next and those expectations are used to guide our understanding of what we hear or see. We comprehend new information by finding a place for that information in a structure of normal event flow provided by the script. Bower made the assumption that any structure that was used for processing information was naturally a memory structure as well. Actually, I am not sure he knew he was making that assumption. It's just that when the idea of scripts was proposed (by me and my colleague at Yale, Bob Abelson), it seemed to him that they must be memory structures. So, when subjects failed to recall whether an event occurred in a doctor's office or a lawyer's office, he called into question whether different memory structures could have been operating in these situations. In order for subjects to confuse doctor's office with lawyer's office, some more abstract structure, such as *professional's office*, must have been operating in memory.

Here we have the script instantiation problem again, but this time it's even more serious. The earlier version of the problem, as I described it in Chapter 5, had us worrying about which of the many scripts we knew was the one we needed to help provide expectations at any given moment. But the stronger form of the problem is that it is not at all clear that we know exactly what scripts there are. Of course, it is easy when writing a computer program to simply state that there are fifty scripts, to write those scripts in gory detail, and to decide on the distinctive features they would have that would allow us to write rules to determine which script should be active at any given moment.

But with people, computer scientists don't get to determine which scripts are in the head. The problem is to find out which scripts or other abstract structures might actually be in use. I want to know both. I want to build something that works, but I want it to parallel what people do.

So when Bower found that subjects couldn't remember whether Nancy was in the doctor's office or the lawyer's office when she received a phone call, Bower was concerned. He had thought that scripts were a good idea, but now it seemed clear to him that they were not memory structures. That is, they made no prediction about how some event might be stored in memory.

I was supposed to be concerned too, but I was just confused, and confusion can be a very good thing for the creative juices. I had never thought that scripts were supposed to be abstract memory structures. In my mind they were quite specific. We know detailed information about a doctor's office visit, and, while it is similar to what we know about a lawyer's office visit, it is by no means identical. Why shouldn't this information be separate and distinct? Why shouldn't we continue, as we had in SAM and FRUMP, to create detailed scripts, and use them to provide expectations? If these scripts overlapped in some way, well, so what?

Artifical Intelligence research is a funny field. There are no rules. The goal is to produce intelligent computers, but nobody quite knows what that means. It is not clear, really, what intelligence is all about. And, it is not at all clear that intelligent computers ought to have anything to do with human beings at all. After all, the super chess-playing programs that exist today don't do things the way people do. People can't search through millions of possible moves and their ramifications in time to make the next move. The fact that computers can do this may be fun, but it doesn't tell us much about people.

But whether you are interested in human or computer intelligence, if you are interested in doing more than building special-purpose machines, you have to think about doing things that will generalize, doing things in one domain that might work in another as well. It seems clear that we cannot build a conversational machine, for example, that searches through all the millions of possible sentences it might say, and their ramifications, so fast as to not interrupt the flow of the conversation. That seems an odd model of the conversational process.

The same is true of SAM and FRUMP. They, or programs like them, won't tell us much about human intelligence, or even become more comprehensive machine intelligences, unless they do things sensibly. There had to be a good reason why doctor and lawyer information might be stored in memory in such a way as to cause recognition confusions. When Bower told me about his experiments, I began to wonder what it was.

I end with a problem. One day I found myself in Milan with some business types and an evening to kill. Naturally, I looked in my *Guide Michelin*. I found one three-star restaurant listed, Gualtiero Marchesi. I asked whether anyone would like to join me, and one person said sure. I was pleased to have his company. Now, the question is, what were my expectations? Naturally, I expected a three-star restaurant. But, I had never been to one in Italy—this was the only one there was—so I expected a French restaurant. But this was Italy, so I also expected an Italian restaurant. My newfound eating partner added a new problem. He was a vegetarian. It seemed to me that the food would be a waste for him, but then I was reminded of Arthur. I wondered whether this vegetarian ate fish.

So, burdened with confused expectations, I entered the restaurant, prepared to modify my scripts. It turns out that I barely had to. Everything was as you might have expected. The restaurant was wonderful, an Italian restaurant with serious French influences, pasta and nouvelle cuisine. My eating partner announced his preferences and a special menu was prepared for him, the kind of service I had expected, in fact.

Actually, I don't remember all that much about the meal. It hardly violated any expectations at all. No scripts were altered very much. Too bad, script failure is fun.

CHAPTER 7

That Reminds Me of Chicago

A re we likely to have specific kinds of information about how events flow in a restaurant in general, or do we have specific information about particular restaurants or particular kinds of restaurants? Do our memories tell us about how events flow in a three-star restaurant in France, or do we have detailed information about the flow of events in Taillevent? To put this another way, when entering Georges Blanc, another three-star in France, which of these types of information do we bring to mind, ready to help us?

The answer is "all of the above." This must be so, because human beings are learning systems. When we enter Georges Blanc, we must be prepared to create a new memory structure that will capture information about Georges Blanc so that when we return we will be able to rely upon what we have previously experienced.

On the other hand, we must have access to the Taillevent information in order to help make generalizations about three-star restaurants that will help us in the future in the next such restaurant we encounter. And what if we find out something that will be of use in any restaurant, or in another situation in life that has nothing to do with restaurants? We must be ready, as processors of information and as learning systems, to make use of what we find anyplace that it might help. In order to do this, everything we know must be available all the time. This is a tall order, and is enough to make an intelligent system bog down in the face of an overwhelming amount of information.

If we have no expectations of what might be coming next, we will not know what to do with new information. So which is it? Do we have specific expectations generated from one knowledge source, or do we have multiple expectations generated from multiple knowledge sources? The answer to both questions, fortunately, is "yes." Also fortunately, the reason for this can be explained by talking about wine for a bit.

The night we all ate at Taillevent, we had the usual conversation with the wine steward. He came by, asked me if I had selected the wine, and offered advice.

Now, as you might have suspected, I have my very own *ordering-wine-in-a-restaurant* script. It has evolved over time, as scripts tend to do, but basically it goes like this: The wine steward asks if I have made a selection or need help. In France, they ask somewhat contemptuously, assuming an American knows nothing and will either order something ridiculously expensive because he is showing off or order some cheap white wine because he doesn't really like wine. Wine stewards come prepared with a contemptuous question to ask after you have expressed some confusion, namely, *how much did you want to spend?*

The right answer is, of course, *nothing, I want the wine to be free.* Now, as it turns out, this is not only a truthful answer, it is precisely what I am after. I have evolved, over time, a method for getting the wine for free, but it never works in France, so I wasn't using that method on this particular evening. (I will explain the method shortly.)

The reason that question is contemptuous is that no one who likes wine would ever be able to answer it. A wine maven is looking for the best wine at the best price; price is most definitely a factor, but as he has no idea what that will mean with respect to a given wine list before he reads it, he could not know how much he wanted to spend. If, for example, he ordinarily spends fifty dollars for a wine at a nice restaurant, he would not turn down an opportunity to order an unexpected bargain at twenty-five dollars, nor would he fail to order something extraordinary at one hundred dollars, especially if he thought that the wine really should have been four hundred. Wine lovers are really bargain hunters.

Wine lovers are in a constant search for the error of the wine list. A wine bottle is, after all, assuming proper storage, the same no matter where it is served. But the prices of bottles keep changing. The 1970 Bordeaux wines were extraordinarily cheap in 1973 when they became available. No one wanted them. The wine business was doing poorly, the dollar-franc ratio was beginning to worsen, and so on. But today, no good restaurant can fail to have 1970s on their list. This has turned out to be the best vintage of the seventies, and it is ready to drink now. What happens if you didn't buy that wine in 1973 and you are running a restaurant? You buy it now, at perhaps twenty times the price.

So, a wine maven looks for bargains because there are likely to be bargains. When a restaurant buys wine at the right price, it tends, especially in France, to sell that wine according to the price at which it was purchased, rather than according to its current market value. Restaurants in France consider themselves to be in the food business and, in general, are happy to have a good wine list to entice customers into the restaurant.

The game, then, is to find the mistake in the pricing. This "mistake" might be an actual error; the wine steward may not have understood what he was doing. But more likely, a good price is reflective of bargains the owner himself found. Either way, you win if you find it. So the right answer to how much you want to spend is: *I want the best wine at the best price.*

But, one cannot really say that. What I usually do say is that I like old Bordeaux, but I hate to spend a lot of money on wine. Then I suggest one that I think might be a good possibility. In other words, I say to him, in essence, *I am playing the error-of-the-wine-list game, and my choice is X.* Now, the fun part of phrasing it this way is that you put the wine steward into precisely the situation he loves to be in. He is, after all, a wine professional. He wants to believe that he knows more about wine than you do, and certainly more than you do about his own wine list, which, of course, he has actually sampled extensively. He is not concerned that you might find his mistakes; in fact, he might like it if you did (for the right reasons) because wine stewards like to have educated customers to talk wine with, as they appear so rarely (especially in America).

The wine steward loves to win. When you have selected X as your best choice and asked him to beat you, he loves to tell you about "Y, which is much better than X, and at about the same price." And, of course, you win too, unless you misunderstood the game.

Of course, you can't play the game like this unless you know enough about wine to have selected a reasonable X in the first place, one that will make the wine steward appreciate that the game has begun. And one needs to know a great deal about wines to do this. It helps to have tasted a lot of them and have remembered what they tasted like so that you can discuss them with the wine steward as they are suggested. But if you cannot do this, you can always use my simple rule of thumb: Find the oldest, cheapest wine on the list and select it, but always with the tag question, "I am assuming that this is still good?" The wine steward will tell you if it isn't and the game will begin. If it is good, well then, you are done.

On this particular evening, I selected whatever I selected and the wine steward informed me that the 1967 Duhart-Milon-Rothschild was really a better choice, so that's what I had. This story doesn't get any more interesting than this, unfortunately. I had had this particular wine only once before, at the house of a very rich friend who brought it along to drink in the car on the way to a baseball game. I had no idea, initially, if he was bringing along some junk wine, or if he ordinarily treated good wine as if it were a jug wine, except that the wine was a 1967 and of sufficient age and good enough year to be quite fine, which it was. After this experience I now had some idea of my friend's respect for both wine and money, but then, for him, this probably was a cheap wine.

In any case, I now had two experiences with this wine, from two quite different scripts.

Now, let's jump to four years later. I am no longer living in Paris. In fact, I have moved to Chicago, and am busy trying out the good restaurants in town, of which there are quite a few. I am trying out Le Français, a restaurant with a reputation as one of the best in Chicago and perhaps one of the best in America. It also has the reputation of being a stuff-a-thon, which doesn't bode too well, since the object behind eating well is tasting new and interesting tastes rather than a lot of the same taste. Nevertheless, off we went. The food was fine, if not memorable. It was a good place to have a nice meal and be reminded of France.

What I do remember was the wine. As in most fancy restaurants in the United States, the wine list of Le Français is wildly overpriced. I hate to spend more than fifty dollars for a bottle of wine at a fancy restaurant. In fact, I hate to spend even fifty dollars. As I said, I look for the error of the wine list, but I also look to get the wine for free. This is a bit tricky. There are a variety of ways to do it, but they all boil down to the same thing.

Wine stewards in America are a lonely lot. If they work in a restaurant that keeps a large wine list, they are usually in charge of assembling that list, which means that they are primarily wine purchasers. They work hard at getting a good price, at an auction, or from someone's cellar. They make sure that they have enough so that they won't run out. If they stock a particular wine, they try to have a variety of years available. They taste the wine and need to know what's ready and what's not ready. They make sure that their wines are properly stored. Mostly they plan ahead for years at a time, buying wine now that no one will drink for ten years. In short, they work hard at what they do, need to be very expert, and, above all, really appreciate wine. They care about the bottles and, in general, are proud of their cellars.

In a three-star restaurant in France, all this work is appreciated. Having visited Georges Blanc near Lyon a number of times, I have spoken at length with the wine steward there, who is English. He relishes finding an odd bottle in a farmhouse somewhere, spends his time with the other wine stewards at equivalent restaurants in Lyon talking shop, and in general works enormously long days, serving lunch and dinner and shopping beforehand. He takes his job seriously and is well appreciated for it. He is written about in guide books, gets lots of job offers, and is rather pleased with himself.

But in Chicago, things are different. The wine steward at Le Français may not have to work quite as hard as his counterpart in Lyon, but, at least, the Lyon sommelier doesn't have to hear, ten times a night, in response to his request for the wine order, "A nice white wine, not too expensive."

In general, Americans don't know much about wine. They have a preference for white wine because it is rather bland and requires little expertise to order. They have been sold a bill of goods about white wine with fish and red wine with meat, which might make some sense if no fish ever had a sauce on it. Since they don't care for wine all that much, they are happy to drink cheap wine.

Wine stewards in America also have to put up with the opposite problem. There are many businessmen on expense accounts who want to impress their customers. For these people, wine lists are full of 1959 Mouton-Rothschild at one thousand dollars a bottle. Wine stewards have a problem with such people. They happily take their money, of course, but the stewards love these rare bottles and they hate to see them drunk by someone who probably isn't going to appreciate them.

So, all in all, the wine steward in America is a lonely and frustrated man. And, this is how I get free wine.

It's not that I am always trying for free wine. Mostly what I am trying to do is find the best wine at the best price. But I also am looking for something I haven't tried before, or something rare that I have never seen before and might be peculiar to this wine list. For me, reading the wine list is an adventure. My dinner companions need to find someone else to talk to for a while.

Now, as I said, the wine list of Le Français is, as is quite usual for such restaurants, wildly overpriced. Wines that one might pay fifty dollars for at a restaurant with a great wine list that is not overpriced, such as Anthony's Pier 4 in Boston, are one hundred and fifty at Le Français. The only wine I could find even near fifty dollars of a vintage that was both good and ready to drink now was a 1971 Duhart-Milon-Rothschild.

When the wine steward came over, I gave him my opinion of the wine list. I told him that his list was extensive, well thought out, and fun to read, but not useful for the ordinary non-millionaire. I said that the only error I could find was possibly the 1971 Duhart for seventy dollars. He assured me that this was not an error at all, that, in fact, the wine had died a long time ago.

At this point, having established that I knew and appreciated wine by making a variety of comments about which ones on his list I liked but remarking on the difference between what I had paid for them previously and what he was asking for them, I entered phase two of the game. If I insisted that I knew more than he did about wine, this would be wrong for two reasons. First, I don't. Second, the idea is to get him to want to help me, a poor guy who loves but can't afford great wine.

I ask for his help. With a twinkle in his eye he asks me how much I want to spend. I say, "Fifty, I had hoped; in any case no more than seventy." He says: "How about a 1966 Branaire-Ducru?" I say: "Still drinking well?"

Now, I have studied the list. This is a $150 bottle for sure. I ask him how much and he says $70. "How come?" I ask. He says he bought ten cases a while back, but that people at Le Français don't usually order wine of this sort (old but not fancy), so he is stuck. I ask if he will sell me a case when I get settled in Chicago, and he says sure.

The wine was great; 1966 was a great Bordeaux year for non-rich people, good but not as special as some years surrounding it, so not as expensive as it might be some twenty-odd years later. During the meal, the 1971 Duhart showed up. The wine steward, seeing that I was loving the 1966 Branaire, wanted to prove to me he had made the right choice, so he brought the 1971 Duhart for us both to try. We drank it and discussed it. He had been quite right. Wine stewards usually are.

On the other hand, you must be careful that you are actually talking to the wine steward. Not too long after this I visited Café Provençal, which is possibly the best restaurant in Chicago. The wine list there is pricey but nowhere near as pricey as Le Français. I picked three possibilities and asked the wine steward which one he suggested of the three. He was out of two of them, which happens frequently when I order wine. This is sort of the booby prize for wine experts, finding the wine that was so underpriced that everyone who knows wine has already drunk up. Nevertheless, we found something to drink and, in the process, I got some tastes of some special bottles that a customer had brought in that the wine steward thought I might appreciate.

The next time I went back, however, the wine steward was not to be found. In his place was the owner, who responded to my help-me-select-one-of-these question with, well, it depends on what you like and what you are eating, a remark that is useless if you are at dinner with a number of people who are eating different things and in any case misses the point. She went on to describe the differences in the wine, which it was obvious I was quite aware of. What I wanted to know was which one tasted best for what it was, right now, today, but she hadn't drunk them, only bought them. To play the wine game properly, the other player must really like to drink wine.

The next time I went to Le Français, as you might imagine, I asked the steward for the 1966 Branaire and told him I was ready to buy a case now. But, alas, Le Français had been sold. The steward was the same, the cellar was the same, but the policy was different. The wine steward was now only the caretaker, not the buyer and seller of the wines. He no longer had any control of the situation. So sad. It is fun playing the wine game at a great cellar.

It is also fun playing the wine game at a mediocre cellar. On a recent trip to Milan, my hosts, upon discovering that I knew about wine, decided to take me to a special wine restaurant that they knew. They prefaced my visit by telling the owner about the wine-loving visitor from New York who was arriving.

The wine list was presented with a flourish. I selected some older wines, as is my habit, following the general rule of thumb I described previously: Order the oldest, cheapest wine on the list. If it isn't any good, they will tell you; if they don't tell you, and it is bad, send it back.

I tried a variety of older Italian wines (there were a lot of us). Some weren't so good and I got into a long conversation with the owner on the storability of older Italian wines. He claimed that Italian wines didn't age well. I claimed that a 1970 ought to be good to drink if it had been stored properly. All this was done in good fun, with translators jumping into the conversation at every turn. In the end, the owner said that the best wine was something I hadn't ordered, and my host said that he thought the best Italian wine was Venegazzu, a wine I enjoy a lot but is certainly not as good as Sassicaia. The result was that I walked out of the restaurant carrying three bottles of wine, one I had liked, the one I should have ordered, and a Venegazzu, all gifts of the management.

This kind of thing can happen anywhere, even at La Côte Basque in New York. It was my wife's birthday and she was a little drunk before our meal had started. I was still reading the wine list when she demanded to see the chef. She had read in a guide book that La Côte Basque treated you quite differently if they knew you and that the food was spotty when the chef wasn't around. In demanding to meet him she was killing two birds with one stone.

He appeared in ten minutes. I was still reading the list. (It was a long list.) Unfortunately, Diane decided at this moment that she had nothing to say to the chef whatsoever. She was, after all, only trying to establish that he was actually there. So I engaged him in chef talk, where he had trained, where he liked to eat in France, what famous chefs had eaten at La Côte Basque recently and what he had made for them—stuff like that. Then, I complained about the wine list. I don't always complain about the list, of course, but there is quite often something to complain about.

This time the problem was that I had decided to order a Burgundy and the Burgundies on this list were all listed without their *négociant* (the buyer-packager-shipper of the wine), which is kind of like listing Bordeaux without the château. When I pointed this out, the chef apologized and said he would take care of it, which meant, in this case, that a hundred-dollar Burgundy arrived gratis. Complaining has its virtues.

You might wonder why I am telling you all this. Do I just like telling stories about how I get free wine? Well, yes, I do, actually. But the real question is how I find the stories to tell. Do I just say *free wine* to my head and off it goes searching for stories with that label?

I started this discussion at Taillevent, in the last chapter. Eating at Taillevent reminded me of the wine I ordered, which reminded me of other occasions in which I had had that wine, which reminded me of having gotten that wine for free, which reminded me of other times that I had gotten wine for free. We don't search for stories to tell, they just come to mind. The answer to *well, how does that happen*? is also the answer to the problem that I ended that last chapter with, namely the relationship between script failure, recognition, confusions, memory, and learning.

When the maitre d' at Taillevent swiped Diane's fork when she tried to taste something from someone else's plate, I stored away that experience. When she said that she liked the chestnut puree and another one was produced instantly, I recorded this information. When the wine steward suggested the 1975 Duhart, I drank and remembered. The question is: Where did I put these memories?

The answer has to be different in each case. Here's why: When I want to go to another three-star restaurant, I want to be reminded of Taillevent. I want to expect that maitre d's will change my fork and supply infinite puree. But, I also want to know exactly where and when to expect this. I should expect it at Taillevent. I might expect it at Georges Blanc. I should not expect it at Louis' Lunch. This constant adjusting and honing of expectations is very important for learning, but—and this is an important but—it would be very sad if we had to understand every event that deeply. We do not really spend that much time worrying about these things. They just happen. The issue is: how?

One clue to how is to consider the issue of the wine. When I taste 1975 Duhart for the first time, I need to store information about this experience someplace in memory. If I store it as part of the Taillevent script, there will be problems later on. I might see some in a wine store and not recognize it as something I have tasted, for example. To recognize it as itself, I must store it with a label such as: 1975 Duhart. But suppose that I then do recognize it that way. I would also want to recall where I had had it. So some tie to Taillevent must exist in memory as well. Now suppose I go to a wine-tasting party, and someone brings a wine that tastes like the 1975 Duhart. I want to be able to recall the Duhart in order to make the comparison. So some mental labels must also be about taste, color, smell, and so on. Now also suppose that I want to remember the baseball game I went to where we drank 1967 Duhart in the car. I would have to have a great deal of information just about the concept of Duhart. Now further suppose that I had gotten a 1971 Duhart for free. I would want information about getting wine for free to come to mind so that I can compare this experience with other times that I had gotten wine for free. Now further suppose that I was in an auto parts store and wanted to get a certain part for free. Might I not want to use the information that I had gathered about how to get wine for free to see if it worked in an auto parts store?

To make all this happen effectively, the basic unit of storage in memory could not possibly be the script. If drinking 1975 Duhart were stored with respect to the entire situation in which it occurred, it would be rather difficult to retrieve it under other circumstances. If, on the other hand, the scene of ordering and drinking the 1975 were stored as a unit in memory, that unit might be accessible whenever it was needed. It might be labeled in a variety of ways: as part of *Taillevent*, as part of *tasting wine*, and as part of *experiences with Duhart*. The most important part of this arrangement is that it makes learning possible.

When I learn something about how to get wine for free, when I have a good conversation with a wine steward and something better than I expected comes out of it, I cannot afford to store this experience away as a part of the Taillevent script or the Le Français script. I must recall it later when something like it happens, so that I can be reminded of it. I need to be reminded of it so that I can compare the two experiences and form a new generalization, and, hence, a new set of expectations, from the combination of the two experiences. In order to learn, I need to compare. I need to know if this new experience is totally unique or if it is in some way like something that has happened to me before. But one can have experiences that are like each other and be in entirely different scripts. Because this is the case, reminding must be cross-contextual. It must be possible to learn from the combination of two superficially different experiences that are somehow the same.

I was walking along the streets of Chicago one day and I stopped to observe a building being knocked down. It was quite fascinating to watch, and as I was quite close and basically the only one watching, I enjoyed spending some time observing it carefully. A large beam was giving the operator of the wrecking machine particular trouble. It was standing straight up, three stories high, and had wedged itself in the rubble in such a way that it just would not go down, no matter how many times the wrecker swung his iron ball into it. Suddenly, I found myself thinking of Spain. I was seated at a bullfight, with two women, the wives of my hosts on that particular occasion, the husbands having refused to go to the bullfight, having the bullfight explained to me in French, as neither woman spoke English. The women liked the bullfights for two reasons. First, they liked to watch the matadors. They loved their bodies and they loved their elegance and grace. Second, I was told, killing the bull was an art and therefore could be appreciated by how well it was performed. The death of the bull was a foregone conclusion; these women did not fret over that. They worried about whether the killing would be done well. And, in fact, one particular bull was not killed well at all. The bull wouldn't go down, no matter how many times he was stabbed by the matador. My companions had loved this matador when he first appeared, but by the end, they were revolted by him.

And, suddenly, on the streets of Chicago, I found myself thinking of bullfights. The concrete beam became a brave bull, refusing to go down. The wrecker lost face in my eyes for his inability to execute a graceful kill. I felt sorry for the beam and sorry for the wrecker.

All this was quite ridiculous, I realized an instant later. Yet I found myself pondering, nevertheless, the art of doing something well versus the accomplishment of the actual goal. An interesting thought. Another victory for the phenomenon of reminding.

Now we can see why there were recognition confusions in Bower's experiments. People recalled the scene of the woman in the waiting room, but they lost the context, or script, in which that scene was embedded. This happens because scenes, either visual scenes or scenes imagined in the mind's eye, are the basic units in memory.

These scenes can be put together into combinations of scenes. These combinations come in well-known forms. So the restaurant script is really a collection of well-known scenes: for example, the ordering scene, the getting-seated scene, the paying-the-check scene, the tasting-the-wine scene, and so on. What we know about restaurants is what scenes they might include. What we know about scenes is the large number of scripts in which they might fit. This is a key point.

The paying-the-check scene can be part of restaurants, to be sure, but doctors may also demand payment upon leaving, as do stores of all sorts. The process is basically the same in each case, and what one learns about the validity of one's credit card, for example, is useful to know no matter whom one is paying. To generalize effectively, what is learned in one scene within a script must be available when that scene comes up again, even if it comes up in a different script.

So when the label of destroying an object by repeated bashing comes up, when I find myself characterizing a situation that I am viewing in that way, I need to be reminded of other scenes that I may have previously labeled in that way, even if they occurred under entirely different circumstances. The key problem in memory, then, is correctly labeling the scene. Once the 1971 Duhart arrived at Le Français, the scene became a *getting-the-wine-for-free* scene. It was still an *eating-at-a-fancy-restaurant* scene and an *ordering-the-wine* scene as well. Further, there also had to be, as a subpart of the *ordering-the-wine* scene, an *ordering-the-wine-at–Le Français* scene, so that the second time I was there I could expect the 1966 Branaire at a good price and so that I will not expect this the next time I eat at Le Français (although I probably will try nonetheless).

The mind has to have multiple labeling schemes for its various units. Scenes are labeled in terms of the scripts they relate to, but they are also labeled in terms that are rather idiosyncratic. If I see particular scenes as being examples of the work of aliens who are out to get me, then that is how I see them. The important thing about the creation of a workable memory is that the labels that one uses must be consistent. Correctness has nothing to do with it. So, as long as I consistently use the alien label, other scenes will come to mind that have been labeled in that way. This allows one to gather similar events and create generalizations from their similarities. But similarities are in the eyes of the beholder. What I see as the fun of getting wine for free, you might see as an example of outrageous behavior.

Thus, I have a great many wine labels, where you might not

have them. I have many three-star restaurant labels that allow me to make predictions about which food will be good where and what the service will be like and so on. There really is no one restaurant script. There are infinite restaurant scripts possible from the combination of one's own experiences.

The key part of this whole process is reminding. Every time we are reminded of some experience by some other experience, the value is in the potential for learning. We cannot remember every experience that ever happens to us. Instead we remember the exceptions, the oddities, the events that did not conform to expectations. We have standard scenes, our expectations about what happens when the wine steward comes over to take our order, for example. These expectations build up over time by the constant reminding of virtually identical events. One wine-ordering scene looks like another and we gradually merge them all into one generalized set of expectations. But every time something odd happens, we label that event and store it away. When we find ourselves constructing that same label again—presto! up comes the old memory. We are reminded. We then get the chance to modify what we previously thought about wine ordering; often two similar exceptions are reason to revise our expectations. Or we might want to create an entirely new scene, into which we can begin to merge new experiences. The first visit to Taillevent is an exception to the restaurant script, the second ought to remind us of Taillevent itself, and the third ought to make use of the new Taillevent script made up of the Taillevent scenes that we realized were exceptions to those in the normal restaurant script.

In this way, scripts evolve. Scenes change by constant comparison with other scenes. Scenes become packaged by different scripts and are called to mind in different ways. Labels that were once unique, and therefore useful, become old hat, bringing up too many memories and then not enough. Eventually getting the wine for free becomes a script, a package of things to do that usually work, long disassociated from the original events that caused that script to be created and full of memories that are exceptions, times that the standard tricks didn't work, or times that the tricks worked out quite unexpectedly, but wonderfully.

In three of the above experiences, Diane, my wife, was present at dinner. Yet, if I asked her what wine we had at Le Français, or what she thinks of Duhart-Milon-Rothschild, she wouldn't know. Two people can have the same experience, yet encode it differently. We see things in terms of what we have already experienced, and in terms of the problems about which we concern ourselves. Diane likes wine; in fact, she has quite sophisticated knowledge. She knows what tastes she is interested in, but she has no interest in learning one wine from the next. She just doesn't think much about wine.

The structures that one has available in memory embody one's experiences. We understand in terms of the structures that we have available, which reflect how we have understood things in the past. My structures are not hers and vice versa. Because of this we will attend to different aspects of the same experience and remember the same event quite differently.

Ordering Duhart-Milon-Rothschild at Le Français reminded me of Taillevent. What kind of reminding is this? There is no obvious failure here. Basically, there are two possibilities. If the Taillevent ordering of Duhart is encoded in memory as a failure of my normal expectations about ordering wine, the Le Français order would constitute a similar failure, and reminding would occur. On the other hand, ordering Duhart could be encoded in memory as an entity in its own right, apart from knowledge about wine ordering in general. In that case the natural processing of Duhart should lead to the same structure that encoded Taillevent. Use of a structure that has a unique referent (Duhart) will cause one to be reminded of that referent.

Understanding an input means finding the closest approximation in one's past experience to the input and coding it in terms of the previous memory with an index that indicates the difference between the new input and the old memory. Understanding, then, implies using expectation failures driven by prototypical memories or specific memories indexed under prototypical memories. Understanding is reminding (or recognizing, to take that word literally) and reminding is finding the correct memory structure to process an input. Our major problem, then, in formulating a theory of understanding, is to find out what the requisite high-level memory structures might look like.

Children, as we have noted in Schank and Abelson (1977) and as Nelson and Gruendel (1979) show, learn scripts from a very early age. We hypothesize that the basic entity of human understanding is what we have termed the *personal script*. Personal scripts are our private expectations about how things proceed in our own lives on a day-to-day or minute-to-minute basis. In the beginning, a child's world is organized solely in terms of personal scripts, i.e., his private expectations about getting his diaper changed or being fed or going shopping. Such expectations abound for children, and they can be quite vocal when these expectations are violated. The child who has gotten a piece of candy at every grocery store visit will complain wildly when he does not get it at the current grocery store. These expectations are not limited to such positively anticipated experiences, however. Trifles such as taking a different route to the same place or not being placed in the same seat as last time are very important to children and serve as reminders to us of the significance of personal scripts in children's lives.

As time goes on, children begin to notice that other human beings share some, but not all, of their expectations. When a child discovers, for example, that his personal restaurant script is also shared by other people, he can resort to a new method of storage for restaurant information. He can rely on a standardized restaurant script with certain personal markings that store his own idiosyncratic points of view. That is, he can begin to organize his experiences in terms that separate what is peculiar to his experience from what is shared by his culture.

For example, adults know that getting in a car is not part of the restaurant script. However, this may be a very salient feature of a child's personal restaurant script. It is very important for a child to learn that the car experience must be separated from the restaurant experience so that he can recognize a restaurant without having gone there by car and so he can understand and talk about other people's restaurant experiences. Thus, the child must learn to reorganize his memory store according to cultural norms.

Adults do not abandon personal scripts as important organizational entities. We still expect the doorman to say good morning as he opens the door or expect the children to demand to be played with immediately after dinner, or whatever sequences we are used to. We may no longer cry when these things do not happen, but we expect them nonetheless. These expectations pervade our lives just as they did when we were children.

We continue to reorganize information that we have stored indefinitely. New experiences are constantly being reorganized on the basis of similar experiences and cultural norms. The abstraction and generalization process for knowledge acquired through experience is thus a fundamental part of adult understanding. When you order a wine for the first time, everything in that experience is stored either as a single, isolated chunk or in terms of experiences (ordering food, for example) that seem similar. Repeated experiences with the same wine, or other wines, and descriptions of others' experiences with wine stewards serve to reorganize the original information in terms of what is peculiar to your first wine-ordering experience, ordering wine in general, yourself with respect to wine stewards, and so on. The reorganization process never stops. When similarities between wine ordering and buying cheese in a cheese shop are seen, a further reorganization can be made in terms of *ordering specialty items where the seller knows far more than the buyer.*

What we are proposing, then, is that a lot of the knowledge that we would previously have stored as part of the restaurant script is, in reality, part of other memory structures that are used in understanding a story involving a visit to a restaurant. Such a proposal has two obvious ramifications. First, this view implies that scripts do not exist as an inviolate unit. While it may be possible to collect all the expectations that we have about a complex event into one complex structure that contains everything we know about restaurants, such a structure does not actually exist in memory. Instead, the expectations are distributed in smaller, sharable units. Second, if a diverse set of memory structures is used for processing a story about a restaurant, and if memory structures are the same as processing structures, then it follows that a story about a visit to a restaurant will get broken up by memory into several distinct pieces. That is, whatever happens in driving to the restaurant, if it is of interest to memory, will be stored as a modification of what we know about driving, not restaurants. Each event will be processed by, and stored in terms of, the structure that relates most closely to that event.

Such a scheme has the negative effect of forcing us to use a reconstructive memory to help us recall events that have happened to us. (And, of course, we may not be able to reconstruct everything.) But this negative effect is more than outweighed by the powerful advantage of enabling us to learn by generalizing from experiences once we notice their commonalities.

A third important implication is that there must be some memory structures available whose job it is to connect other memory structures together. In order to reconstruct what has happened to us, and in order to have the relevant structures available for processing when they are needed, memory structures must exist that tie other structures together in the proper order. Even though we have learned to disassociate memories about *wine ordering* from those specific to *restaurant visits*, we still need to know that restaurant visits might involve wine ordering.

Information about how memory structures are ordinarily linked in frequently occurring combinations is held in a *memory organization packet*, or MOP.

In order to account for reconstructive memory, and the ability to generalize and learn from past experience, structures such as MOPs must exist in the mind. As a memory structure, the role of a MOP is to provide a place to store new inputs. As a processing structure, the role of a MOP is to provide expectations that enable the prediction of future inputs or inference of implicit events on the basis of previously encountered, structurally similar, events. A MOP processes new inputs by taking the aspects of those inputs that relate to that MOP and interpreting those aspects in terms of the past experiences most closely related to them. Many different high-level memory structures can be relevant at any given time in processing an input, i.e., any of a number of different MOPs may be applicable at one time.

However, memories are actually held in scenes, not MOPS. Scenes are general structures that describe how and where a particular set of actions takes place. WINE ORDERING and AIRPORT RENT-A-CAR COUNTER are possible scenes. Scripts (in this narrower formulation of them) embody specific predictions connected to the more general scene that dominates them. Thus, an individual might have an *ORDERING WINE AT LE FRANÇAIS* scene that differs in some way from the more general WINE ORDERING scene. Scenes, therefore, can point to scripts that embody specific aspects of those scenes. I was trying to develop a script about wine ordering at Le Français after one trial, but found that I couldn't repeat the experience. I remembered the first experience clearly, but it is doubtful that Diane did. She was not interested in creating this new script or elaborating on this particular scene for the obvious reason that she never orders the wine.

MOPs differ from scenes and scripts in the amount of knowledge they cover and the generality of that knowledge. A script must be limited to a sequence of actions that take place in one physical setting. Similarly, a scene is setting-bounded. But a MOP can contain information that covers many settings. Furthermore, a MOP has a purpose that is not readily inferable from each of the scenes or scripts that it contains. Because of this, memory confusions can take place when it is forgotten which MOP a particular scene-based memory was connected to. This is like remembering what you did without remembering exactly why you were doing it. Some examples of this include remembering an incident that took place while you were driving and being unable to recall where you were driving to, or remembering a waiting room without being able to recall exactly why you were there.

The primary job of a MOP in processing new inputs is to provide relevant memory structures that will in turn provide expectations necessary to understand what is being received. Thus MOPs are responsible for filling in implicit information about what events must have happened but were unstated. At least three MOPs are relevant to processing, memory, and understanding of what ordering wine entails. They are: M-RESTAURANT, M-ADVICE-GETTING, and M-CONTRACT.

Each of these MOPs organizes scenes and scripts relevant to the processing of any story involving wine ordering. Any given action while ordering wine might be done because it is expected due to the MOP that is driving the action. When the wine steward suggests a wine, it is because he has assumed that his role of advice giver expects this action of him. When I respond with a discussion of exactly how much he is charging me, I am both haggling and implicitly acknowledging that we are about to enter into a contract. The primary function of any MOP is to let an understander know the role of any given action with respect to his expectations, thus providing the correct sequencing of the scenes that provide the appropriate expectations for use in processing.

In order to create the proper set of expectations, we must recognize what MOPs are applicable. How do we do this? M-RESTAURANT has information attached to it concerning what other MOPs might also be active when it is active. In addition to what we know about restaurants, we also know quite a bit about why the actors in the various scenes of that MOP do what they do. Knowing this allows us to predict further actions not explicitly part of M-RESTAURANT. It is in no sense a requisite part of M-RESTAURANT, for example, that people may pay for the service they get. Services can, of course, be free (as in a soup kitchen). Included as part of M-RESTAURANT, then, is information that, in this person's experience, the MOP M-CONTRACT is activated when M-RESTAURANT is activated. That is, we know that an implicit contract has been made by the diner and proprietor, and trouble will ensue if the diner doesn't pay. All of this information is part of M-CONTRACT, not M-RESTAURANT. In my M-RES-

TAURANT, the WINE ORDERING scene is always called into play, as is my particular version of M-ADVICE-GETTING, which is called up by the WINE ORDERING scene. Diane's versions of these MOPs are quite different.

A MOP carries with it at least two kinds of information: an ordered set of scenes (or place holders for scenes) and other MOPs that frequently occur with it. A MOP serves to organize a set of scenes and scripts commonly associated with a goal in memory.

A scene defines a setting, an instrumental goal, and actions that take place in that setting in service of that goal. These actions are defined in terms of specific and generalized memories relating to that setting and goal. For example, *paying in a restaurant and getting your baggage in an airport* are scenes. As long as there is an identifiable physical setting and a goal being pursued with that setting, we have a scene. First, we have physical information about what the scene looks like. Information about what was in one's line of sight can be part of one's remembrance of a scene. Second, we have information about the activities that go on in a scene.

The most important aspect of the structures organized by a MOP is that they be general enough to be used by other MOPs. This is a key point. Scenes and scripts organized by one MOP can also be organized by others. For example, the PAY scene is used by a great many MOPs in addition to M-RESTAURANT. If you lost your wallet, you might attempt to figure out where you had it last. You might remember putting it down near a cash register while paying. The problem then would be to differentiate one PAY event from another. The fact that this is difficult indicates that PAY is a shared structure.

There is another way in which sharing memory structures can cause memory confusion. An event that takes place in WINE OR-DERING will be stored in the WINE ORDERING scene and thus will be linked to M-RESTAURANT. An event that takes place in a WINE ORDERING may easily become disassociated from the particular restaurant that scene took place in. A person may be able to recall that a particular wine was ordered under certain circumstances but forget the restaurant that the event occurred in.

So the disadvantage of sharing memory structures is that it creates possibilities for memory confusion. This is outweighed, however, by the advantage gained in allowing generalizations. At the cost of being unable, on occasion, to remember the restaurant in which a particular wine was ordered, or where a certain food was tasted, we gain the advantage of having all the knowledge we

have acquired about particular foods or wines from all our restaurant visits, or from all the situations in which we have had to
order anything, available to us to deal with a new situation.

New events that we experience do not enter memory as a unit.
Various knowledge sources are used in the processing of any event.
As I order a wine, I learn about that wine, ordering in that restaurant, interactions with certain types of people, the feelings that
I have that particular day, and a great many other issues. No single
event is only one thing at one time. During the processing of such
an event, therefore, the knowledge sources that come into play
are changed by the event. What we know about each subject that
is germane to the event is altered by new information about that
subject. Any event that we experience provides such new information. Since a new event carries information of many different
types, and since the whole experience of spending an evening at
a restaurant, for example, has many different events within it, this
implies that an evening at a restaurant will be *broken up*, with its
various pieces being assigned different locations in memory depending on the knowledge used to process them.

According to this view, then, memory would seem to have a
set of knowledge structures, each of which contains pieces of various episodes. However, it seems unlikely that this is exactly the
case. Under some circumstances when an episode breaks into
pieces, each piece is useless in retrieving the other pieces of that
episode. At other times, an entire episode is retrievable through a
piece of that episode.

This difference is related to the problem of reconstructive memory. Consider an argument that one has in a restaurant. Is it possible to retrieve the food or the wine when thinking about the
particulars of the argument? The answer depends upon the re-
constructibility of the episode given a scene from that episode. An
episode is reconstructible if there are events or objects present in
a scene from that episode that in some sense depend on prior or
subsequent scenes. Such dependence can be of two types. The
dependence may occur because a particular element is present in
the given scene that directly correlates with a specific element in
a prior or subsequent scene. Or, the dependence may occur because
general information is available by which the prior and subsequent
scenes can be *figured out* (perhaps the argument was about the
wine).

In the latter case, we have an instance of the use of MOPs.
MOPs provide, among other things, the temporal precedence

among scenes in a standard situation. We know that an airplane trip involves arrival at the airport, followed by checking in, followed by waiting in the waiting area and so on. This information is all part of M-AIRPLANE TRIP.

We can use this information to reconstruct episodes based on the memory of some portion of them. That is, given a scene, by examining a MOP that it might belong to, we can infer what other scenes must also have occurred. When any memory structure is considered as a possible holder of a memory that we are seeking, we can search that structure by using indices that were found in the initial scene. Events are broken apart in terms of the structures employed in understanding them, are stored in terms of those structures in memory, and are reconstructible by various search techniques. Events are not remembered as wholes but as pieces.

The first time I met Jean-François we ate at Laserre, a former three-star restaurant that was now a two-star. The food was as one might expect at a two-star, so I don't remember it. What I do remember was the roof opening and closing in the middle of dinner, not something Taillevent had taught me to expect. I also remember the wine, a 1962 L'Enfant Jésus that Jean-François, who is a Burgundy man, had ordered. I didn't drink Burgundy much until I met Jean-François, so I had very few expectations about the wine. I remember drinking it, but I remember the taste poorly because my comparison set, the wines I might have been reasonably reminded of, was so impoverished. But I have eaten at a lot of restaurants, and the roof always stayed put in those. So I will be reminded of Laserre every time I drink L'Enfant Jésus or see a roof open up. I am ready to learn from these experiences. But I will not be able to learn from these experiences unless I can recall them. I must be able to find Laserre or L'Enfant Jésus if I need them. This turns out to be rather difficult to do.

It is much easier to learn about restaurants, because I know so much about them already. It is also easy to learn about entirely new things, such as restaurant ceilings that open, because we can create new categories for them. But to learn about new things that are small variations on old things, that violate no expectations, is rather tricky. To do this we must develop MOPs that allow remindings to take place. This means understanding how the new experience differs from other similar experiences. Reminding is a great facilitator of learning, but reminding will not take place unless, when something tastes very good, we wonder why. We cannot remember a bullfight as a valiant triumph against dying unless we thought about it that way at the time. In general, I remember when I got a particular wine that was good, for a particularly good price. Why do I remember such events? Because I care enough about them to think about them. Thinking produces indices and indices produce remindings. Remindings encourage us to think about the relationship between what has just happened and what we were reminded of. In this way, thinking causes more thinking.

CHAPTER 8

Cases, Suitcases, and Reasoning Spaces

I usually try to arrange my travels so that when I arrive at the airport, I can go straight onto the plane. Carrying little baggage, having my ticket in order, and arriving minutes before the flight is scheduled to depart facilitate this process. On one sad trip, however, all this was not possible. The Spanish government—well, actually the Catalan government; they are sticky about such things over there—had sent me a ticket to Barcelona so that I could give a lecture. Never one to miss the opportunity for a good meal and having been warned about Spanish food, I decided to stop over in Paris on the way. My problem was that my ticket needed to be rewritten, and as the ticket had not been generated by my travel agent, the only party who could rewrite it was TWA at the airport. This meant arriving early for my flight to Paris.

So here I am, with a reservation on the eight o'clock plane to

Paris, and a ticket in hand to Barcelona with a stop in Madrid (because the TWA flight goes that way, not my choice). It is 6:30, which is so early I am sweating from just thinking about being in an airport all that time. I hand my ticket to the lady at the ticket counter, tell her I need it rewritten to include a stop in Paris, and her response is, "Impossible." "Not impossible," I respond, "in fact, quite possible. In fact, quite ordinary. What do you mean, impossible?" She says something about the ticket having been issued not by TWA but by some Spanish travel agency, and so we have to send my ticket back to Spain to be rewritten. As it is now 6:45, she probably doesn't have time to do this.

Of course, one always has an out in these cases: Yell for the supervisor. In this case, I know that I am on pretty safe ground since TWA already said they could do this when my secretary talked to them on the phone, and, although airlines can behave rather oddly some of the time, they rarely turn away business. They know how to rewrite tickets because they are usually re-writing them in such a way as to make money in the process. So I trudge off to the supervisor, who is, needless to say, on the other side of the terminal.

The supervisor was a pleasant woman who gave me one of those *you-must-be-kidding* looks that made it clear that she can't find good help these days either, and the two of us trudged back to the original lady, who now had another customer. Her words to her charge were "of course, you can do it," which left the original lady and me knowing we had a problem. It wasn't that she thought that a ticket couldn't be rewritten, I realized, it was that she thought that *she* couldn't rewrite a ticket, and clearly she was right.

Her first remark to me was "of course, it will cost more," which is the kind of remark that makes you feel that she was going to get me for exposing her ignorance. Of course it was going to cost more. It would be nice if they gave you a cut rate, should you only agree to take a side trip to Paris.

I then watched her play with her computer for half an hour while she presumably calculated the new fare. I say "presumably" because she announced, "You owe us one hundred dollars." Now think of that! The price on my ticket read 25,647 pesetas (I am guessing here, but it was something like that) and the cost of the extra leg of the flight was exactly one hundred dollars, no more and no less. What a mathematical whiz this lady must have been to get it to all work out so evenly. A horrible thought crossed my mind: Do you think she made it up? What a way to run an airline.

Since my guess was that the extra fare she was going to make up was higher than the one she actually made up, I gladly paid it and happily received the new ticket, with twenty minutes left to spare before my flight. For some reason of vague distrust, I looked at the ticket. She got me to Paris on the right flight, but the next section of the ticket read Paris-Madrid and then Madrid-Barcelona. I pointed out that I already had a reservation on a non-stop flight from Paris to Barcelona, and I asked why she had written the ticket this way. She replied that as I had stopped in Madrid on my original routing, she assumed that I had wanted to stop there this time, too. I must have missed some attraction in the Madrid airport, I thought, since neither my original ticket nor her new one gave me more than an hour to change planes. I pointed out that I liked my own arrangements better and asked her to try again one more time. She said that that would be unnecessary, and that I could just use the ticket she had given me for the Paris-Barcelona flight.

Suddenly, I realized what was going on here. I had this image of me handing the Paris gate agent a ticket to Madrid for a flight to Barcelona, which I would have found very funny to watch if it had not been me who was trying to do this. The problem here was that she had no such image herself. I asked her if she had ever flown anywhere with a ticket to someplace else, and she admitted, as I had suspected, that she had never flown anywhere at all.

People who need to reason about things are not very good at trying new things. They reason from old things. They reason, as the Harvard law and business schools will happily tell you, from cases. In order to reason from cases, you must have some to reason from. What we had here was a particularly dreadful example of what happens when someone has no script, no case, nothing. Reasoning from first principles is darned tricky for the swiftest minds. When a reasoner is in trouble, he has to find the best case he can find, even if it is one that doesn't match the current situation, and apply whatever principles he can from the first case to the new one. When you get on a plane for the first time and your only prior experience with public transportation is Greyhound, then you will have to assume that planes are like buses. And, in some way, they are. You must do a partial match from the current case to the one in your memory that looks the most like it. It won't be perfect, but it's the best chance you have to predict and cope with whatever will happen next.

Our TWA lady didn't seem to have any prior cases to match. She didn't get reminded of the last time a similar thing had happened to her. My situation matched nothing she knew about initially, so she sent me away with an authoritarian *impossible*. When that didn't work, she matched two prior situations that she knew about, fare raising and simple ticket rewriting. She clearly wasn't familiar with very many of the nuances of either of these situations, so she faked it. Actually, when it comes to partial matching, we are all faking it most of the time. If you've never been to a three-star restaurant, you can match only to the best you have been to and hope you don't embarrass yourself by missing too much. You might, for example, demand to smell the cork of a bottle of wine, since you have come to expect that in a fancy American restaurant. How are you to know that a three-star restaurant is unlikely to let you come near the cork unless the bottle is very old, and the state of the cork is in question?

When you can't reason from a substantially similar case, you do the best you can and hope to muddle by. The real issue in such circumstances, which arises when the case you have selected by partial match to serve as your baseline experience is going to fail you, is whether you will recognize that it has and be able to recover. Clearly the TWA lady didn't recognize that her partial match was failing her, or at least didn't know what to do when it failed. Of course, you have to give her credit for the hundred-dollar part, but I suspect she got caught by somebody at TWA for that one later on. In any case, reasoning depends upon having cases to reason from. Matches are rarely perfect, so intelligence in the matching business is in knowing when one can substitute what for what. When the recipe calls for paprika, will cayenne pepper do?

We need to remember cases, especially paradigmatic cases—those that are somehow critical in influencing our perception of a certain type of thing for years to come, in order to build up a base of experiences to reason from when we encounter something like them in the future and want to be able to base our behavior on what happened in the prior situation. If what we did last time worked out, we want to do it again. If what we did last time didn't work, we want to do something else. And, we want to remember the outcome of this new situation so we can keep on improving.

Memory of this type, which concentrates on our own actions so that we can keep learning from them, is very basic to survival. Dogs and cats have this kind of memory as well. They recall actions that have worked out well for them—following a certain route or rolling over or purring—and they recall those that have failed—knocking over the garbage can or going near the house with the big grouchy dog. They may not always be able to modify their behaviors so easily because they may have other concerns when looking for the food in the garbage pail, or they may think they can get away with it. But when the pail falls over, if they have been punished before, they hit the road.

What do they do when they knock over something that isn't a garbage pail? Should they run or not? They might just get ready to run and see what happens. They are trying to learn. The method of learning that they are using is generalization from prior cases. But which case is appropriate, the one where they got hit or the one where they got laughed at? Knowing the difference between the two, knowing when and how to make a generalization, is at the heart of intelligence. One important role of memory is to provide the right case at the right time to reason from.

Although we reason from prior cases all the time, the method is fraught with peril. Neustadt and May, two Harvard government professors who teach future leaders to reason in affairs of state, cite many examples of reasoning from cases that actually have occurred. My favorite (from *Thinking in Time*) is the *Mayaguez* incident. The *Mayaguez* was an American freighter that carried cargo in Southeast Asia and was seized by the Cambodians. Gerald Ford, who was president at the time, attempted to get back the ship and crew. He was reminded of the *Pueblo* incident, from a few years before.

During all that early period, Ford had the earlier *Pueblo* incident much in his mind. He was to write afterward (in *A Time to Heal*, 1979): "Back in 1968, I remembered, the North Koreans had captured the intelligence ship *U.S.S. Pueblo* in international waters and forced her and her crew into the port of Wonsan. The U.S. had not been able to respond fast enough to prevent the transfer, and as a result, *Pueblo*'s crew had languished in a North Korean prison camp for nearly a year. I was determined not to allow a repetition of that incident."

But as Neustadt and May point out, the *Pueblo* was like the *Mayaguez* only in the fact that they were both Spanish-named, American-owned ships:

The *Pueblo* had been a Navy vessel, not a merchant man. She had carried sensitive intelligence-gathering gear. Her captain and crew knew secrets that North Korean investigators might discover. And there had been little doubt of the North Korean government's deliberately planning the provocation. . . . The *Pueblo* had been a prize in its own right. The *Mayaguez* was not.

Nevertheless, Ford used the *Pueblo* incident as his model and thus decided not to make the same mistakes. He decided to recapture the crew of the *Mayaguez* because we had not attempted to recapture the crew of the *Pueblo*. In the rescue attempt he almost caused a serious disaster, precisely because the incidents were not really very similar at all. Neustadt and May point out many instances of how people in government make decisions by making analogies to prior cases. Their concern is how to evaluate the effectiveness of the analogy. Anyone who wants to rely upon his memory to help him do anything at all also has this concern. How relevant is the memory that just came to mind? Will it help me formulate a plan of action? We all use prior cases to reason with. But we don't always know readily which of our prior cases are the most relevant. Our memories help by finding cases we didn't know we were looking for to use at critical times. Case-based reasoning is not necessarily a conscious process.

A French movie I rather like is called *La Grande Bouffe*. It is the story of a group of gourmets who get together for an eat-a-thon, a perpetual gourmet feast, at the end of which they are all supposed to die, and in fact do. I am often reminded of this movie by events in my own life. I have never eaten myself to death, of course, but I have thought, at times, that I might just do that.

When I was busy starting a software company, my friend Tolya and I traveled in Europe, looking for business. We arrived in Brussels on Saturday morning, and we couldn't wait to have a great French meal. So off we went to stuff ourselves with mussels, a specialty of Brussels, which is also nice because of the rhyme. That night, some potential clients held a party in our honor. We weren't that hungry, but we were guests; so, of course, we ate. At the party, another person interested in our work invited us for "a country lunch" at his home.

The next morning, we arrived to find that our French-speaking host had a Vietnamese wife. We thought this was also very nice since Vietnamese food is quite pleasant. She was an excellent cook, and had made spring rolls, various dumplings, and a variety of

Vietnamese finger foods. We had eaten quite a bit, assuming that this expansive array was lunch, when our hostess asked us to sit down for lunch. We were now served a full French dinner. We didn't have much room for any of it, but again, not wanting to offend, we ate. All along, we knew that a man who might possibly give us a large contract was expecting us for dinner that evening.

We arrived at the restaurant without an iota of appetite. The restaurant was one of those Michelin one-stars, good without being great. We tried to order lightly. We couldn't say we were too full to eat. This was an expensive place, and it would have been awfully rude to arrive without an appetite. Our host, knowing that we really enjoyed French food, apologized for the restaurant, which he assumed had displeased us. He said finding a good restaurant open on Sunday was difficult, and he promised to treat us better the next day at lunch after our business meeting.

Lunch. Now that is a word without meaning in French. The French have never heard of lunch. There are meals, and then there aren't meals. What one eats at noontime is a full three-course meal, and what one eats at nighttime is a full three-course meal as well. How the French manage this constant and prolonged eating without weighing three hundred pounds each has always been a mystery to me. The answer is, I think, that they don't always eat each meal, but when they go out to eat, a meal is a meal.

Our host knew his restaurants. He selected a superb place where the best thing on the menu was foie gras. I really like foie gras or did at the time, so I enjoyed the place a great deal. I was still full from Sunday, but I do like to eat.

I forgot one thing. We had promised a woman who had made some of our business contacts a meal at one of Brussels's great restaurants as recompense for her efforts. This restaurant also specialized in foie gras. We had selected the date for this dinner some time ago—Monday night. So, on we went to dinner. More foie gras. At this point, looking at anything resembling food was difficult, but we ate.

The next day, we had a meeting arranged with the South Belgium planning commission, Belgium's attempt to raise the economic status of the French region of the country. We drove an hour south of Brussels to have our meeting. I didn't feel too well on the trip. I wondered why.

We met and then were told that, naturally, a banquet had been planned. The planning commission had reserved an entire restaurant and arranged a six-course meal for their honored American guests. For lunch! The specialty was foie gras. I tried; I really did. I got through two courses when suddenly I had to get out of that place. Somewhere, on the streets of a little town in South Belgium, are the remains of a lot of geese who died for no particular reason at all. We didn't get the contract.

This experience has become a paradigmatic case for me. I am reminded of it when I overeat, I am reminded of it when I have business lunches and dinners scheduled on a trip to Europe, and I am reminded of it when I eat foie gras. Each time that I am reminded of it, I alter my plans slightly. I avoid scheduling business lunches and dinners on the same day. I never eat foie gras more than once per European trip. I have learned from my experience. Even if I don't change my behavior, I get reminded of that experience anyway, despite the fact that what I really want to do is eat, not remember.

Prior cases primarily influence planning. When you have to plan something—a trip, a meal, a route—the easiest way to do so is to copy a previous plan that has worked. Computer programmers use this trick all the time. When they write a new program, they start by copying an old one, and they attempt to modify the old to make it do something new. This reasoning method is quite pervasive. Real experts are just individuals with collections of experiences and the ability to find those cases when they need them to help them solve new problems. Although case-based reasoning may not be a conscious process, it is a very important part of our thinking ability. We have built a number of case-based reasoning programs in our lab, which created new football plays from old ones, mimicked judges in their sentencing behavior by comparing new cases to old ones, and diagnosed lung cancer by comparing new examples of lung tissue to a memory filled with pictures of lung cancers of various types.

When I was encouraging graduate students to work on case-based reasoning, my favorite ploy was to ask them whether they could do something well or knew some field really well. When they told me something that involved knowing a set of cases and adapting those cases in some way for novel circumstances, I encouraged them to model themselves. I was overjoyed one day when Kris Hammond told me that what he did well was cook Chinese food. "You're my boy," I said.

The program that Hammond built was called CHEF. It was an expert on stir-fry cooking and soufflés. The premise behind CHEF was the practical cooking problem that most chefs at home face, namely, *I am home, now let's see what's in the refrigerator that I can cook up into something interesting.* Cookbooks tell you what you could cook if you had the proper ingredients. The intent of CHEF was to tell you what you could cook with what you actually had available. CHEF's goal was to create a new recipe, appropriate to the user's needs, by adapting an old recipe. The idea then was to reason from cases it knew about in order to create what were, in essence, new plans to deal with circumstances differing from those in its library of cases.

The input to CHEF is a list of goals, such as "give me a spicy stir-fry dish with beef and broccoli." The output is a new recipe, based on some old one, modified to meet the input goals. Although the original recipe produced a tasty dish, the new derivative dishes that CHEF created initially could easily have unexpected problems, because different ingredients interact in subtle ways. But CHEF could repair the recipe, because it knew a set of general strategies. It would attempt to analyze what might have gone wrong and proceed to fix it in its next version of the recipe.

CHEF got smarter over time in at least two important ways. First, its case library kept growing as a result of its own efforts. It remembered its new creations and could use them for adapting in new ways. Second, when a failure occurred, CHEF would remember it if the same circumstances were ever encountered again. CHEF could be reminded of its own mistakes in the course of creating a new recipe.

Let's look at an example of CHEF planning for the problem of building a stir-fry dish with beef and broccoli. CHEF has three goals: to have a stir-fried dish, to include beef, and to include broccoli. CHEF searches its memory for a single plan that matches or partially matches as many of the goals as possible. Below is the output that CHEF produces to tell the user what it is doing while it works:

Searching for plan that satisfies
  Include beef in the dish.
  Include broccoli in the dish.
  Make a stir-fry dish.

Found recipe → REC2 Beef-with-Green-Beans

Recipe exactly satisfies goals
  Make a stir-fry dish.
  Include beef in the dish.

Recipe partially matches
    Include broccoli in the dish.

When CHEF finds a reasonably relevant recipe, its next problem is to modify the recipe so that it satisfies whatever goals haven't already been satisfied.

Building new name for copy of Beef-with-Green-Beans
Calling recipe Beef-and-Broccoli

Modifying recipe: Beef-and-Broccoli
to satisfy: Include broccoli in the dish.

Placing some broccoli in recipe Beef-and-Broccoli

—Considering ingredient-critic:
    Before stir-frying an object, chop the object into pieces the size of chunks.
—ingredient-critic applied.

Here, CHEF has decided to modify the recipe it found by substituting broccoli for green beans. When it decided this and was about to start stir-frying in its mind, rather than in the wok, it remembered that stir-fry dishes need small objects, and that broccoli is big. So it adds a step to the original recipe. Here is the new recipe that CHEF first creates:

Beef-and-Broccoli

A half pound of beef
Two tablespoons of soy sauce
One teaspoon of rice wine
A half tablespoon of cornstarch
One teaspoon of sugar
A half pound of broccoli
One teaspoon of salt
One chunk of garlic

Chop the garlic into pieces the size of matchheads.
Shred the beef.
Marinate the beef in the garlic, sugar, cornstarch, rice wine, and soy sauce.
Chop the broccoli into pieces the size of chunks.
Stir-fry the spices, rice wine, and beef for one minute.

Add the broccoli to the spices, rice wine, and beef.
Stir-fry the spices, rice wine, broccoli, and beef for three minutes.
Add the salt to the spices, rice wine, broccoli, and beef.

In cooking, as in life, the best plans rarely work the first time. This recipe is actually not any good. Cooking broccoli causes different problems than cooking green beans. Broccoli gets soggy when it is cooked in the liquid that the beef produces. CHEF discovers the failure by simulating the execution of the plan:

Checking goals of recipe → Beef-and-Broccoli

Recipe → Beef-and-Broccoli has failed goals.

The goal: The broccoli is now crisp is not satisfied.
It is instead the case that: the broccoli is now soggy.

Unfortunately: The broccoli is now a bad texture.
In that: The broccoli is now soggy.

Changing name of recipe Beef-and-Broccoli to Bad-Beef-and-Broccoli

CHEF's first problem is to make sure that this recipe is not taken seriously, so that it doesn't copy it in the future. It then attempts to fix the plan. CHEF knows what steps and states combined to cause the current failure. It also knows which goals were being pursued in taking the actions and creating the states that led to its failure.

Because CHEF has experience with failure, its case library includes not only past successes, but also past failures. Attached to these failures are the tricks it has learned about what things can be fixed in a recipe to make it better. For example, it knows about reordering steps as a way of recovering from the side effects of some steps.

The problem for CHEF, then, as for any intelligent system, is to organize its memory in such a way that it can find what it needs when it needs it. One way of doing this is to compose the labels of past experiences out of the combinations of goals and plans that characterized that experience. In other words, if you remember why you were doing what you were doing and what you did to fix it, when those same goals and plans reappear you can get appropriately reminded. The memory structure that is relevant here we call a side-effect (SE); specifically:

SIDE-EFFECT:DISABLED-CONDITION:CONCURRENT (SE:DC:C)

This is the name of a memory structure related to the interaction between concurrent plans in which a side effect of one violates a precondition of the other. This happens because the side effect of liquid coming from the stir-frying of the beef is disabling a precondition attached to the broccoli stir-fry plan that the pan being used be dry.

Here is what happens next:

Found → SIDE-EFFECT:DISABLED-CONDITION:CONCURRENT SIDE-EFFECT:DISABLED-CONDITION:CONCURRENT has 3 strategies associated with it:
SPLIT-AND-REFORM
ALTER-PLAN:SIDE-EFFECT
ADJUNCT-PLAN

The memory structure SIDE-EFFECT:DISABLED-CONDITION: CONCURRENT has three strategies associated with it. SPLIT-AND-REFORM suggests breaking a problematic step into several separates steps. ALTER-PLAN:SIDE-EFFECT suggests replacing the problematic step with a different plan. ADJUNCT-PLAN suggests adding a new step to counteract the effects of the problematic step. CHEF tries to apply each strategy to the current example. Only SPLIT-AND-REFORM works out:

Applying → SIDE-EFFECT:DISABLED-CONDITION:CONCURRENT to failure it is not the case that: The broccoli is now crisp in recipe Bad-Beef-and-Broccoli

Asking questions needed for evaluating strategy:
SPLIT-AND-REFORM

Asking → Can plan
Stir-fry the sugar, soy sauce, rice wine, garlic, cornstarch, broccoli, and beef for three minutes.
be split and rejoined

Found plan: Instead of doing step:
Stir-fry the sugar, soy sauce, rice wine, garlic, cornstarch, broccoli, and beef for three minutes

substitute:S1 = Stir-fry the broccoli for three minutes.
S2 = Remove the broccoli from the result of action S1.
S3 = Stir-fry the sugar, soy sauce, rice wine, garlic, cornstarch, and beef for three minutes.

S4 = Add the result of action S2 to the result of action S3.
S5 = Stir-fry the result of action S4 for a half minute.

And so, CHEF creates a new recipe. Of course, you are wondering
if this new recipe tastes good. Computers, after all, are not well-
known gourmets. Fortunately, for Hammond, his advisor liked to
eat quite a bit, so he cooked up the dishes that CHEF suggested
from time to time and served them to me.

I wish I could say that Hammond became the owner of a very
well-known inventive Chinese restaurant with a computer chef,
but actually the food just wasn't that good. Hammond had to settle
for being a professor of computer science at a well-known university. Hammond's attempt at a case-based reasoner was very
important, nevertheless, as it taught us about the complexities
involved in actually doing reasoning of this sort by computers or
by people.

Chapter 9

Vintage Indexing

J ean-François and I frequently go to a restaurant in Paris where the wine list is great fun. They have many old bottles, and the prices are rather low, even with the dollar-franc rate being as lousy as it is. Actually we go there for the truffle-egg dish as well, but I'll get to that later. This restaurant has the atmosphere of something from the twenties. In fact, it *is* something from the twenties—hasn't changed a lick. This may well be why the place is full of old bottles at reasonable prices. Restaurant owners don't always think to update their prices. These bottles cost them only a couple of dollars originally after all, probably not even that. When they sell a two-dollar bottle for seventy-five dollars, it seems to them that they have updated their prices. It is great fun to order a 1934 Bordeaux, especially at this restaurant, because not only has one found something rare, but one doesn't really have to pay anything close to what one might have expected. I know most of the good years of Bordeaux; in fact, I know all the years back to 1945 quite well, but 1934? I don't carry around all these massive wine books; 1934 means nothing to me. One thing I can figure about 1934 is that this restaurant was here then, and so were the Nazis shortly after the 1934 bottles arrived—this is one they didn't get. Puts more fun into it in a creepy sort of way.

Anyway, the bottle arrives. We drink. But, how do we know what the thing is supposed to taste like? Well, we have some expectations about what old Bordeaux is like, and this one exceeds our expectations. We both like it a great deal. The point here is merely that it was good enough that the next time I was in Paris, I called Jean-François, and off we went again to this wonderful place.

This time we order the Grand-Puy-Lacoste 1945, which is cheap, but when we are ready to order it, we notice a star next to it on the wine list. We ask what the star means, and they say it means that, if we don't like the wine, it's "our tough" (as my teenage daughter used to say)—they won't replace it.

Now you never know the policy on the replacement of bad bottles at a restaurant, partially because your idea of a bad bottle might not be the same as the management's. Good restaurants stand by their bottles, but you can't always count on them to replace them if you disagree with their taste. Fancy restaurants as a rule will replace them, but this is sort of a mom-and-pop affair, and who knows? Well, now we know. They will replace them if there is no star next to the name on the wine list. So we order the Grand-Puy-Lacoste 1947, not as good a year as 1945 but pretty good, nevertheless. It is the same price, but no star.

We taste it. It doesn't taste great. It doesn't taste bad. It tastes, well, different. We discuss it with each other. We discuss it with the waiter. He discusses it with the manager. The boss, we discover, is not around. This matters.

One problem is that it is cloudy. We send it back. Cloudy. Ha! They must have shaken it up on the way here from the cellar. And no star. "Give us another." The waiter agrees that it is cloudy. No manager to ask, and why should he? Guess who gets to drink the returned bottles? They don't get sent back to the manufacturer for a refund, you know. The next '47 Grand-Puy-Lacoste arrives. Guess what? It tastes the same as the last one except it isn't cloudy. We marvel at its color. We sniff the bouquet. We swirl and drink. We say how great it is. We don't like it.

Now, it is hard to say you don't like it too loud, even to each other. I mean, this bottle may have been cheap, but that was a relative cheap. And they are not going to take this one back. The waiter has already polished off the cloudy one. He isn't thirsty.

I am trying to figure out what to compare this to—to understand what exactly it tastes like. Jean-François isn't talking, he is just looking at the wine list to see if they still have the 1934. It isn't that we didn't like the 1947. It is just that we were supposed to love it. We were there for *it*. Great connoisseurs I am sure would say that this is exactly what this wine should taste like, but you have to have tasted a lot of this stuff in order to feel confident about that sort of judgment. With so many different types and years of wines out there, not many people besides wine professionals are that confident.

The only thing that I have to compare it to is some 1916 Smith-Haut-Lafitte I recently acquired. I have since looked up 1916, and it was only a mediocre year. Smith-Haut-Lafitte is not now the greatest Bordeaux being made, and it probably wasn't then, but it is okay. I've tasted some of the more recent vintages, but the 1916 was bizarre. It didn't really taste like wine. Not that it was vinegar; it was just—well, different. Suddenly, I am reminded of my mother. *Why?* you ask.

I bought the wine for her birthday. She was born in 1916 and will probably cringe when she sees that in print. Birth-year wine imbibed on your birthday is a French tradition I kind of like, so when I saw the Smith-Haut-Lafitte, I snatched it up. My mother doesn't especially like wine, in the sense that she drinks wine all the time but, like most people, orders the few white wines she knows and only drinks red wine when I am around and have ordered it for her.

So it's her birthday, and we are drinking this stuff, which tastes nothing at all like wine, and I hear her say that it is, well, different, and interesting. Actually, it was so dry that your mouth puckered from drinking it, and the color was more pink than it was red; but it really was interesting.

Now having been appropriately reminded, I realize that I have the requisite two experiences from which all human beings and no scientists are happy to make a generalization. I have something to think about here. I am ready to learn something about old wine. But what generalization to make? How about: *Old wine stinks?* But I really love old wine; I am sure of this. How about: *Some old wine doesn't taste like wine exactly but tastes like something else, which is reason enough to drink it, although I wouldn't go out of my way?*

I try this one on for size, but something is missing. The 1934. I liked the 1934. I loved the 1934. Why? Well, Nazis and Paris bistros, and all that. Also, it tasted good. And I realize that my mother wasn't just being polite. Polite isn't her style. She really loved the 1916. She loved it because it was hers. How many people her age were drinking their birth-year wine? No one she knew in Florida, I'll tell you that.

Wine isn't just taste. People don't go to all this fuss just for taste. There is a whole lot more going on that translates in terms of ego and love and power and how one looks to others and how one feels about oneself. Suddenly, I have my generalization. I have explained my failure to like these wines. The fault is not in me but in my expectations about what these wines were supposed to be. If I had realized that they were supposed to be neat and weird experiences noted primarily for the ambiance of the moment rather than for taste, then I wouldn't have been disappointed. I will revise my expectations accordingly. Next time I won't be surprised. Next time I will expect ambiance.

Actually ambiance is fine to get, but it's nicer if you expected it or were pleasantly surprised by it as an additional feature beyond your other expectations. Here, I got ambiance instead of taste. The only value to an expectation failure is the hope that you can learn enough not to be surprised next time. Certainly I won't be surprised by the taste of the 1916 Smith-Haut-Lafitte that is still waiting in my cellar. But what have I learned about old Bordeaux in general that will allow me to have better expectations the next time a very old bottle is opened?

I am, of course, thankful for this bad experience. Now I have something to think about. I have become more of a connoisseur because now I know that I don't like all old Bordeaux. I am ready to learn to discriminate better. To do this, I need more expectations and more expectation failures.

How do you learn to expect anything? And, why does it matter to expect anything at all? Much of the human learning scheme is built upon expectations. Imagine a small baby at its mother's breast. It may not know what to expect the first time it starts to suck, but after a number of tries at getting and receiving milk from Mom, Baby will be damned surprised if one day it gets chocolate milk. And, you can be sure, Baby will cry. Baby will cry because of expectation violation, not pain. Babies usually like chocolate milk, after all. But babies, like everyone else except connoisseurs, don't want their expectations violated. They are practicing getting the world right and object every time that they discover that the world has fooled them again.

Wondering what babies do when their expectations fail is a reasonable consideration. Babies don't fall apart for very long. Children learn to adapt to all kinds of things by noting the expectation failure and adjusting to it. A baby may cry the first time it is exposed to something new, when it had expectations to the contrary, but if that something new is pleasant, the baby will quickly adapt. In fact, the baby adapts even if the new thing is unpleasant. Just knowing what kind of unpleasantness is coming makes it a little easier to take.

Now, let's imagine that instead of chocolate milk from mama's breast, Baby suddenly finds Château Mouton-Rothschild 1966. Does Baby say, "Hmm, not quite ready to drink" or "Wah"? If you selected "Wah," then, assuming you weren't prejudiced by the trifle that Baby cannot talk, you may understand something about learning. Learning depends upon having expectations and upon having them fail. No one will find Mouton-Rothschild to be a great wine if it is the first wine that he has ever drunk. Before you can discriminate great wine, you have to have first drunk wine. Very few of us drink our first glass of wine and say much more than "Wah." Wine is, after all, not what you expected. Few of us like our first taste of wine or beer or anything alcoholic, for that matter. We all know that we have to learn to develop a taste for such things, but what does it mean to develop a taste? The first time we have a new experience, we have only prior experiences to work with. If we want to learn important discriminations in a taste, for instance, it is helpful if those discriminations are rather on the fine side. If the discriminations are rather gross, then little will be learned from the connoisseur's point of view. How different does Mouton-Rothschild taste from milk? Does it taste more different from milk than Gruaud-Larose does? The fact is that these questions aren't as silly as they seem. You have to have some expectations if you want them to fail. If expectations don't fail, learning is hard because no learning is needed. If everything happens the way you expected it to happen, you may well be happy, but you won't learn a thing. To learn, we need expectation failure. Further, we need expectation failure that we can cope with. The failures have to be small rather than large.

Rather than talk about babies, then, since we are talking about wine, let's talk about someone who has drunk wine over a number of years, likes it, but has never paid attention to it much. Now he wants to learn more. What should he do? Actually, this is too abstract a question. Instead, let's talk about me. How did I get to be a wine expert?

Well, the first thing to say is that I am not a wine expert. But I know more about wine than any of my friends do, and much more important—especially to my friends—I *have* more wine than any of my friends do. So let's talk about me.

My first experience with wine was not unlike that of many Jewish lads. At Passover, everyone drinks wine. Four glasses are required of everyone at the table, even little ones. Of course, most people cheat, but four glasses are the rule. Up until recently, one had no choice in what wine to drink. In this country, it was Sweet Concord Grape, made by Manischewitz or by Mogen David. Now you might think that kids would like a sweet syrupy wine, but no matter how much we cut it with seltzer or water or even apple juice, nothing could help. Just the thought of it now makes my stomach queasy.

So wine wasn't my thing. In fact, I have always suspected that the major reason why Jews have such a low alcoholism rate is that once you have started drinking Manischewitz, you can't imagine what the fuss is all about.

My next attempt was beer. Actually, I had no interest at all in things alcoholic. My expectations were that the stuff stunk. But I did have social expectations. I wanted to be accepted. Upon my arrival at college, when the beer keg was tapped at my college fraternity, I certainly did not have the guts to say no. I was sixteen years old and frightened to death that they would discover that I wasn't the eighteen-year-old that I had claimed to be. Admitting to not drinking would have given the game away, and I wasn't prepared to be a social misfit within a week of joining a fraternity. Besides, I was curious. I wanted to know what beer tasted like.

Here is a good point at which to interrupt my life story and ask a question. What should I have expected? What was the beer going to taste like? Would I like it? What effect would it have on me? What would you predict that I would have been thinking before I tasted it, and what would you predict I would have thought afterwards? These are very important questions for anyone interested in how the human mind develops. Knowledge is built only upon prior knowledge.

That having been said, the proper form of the question must be: *What were my expectations, and how were they changed by the actual experience*? I could have had only one of two basic expectations. Expectations come from prior generalizations. We can expect only what we already have experienced. We cannot expect something different. Oh, we can say that we expect something different, but different from what? We have to have a basis of comparison, and this comes from the prior experience that we have chosen as the best expectation we can muster at the time. For me, there were only two possibilities: either beer tasted like soda, the thing it most resembled physically in my experience, or it tasted like Manischewitz Concord Grape, the only other alcoholic beverage in my experience. Of course, one can merge the expectations and get a combined expectation, sodalike sweet wine in this case. But, as you recall, I actually had had some of that when I mixed the seltzer with the wine, and besides, I knew that beer wasn't supposed to be sweet. Actually, the only drink I drank regularly that wasn't sweet was milk, but somehow that seemed wrong, too.

Actually, my expectations weren't that far off. I had a great many expectations, most of them right and most of them derived from knowing a great deal about the subject without having experienced it. I expected a liquid, for example. I expected a non-poisonous, maybe slightly nourishing liquid, probably a refreshing-on-a-hot-day kind of liquid. I had seen beer commercials, after all. I wasn't expecting something that tasted like soap or felt like steel wool or made me depressed afterwards. I had brought in a great deal of prior knowledge about classes of things that beer was likely to resemble. Expectations come from likely generalizations along a broad spectrum of categories.

Well, I had my first beer, and I hated it. It tasted bitter, and it wasn't sweet, and I said I didn't like it, and my fraternity brothers said I would soon acquire a taste for it. What kind of criticism was it of beer to say that it wasn't sweet? This was actually the only legitimate criticism I could make. I expected sweet. I had always gotten sweet before. The taste I got now was different, but not just marginally different. It was very different. It was too different to like.

Every time we experience an expectation failure, we need to explain it so that it doesn't keep happening. You can't go through your life always expecting there to be a parking lot on the corner of Fourth and Maple. The day they start construction on a new office building on that corner, you must decide whether this is temporary, like a carnival (maybe it will go away), and if it isn't, you begin to update your expectations. No elaborate explanation is needed; in fact, we can explain it simply by saying to ourselves that, yes, buildings do tend to get built where parking lots once were. But when they tear down a beautiful old house to make way for a parking lot, a slightly more elaborate explanation must be constructed, one that talks about the insensitivity of our times perhaps or maybe one about the money needed being just too much for anyone to repair the grand old structure.

But when expectations fail horribly, when beer just doesn't taste anything like Coca-Cola, we have no explanations that are satisfactory. What can you say? Beer just isn't Coke, and it isn't Manischewitz. It is something else. When this happens, the answer is easy: Create a new category. Beer is a something else.

Once that is done, we are on our way to becoming an instant expert. The next time someone serves us a beer, we can announce proudly that Miller just doesn't have the flavor of Budweiser, you know. In fact, pronouncements like that, made by amateurs after having had only two beers in their lives, are usually quite accurate. You remember your first beer and can easily distinguish the taste of the second from the first. After you have drunk hundreds of beers of many different sorts, it becomes harder and harder to distinguish one from the other. You have just too much information. Unless, of course, you are paying attention, careful attention. You have to care about what you are going to learn in order to learn anything at all.

To get back to my story—I didn't like the beer. I persisted in the social world of drinking a beer every now and then until the December Champagne Formal, a few months later. This dance involved, as you might guess, champagne. It also involved, as it turned out, a blind date whom I found somewhat less pleasing than the champagne. Can you guess how the champagne tasted to me?

Recall that I now had beer to compare it to. In fact, beer was now in a category by itself, but, since it was the only non-sweet alcoholic drink I had experienced, I expected something beerlike of champagne, which even looked like beer. But it was more flavorful than beer, seemingly lighter than beer, and tasted better than beer. I liked it.

I discovered more than the taste of champagne that night. I also discovered it was easy to drink, and thus I learned how nice it felt to drink alcohol. I discovered inebriation. And since inebriation felt great, I found no reason to stop until I discovered the twin effects of wild drunkenness and hangover. I couldn't get myself home that night, someone had to carry me. The next morning I was so sick I wanted to die. What did I learn about champagne? I learned never to drink it again. And I didn't for many, many years.

How exactly did all this learning take place? Expectations were set and reset. In my mind was an expectation that, after drinking champagne, you get sick. But when I awoke out of my stupor two days later, the questions were: Never drink again? Never drink champagne again? Never drink too much champagne again? Never drink champagne in December? Never go on a blind date? I had a lot to think about.

Someone older might easily understand which of the above questions was the right one, but for me the issue wasn't so simple. Deciding which generalization to make, and thus which new expectation to generate, requires knowing more than you actually can know on your own. Let me put this a different way so that you see what I mean. Suppose that we go to eat in a fine restaurant that serves Thai food. You have never eaten Thai food before and you like the meal, but the next day you are sick. Should you avoid Thai food in the future or just that restaurant or just squid, which you ate there for the first time? Or should you never go out to eat with the people who took you to that restaurant? In real life, we have no easy answers to such questions. In science, we can run an experiment and control the variables. You can eat at another Thai restaurant, you can go back to the same one and avoid the squid, and you can also go out to another restaurant that is not Thai with the same company. But you are really unlikely to do all this, and even if you did, it would prove nothing. Suppose you got sick at the non-Thai restaurant. Does that really mean that the company made you sick? And suppose that you ate the squid, and it was okay. Does that mean it was okay the first time too? Being scientific in real life is very difficult, and, in fact, none of us tries to be. We just make the generalizations that we want to make anyway. We don't worry a great deal about facts. And so I didn't drink champagne for many years. I also never got drunk again, at least not like that.

For the rest of my college years, I never drank wine except at Passover. I did learn to drink hard liquor, mixed with soda. So, as I graduated college, my expectations about wine were still simple. I didn't like it. I liked champagne, but it always reminded me of the time I got sick, and that made it unpleasant to drink. Expectations often come in the form of remindings, although reminding and expectation are not identical. I didn't expect to get sick when I next drank champagne, but I sure thought about it.

In short, my expectations about wine were simple enough. I didn't really think about it. Some years later, I moved to California. In California, people think about wine and talk about wine, and it is available in every supermarket. So, willing to try the California life, I began to bring home a jug of Almaden Mountain Rhine wine every now and then. It was pleasant enough to drink and, after the initial realization that wine wasn't always sweet, I now expected white wine, at least, to be a kind of alcoholic flavorful water.

It would be nice to say that five years in California produced a California wine maven, but that didn't happen. I had never heard of really good wine, California or otherwise. I had never had a bottle of French wine, except for whatever house wine came with the price-fixed dinners that I consumed on my studentlike tours through France. When I actually began to earn enough money for good wine, it would never have crossed my mind to try some. I didn't know anything about the subject. No one I knew drank good wine. I had never been offered any. You can't want what you don't know about.

Had someone told me about, or served me, Château Mouton-Rothschild at that time, I wouldn't have cared. Would the taste of it have driven me to ecstasy, forever making me a wine nut? Certainly not. Why not? Ah, that's where expectations come in.

Today's me, when offered Mouton-Rothschild from a good vintage properly aged, would go into raptures. On a blind taste test, I might not know that it was Mouton-Rothschild, but I would like it a lot, I assure you. Yesterday's me wouldn't have noticed anything more than something that tasted nice enough. How does this kind of transformation take place? First, let me point out that time is an important consideration. The yesterday of which I speak was more than fifteen years from the today I am writing about. Changes in expectations don't happen overnight. More important, they almost cannot happen overnight.

To model this type of learning, a graduate student of mine named Bill Bain built a program called JUDGE. We tracked two trial judges, trying to discover the rules they used in sentencing criminals. How do judges form sentences? What knowledge do they bring to bear on the task? What processes do they use?

To facilitate building a sentencing model, we talked with two judges who were sitting in Connecticut Superior Court. Our initial discussions concerned cases that they had heard or adjudicated, and for which they were expected to fashion sentences.

JUDGE stored its cases as experiences in memory and occasionally formed general rules for giving sentences in similar situations. Because of this, the order in which it received cases was crucial. The program did not always give the same sentences for crimes when they were presented in a different sequence, nor did it necessarily form the same rules or generalize rules that related to the same crimes. Both the sentences that it gave and the rules that it formed depended upon what it retrieved from memory, and when. Thus, if memory was arranged differently, the system would retrieve different cases, which would cause its behavior to change.

In fact, we reversed the order of presentation of twenty cases we gave to the system to observe the effects. The outcome was that the system made generalizations in different places. One cannot be reminded of something that one has not yet seen. Sentencing differences between the two conditions depends on different remindings that might be available as each decision is made.

Below is output from the JUDGE program that shows the system choosing and instantiating interpretations for each action in a crime (Crime1). At the time the program ran the case below, it had previously seen only one other case (Crime0). During the interpretation phase, JUDGE instantiates interpretation structures to describe each "event" in the input. An event consists of a description of an action and its direct and indirect effects.

The events in Crime1 were:

First, Randy struck Chuck with his fists several times.
Chuck was only slightly hurt.
Next, Chuck struck Randy with his fists several times.
Randy was only slightly hurt.
Then, Randy slashed at Chuck with a knife one time.
Chuck's skin was cut.
Next, Chuck slashed at Randy with a knife one time.
Randy's skin was cut.
Finally, Randy stabbed Chuck with a knife several times.
Chuck died.

The program analyzes each action in the input in temporal order. The analysis finds one interpretation for the action, and one for the result. Here, the action is that Randy struck Chuck and the result is that Chuck was hurt slightly. Interpretations are indexed in the system in terms of action-result pairs.

Searching memory for episode-units that have an action similar to that in EVENT 3 . . .

Exact match found with initial action of previous episodes in memory: (RAW-EPISODE-21 RAW-EPISODE-20 RAW-EPISODE-18 RAW-EPISODE-15 RAW-EPISODE-14 RAW-EPISODE-13 RAW-EPISODE-11 RAW-EPISODE-10 RAW-EPISODE-7)

Found RAW-EPISODE-21 in memory, an episode that matches EVENT 3 exactly. EVENT 3 will therefore initially be considered an UNPROVOKED VIOLATION.

RAW-EPISODE-21 matches the initial action of EVENT 3, giving EVENT 3 the unfavorable interpretation UNPROVOKED VIOLA-TION, because the offender acted first. A test stored with the UN-PROVOKED VIOLATION interpretation checks the applicability of this interpretation to this instance. The test simply checks to be sure that no violative incident preceded the current action. Applicability checks for other interpretations are typically more complex.

The interpretation phase in JUDGE assigns an interpretation to each set of input actions and results. The interpretations provide the system with inferences about the motivations of actors; they also serve as indexes to cases in memory.

The first feature used is the statute the offender violated. JUDGE tries to find in memory other instances of violations of the same statute. The next feature used is who started the fight: the defendant or the victim.

The next feature is the final (violent) result that accounts for the statutory violation. Then the elements of the interpretation are used, in reverse order. That is, the system first indexes with the final result in the crime, then with the actions that led to that result, then with the motive assigned by the interpretation phase, and so on. Program output presented below continues with the same sample case examined in the interpretation phase. The facts of Crime0, which is already in JUDGE's memory, are:

First, Ted slashed at Al with a knife one time.
Al's skin was slightly cut.
Next, Al slashed at Ted with a knife one time.
Ted's skin was slightly cut.
Finally, Ted stabbed Al with a knife several times.
Al died.

This is the only case in memory for this example. At this point in the processing, the system describes the reminding it has retrieved and how it compares superficially with the input case.

> (Retrieve-Mem Crime1)

Now processing Crime1:

Statutory similarity of murder found with indexed crime: Crime0.

Found previous crimes in which the same final action and result was also perpetrated against an INITIAL DEFENDER: (Crime0)

Crime0 was also a murder and the victim also did not start the fight (the victim was the "INITIAL DEFENDER"). JUDGE starts working back through the interpretation structure for Crime1.

Collecting indices for Crime1 in reverse order . . .

Collecting indices for final event:

Finally, Randy caused Chuck to be killed.

Recent previous instance found with same final result as final result in current case—Kill: Crime0

Recent previous instance found with same final action as final action in current case—Stab-Knife: Crime0

Recent previous instance found with same final result interpretation as final interpretation in current case—Achieved-Result: Crime0

Recent previous instance found with same final intent interpretation level as final interpretation in current case—ESCALATED RETAL-IATION: Crime0

Crime0 matched on each one of the indexes. The program proceeds by searching for features related to the event that preceded Crime1's final event, then the next earlier event, and so on until it reaches the first event in the crime. The search for old situations that match the features of the initial event in Crime1 comes up empty. None of the features of Crime0 match it and Crime0 is the only other crime in memory.

Collecting indices for preceding event:

———

Collecting indices for initial event in crime:

The first violative action occurred when Randy hit Chuck several times; Chuck was only slightly hurt.

No previous instances found with same result as intermediate harm in current case—Violated-Bruise.

No previous instances found with same action as intermediate harm in current case—Hit-Body.

No previous instances found with same intent interpretation level as that in current event—UNPROVOKED VIOLATION.

Crime0 involved an UNPROVOKED VIOLATION too, but it was an unprovoked stabbing, not an unprovoked hitting. This system distinguishes between such interactions in its storage and retrieval.

A previous situation involving similar actions and a Kill result, Crime0, was quite similar to the current case.

Crime1 contained the same sequence of actions and results as Crime0, except that it was preceded by hitting.

JUDGE looks for matches between the current case and the previous cases it knows about. Obviously, with only one previous case, Crime1 is going to look a lot like Crime0. But, gradually, JUDGE learned more and more cases, each time comparing the one it was judging to the previous cases it had seen and looking for the best match. Here is an example of JUDGE finding two cases to be similar and then trying to reconcile their differences:

Failure to match on whether victim started things combined with failed-act interpretation is too large to modify. Will recover by sending input crime to comparator.

In both crimes, the victim was killed. Not only were both of these outcomes the result of direct intentions, but the actors intended and caused the same amount of harm.

Ron demonstrated an extreme use of force against Biff when he acted to stab Biff to death in response to being hit hard.

Mike demonstrated an extreme use of force against Bob when he acted to stab Bob to death in response to being hit hard.

Unable to distinguish whether the extreme force used in either crime was worse.

Although the program at this point cannot distinguish between the extent of force each offénder used, it determines that one of them had some justification for acting violatively.

The intent of both offenders was to act repeatedly to stab the victim to death. However, Mike was justified for preventing further harm by causing Bob to be stabbed while Ron was not justified in his intention to stab Biff to death.

Once the program finds a difference in the justification behind the offenders' intentions, it attempts to account for the disparity.

Ron's lack of justification stemmed from earlier in the case when he bumped Biff several times. This was the first use of force in the case. Ron's action constituted an unjustified use of force because Ron was the initial aggressor.

Comparison finished with result that the old crime, Crime21, is substantially worse.

JUDGE now has two important pieces of information at hand. First, it knows that one offender was more justified in intending to stab his victim than the other actor. Second, it knows that this difference occurred between intentions that had a direct causal bearing on the end of the crimes, and thus that it is a rather salient difference. The sentence that the program gives to the input case is now based on what it gave to the old case and on this new information.

The sentence originally given for Crime21, for violation of murder as defined in Section 53A-45 in the Connecticut Penal Code, was a term of imprisonment of not less than 50 years to be served in the state's prison. According to state law, 25 years of the sentence could not be reduced or suspended. Since the circumstances of Crime21 are found to be worse than Crime27, due to more severe actions at the end of the crime, the offender will get a sentence which is more lenient than the sentence for Crime21.

The sentence to be given for Crime27, for violation of murder as defined in Section 53A-45 in the Connecticut Penal Code, will be a term of imprisonment of not less than 25 years to be served in the state's prison. Of this sentence, 25 years may not be reduced or suspended, according to state law. The maximum period of incarceration allowed for violation of this statute is 50 years.

JUDGE learned to make judgments by comparing old judgments to new situations. This is what we do with respect to every experience we have. We learn everything in terms of something we have already learned. To get back to the more palatable job of judging wine rather than criminals, we can learn about the taste of Mouton-Rothschild, with respect to how it differs from milk, how it differs from Manischewitz, how it differs from a Rhône wine, how it differs from an ordinary Bordeaux, how it differs from a Latour of the same year, or how it differs from a Mouton-Rothschild of a different year. These differences are expressed in terms of prior expectations. We don't seriously expect that the Mouton will taste like Manischewitz; we may know better for all sorts of intelligent reasons, but if we have never tasted any other wine, we cannot help drawing the comparison.

What we are doing is updating our knowledge structures that pertain to wine. Contained within such structures are the detailed expectations about smell, color, and various aspects of taste that one must compare and contrast in order to come up with a new idea, a modification of the existing expectations within the knowledge structure. New ideas are inherently modifications of old ideas.

Being able to add new information without regard for the old information it replaces might seem appealing on the assumption that we have empty spaces in the mind that would somehow be filled up by the new stuff. But, how would we ever find the new information we have just added? For information to be useful you must know how to find it.

Imagine adding a new book to your library. You might as well not own it if you place it somewhere and forget where. In a small enough library, you could count on stumbling upon it, but as the library got larger, it would be necessary to have an effective indexing system that would allow you to find something on the basis of some scheme connected to important information about what is contained in the book, such as its author or its subject matter.

The same situation exists in the mind. A new fact must be placed somewhere. People are not usually aware that they place new facts, experiences, ideas, and such someplace in memory, but in a metaphorical sense, they do. There may not be actual spots where one can find George Washington, but there has to be an indexing scheme that allows one to hear "president, wore wig, had wooden teeth, chopped down cherry tree" and to know instantly whom we are talking about. But how does this work?

Labels such as "wooden teeth" are indices used by the mind to retrieve information.

Well, then, what indices should we use for Mouton-Rothschild? The answer to this is highly idiosyncratic. No one tells us what indices to use. No agreed-upon set exists. Well, wine perhaps, if you know that Mouton is a wine. But any wine lover would also use "first-growth" because that is an important label that Mouton is correctly identified by. On the other hand, you might never have heard of that label, so you wouldn't use it, nor are you likely to remember it if this is the first you've heard of it. The only way that you can find labels to use is to find labels that you have used before. No one can hand you a set with any reasonable expectation that they will be remembered, let alone used. The labels must be meaningful to the person who uses them.

The value of all this labeling is to be able to say, when tasting a 1959 Mouton, that it is better than the '61 but not as good as the '59 Latour. Of course, you might not care enough about wine to say this, nor have enough knowledge to say it, but if you both cared and had the relevant experiences, you would want to be able to say it. The only way to do this is to be continually re-examining and re-using the labels that you have previously used. To do this, you must have myriad expectations and be able to deal with the failure of those expectations. When expectations fail, you must be able to explain why. This is the basis of learning.

In order to learn about anything, then, we must have expectations, notice when they fail, wonder why they fail, find an explanation, and get reminded of previous situations that failed in the same way. Clever indexing allows for useful and relevant remindings to take place. When you have encountered something new, something unexpected, something in need of explanation, you need to get reminded of your most relevant prior experience to make a comparison between that experience and your current experience. It is the only way to learn.

If you want to know how 1959 Mouton-Rothschild tastes, therefore, drinking a bottle of it isn't all you need to do. You need to work up to it with lesser wines, taste both younger and older wines, taste wines of the same year or châteaux or equivalent quality, and taste other Moutons. If you fail to do this, you will taste it, but you won't learn a whole lot from the experience. Well, there are worse problems in life.

CHAPTER 10

Trying to Believe Champagne and Armagnac

I find myself in France again. I call to say hello to Laurance. Laurance has nothing to do this particular Saturday. Laurance likes to drink. She says we must go to Champagne. "Why do you need me for this?" I ask. "You have a car," she says. "I do?" I ask. "You can rent one," she responds. An hour later, we are off to Champagne.

Champagne is a pretty part of the world, rolling hills, scenic little towns, and a few great wineries, complete with tasting rooms, tours of the cellars, and films about how champagne is made. I am not much of a tourist—I travel too much to be any good at sightseeing—but, as long as we are in Champagne, I guess we should take the tour and get the free glass at the end of the hour. Laurance is not all that eager to do this, but I can't figure out exactly what it is that she is eager to do, and I assume that this is why we came, so we turn left at the large sign and enter. The tour is uneventful and pretty uninteresting, exactly how I had imagined it would be. There are long speeches about how bottles are turned just so, and long damp cellars to walk through. I look forward to the glass of champagne at the end. I assume there will be one because I am a case-based reasoner like everyone else, and the last tour I took like this one, namely the Hershey's chocolate factory tour when I was twelve, gave out free chocolate at the end.

Well, case-based reasoners will often be disappointed, especially when they have selected the wrong case to reason from. There is no champagne at the end. There is an apology about how there used to be champagne, but now there are too many tourists. Of course, they are willing to sell us some. Instantly, I realize that I had a better case to choose for comparison purposes. I had been back to Hershey, Pennsylvania, to take my own kids on the tour, and found that not only were we not given chocolate, but we weren't even going through the real factory, just some tourist facsimile. I hadn't been reminded of that tour because it was so uninteresting I had forgotten it. But now, I am beginning to spot a trend. Apparently there is no longer any free Hershey Kiss or champagne. It just doesn't pay, according to the marketing folks.

Suddenly I panic, realizing that I have driven one hundred miles to Champagne and I am not going to taste anything except whatever I buy, which I could have bought for the same price in Paris. I wonder why Laurance wanted us to come here, and she says she remembers that there always was free champagne at the end of the tour. I suggest another tour of a less well known winery.

But, alas, the story is the same there, another hour-long tour, and no freebies.

I am depressed. Laurance suggests that we tour the countryside, going to the little towns that surround Reims, which is the city in which we have not been properly treated, and which I avoided mentioning at all so far, since I not only don't remember it fondly, I also cannot pronounce it in any way recognizable to a Frenchman, despite an entire day of trying and Laurance laughing. So we begin to drive along a road that is marked "route de champagne." The name of this road is promising, and I am hopeful that we will pass by smaller wineries that will be more hospitable.

We see lots of grapes, but no wineries, nothing but small towns and small houses. Finally Laurance suggests that we stop and ask some people in the street if they know where we can taste some wine. I am appalled by this suggestion in so many ways that I don't know where to start my complaints. I hate to ask for directions, they are usually wrong, and who knows what kind of answer we might get to this crazy question. But Laurance insists and we approach a group of women who are yakking in the town square and ask them a question that I am certain will subject us to instant ridicule either as ridiculous Parisians or ridiculous Americans, depending upon which one of us they choose to make fun of.

But, no. The woman's answer is that we should follow her. She begins to leave the town square and walk towards one of the houses on a hill. We follow slowly in the car. I am reminded of movies where people try to buy drugs in foreign countries. I wonder if we are doing something illegal, but decide that I have been again inappropriately reminded. Inappropriate remindings are confusing. Learning gets more difficult; you have to think. I am trying to think, but I really can't figure out what is going on.

The woman opens the door of what is by now obviously her house, and invites us in, yelling "André" or "Pierre" or some other male name, which instantly produces her husband. We are ushered into the front room of a very well kept little house. In the front room are some chairs, and a table with four champagne glasses. Pierre enters, says hello, and asks us if we want to taste the good champagne or the less good champagne. The answer to that one is easy, and the next thing I know, Pierre is pouring four glasses of champagne. We all drink, Mrs. Pierre says good-bye, and we try the less good champagne. We make polite conversation and Pierre feels called upon to bring us last year's vintage, which he says is better than this year's, which he has been pouring. It is, we agree, and we all have another.

I ask Laurance what is going on here, and she says that this is this man's own little winery, that he makes a small amount of champagne. I ask her to find out what he does for a living then, and she says she assumes that this is what he does, but she will ask. Sure enough, this is what he does. He makes a few thousand bottles of his own champagne. I ask her how he sells this champagne and she says she assumes like this, and I say that that is ridiculous and could she make sure.

Sure enough, she knew what she was talking about. He makes champagne and his marketing technique is hoping someone might ask his wife while she is in the town square if she knows where one might taste champagne. "From this he makes a living?" I ask.

It seems he does. He sells the champagne to us for a whopping four dollars a bottle. We buy six bottles of the good stuff, and off we go, happier for the whole experience. I wonder not only how he makes a living, but also if he drinks his own champagne with every customer. I am still confused.

Laurance has a remedy for my confusion. She suggests we try another house. You mean, I ask, that we should just knock on the door of a random house? This is precisely what she means. I am mortified yet again, but I am also slightly drunk, so what the hell. She picks a nice house in the next town and rings the bell. The door opens. "Can we taste some champagne?" she asks. "Of course" is the reply.

You think I was confused before? This is a completely random choice. There is nothing to indicate that the people in this house make champagne. Does everybody in Champagne make champagne? Laurance says yes. I am beginning to think that she understands her country better than I do. No surprise there, I guess.

The procedure that we followed before is the one we follow in this house as well. We have stumbled upon a script. The wife has one glass and leaves, the husband drinks with us and talks about the current vintage. The only difference is that this time the prices of his various champagnes are posted on a small card on the table. This reassures me somewhat; at least this guy seems to be aware that he is in business. This champagne is noticeably not as good as the stuff at the last guy's house. But, we buy three bottles. Buying none is out of the question, says Laurance. He is also more expensive. His champagne is going for $4.50.

At this point, even I am ready to try another house in the next town. Laurance points out that we really cannot choose just any house, we must choose one that has the name of the owner on a brass plate on the front gate. This, it appears, is the underground code. So we choose a house with a brass sign.

We have chosen wisely. As we enter the courtyard of this house, the whole family is gathered around—guess what?—drinking champagne. At least they like the stuff. They invite us to join them. It is late in the afternoon and it is time to drink. Soon we are having a party with people we couldn't talk to under any other circumstances. There is little to talk about except champagne. We say we are from Paris, for example, and these people have never been to Paris, but, there is a great deal to say about the champagne.

We are delighted to find out that this champagne is going for only $3.50 a bottle. We are also delighted because this is the best stuff we have tasted yet, although we are hardly reliable sources of information at this point. We walk away with many bottles and

I am left wondering, when I sober up, just what exactly is going on in Champagne. I found Champagne confusing, although I found the champagne delightful.

We assume that we know why people do what they do. When we buy a hamburger at McDonald's, we assume that the person who serves us the hamburger is willing to work hard but is not too skilled, that he does this job for money, and that although it is not the best job in the world, it is probably the best job he can get. He probably will change jobs as soon as he finds a higher-paying one. He might be looking forward to becoming a supervisor one day. Perhaps he would even like to own a franchise if he can figure out how. But, more likely, we expect that this is a temporary job that our server would quickly abandon.

We can assume all this because we know something of human goals. We know, for example, that people need to eat, that they need homes, that they often have families to support, and that these needs translate into goals to earn money. We know also that people have desires that cause other goals to arise in addition to the ones above. For example, people like to win at bowling, go to the movies, and get to be the supervisor at McDonald's. Each of these goals could be related to money, but there are other factors at work as well. People desire success, power, entertainment, happiness, job satisfaction, and relationships with other people, in addition to the more basic needs.

Our ability to anticipate these desires helps us to understand the world around us. It also helps us to understand English. Compare the sentence pairs:

John hated Mary.	John loved Mary.
A truck was headed towards her.	A truck was headed towards her.
John pushed Mary.	John pushed Mary.

In which direction did John push Mary in each case? Knowing what someone believes can help us predict his goals. Knowing someone's goals can help us predict his plans. And knowing someone's plans can help us predict his actions. Understanding the actions of any person means understanding where his actions fit in the belief-goal-plan-action chain.

When people do something that we cannot understand, we attempt to explain their actions to ourselves. What does it mean to fail to understand something in this sense? Understanding the actions of a person that we care about means identifying the beliefs under which he was operating. An action fits, ordinarily, into the following paradigm:

belief
|
goal
|
plan
|
action

We might have, as an example, the action John hit Mary and the following underlying structure:

Beliefs
Children should be taught what behavior is unacceptable.
Mary is the child of John.
Parents are responsible for their children's upbringing.
Pain teaches avoidance of the behavior that led to the pain.
|
Goal
Teach Mary not to repeat her action
|
Plan
Cause pain to Mary
|
Action
John hit Mary.

When John hits Mary, or when we hear that John has hit Mary, we attempt to understand what is going on. This means, in effect, attempting to fill out the implicit beliefs, goals, and plans that underlie the action. We set up a knowledge structure with these empty slots, and attempt to fill in the slots by whatever means are available. When we say that we don't understand why something happened, we mean that we are having trouble filling in the slots and need some help.

Lack of understanding means a lack of knowing or being able to infer any of the fillers for these slots. But where to start? Normally, serious lack of understanding comes from differing beliefs. We do not easily understand that other people fail to see the world the way we do. Possible explanations of our own misunderstandings can focus on each and every item shown above, with some being more reasonable than others. Below, following each item from the above diagram, I have given an explanation of John hitting Mary that might have been made with that particular belief or plan in mind. In other words, if someone asked, "Why did John hit Mary?" any of the answers shown below would be acceptable in principle, although some are clearly better than others:

BELIEFS
Children should be taught what behavior is unacceptable.
John believes that children must learn what they should and
    shouldn't do.
Mary is the child of John.
John is Mary's father.
Parents are responsible for their children's upbringing.
John believes that he must teach his children about behavior.
Pain teaches avoidance of the behavior that led to the pain.
John believes in negative reinforcement, and he thinks pain is a
    good negative reinforcer.
    |
GOAL
Punish Mary
John wanted to punish Mary.
    |
PLAN
Cause pain to Mary
John believes that pain is a punishment.
    |
ACTION
John hit Mary.
John believes that hitting is a way to cause pain.

The sentences in the above diagram are all explanations of John's behavior. Some of them seem like good explanations, and some of them seem stupid or obvious. Such judgments are entirely in the eye of the beholder. The explanations that seem best to us as explanations are those that refer to a belief that we do not actually agree with. When an explanation is focused upon something that we not only agree with, but believe that everyone agrees with, it seems silly. That is why *John believes that hitting is a way to cause* way ourselves, so the person whose behavior we are trying to understand must hold some belief we don't.

It is actually rather easy to determine the beliefs that people hold. To see this, try figuring out the beliefs held by the respondents to this 1981 "man on the street" interview conducted by a Hartford radio station (WHCN):

If you could live anywhere, where would it be?
1. Right here in Connecticut 'cause I like having all four seasons.
2. Boulder, Colorado. That's where my man is.
3. I want to live in a sand trap at the third hole of golf acres.
4. I'd live in New England because it has everything in it. It has all the culture, tradition, history.
5. A tropical island with a mountain for skiing and a beach for swimming.
6. I'd like to live in an enchanted castle with goblets of wine, joints of beef, and wenches at hand.
7. Essex, Connecticut. I could dock my yacht there.
8. Hawaii. It's still in the U.S. and I wouldn't want to go out of the U.S. I'd like to stay here.
9. Bristol, Connecticut. That's where I live right now and I love it.
10. New York City. It's got a lot of class.
11. Estonia, but I can't because it got taken over by the Russians.
12. I think I'd like to live in Disneyland so I would never have to face reality.

Assume that these people are friends of yours and they have just answered your question. It is easy to see that the beliefs inherent in these answers are readily inferable. Each of these people is telling you something about himself, about his priorities in life, about his value system, and about how he makes decisions. Since most of these people do not live where they said they would like to live, they are also telling you something about how they make decisions and why.

Let's look at some of the answers listed. Consider #1. This person believes that weather is a major factor in deciding where you live. So does the person who said he wanted to live in Hawaii (#8). The woman in #2 believes that love ought to be the determining factor, but she can't believe this too strongly or else she'd be there. The people who gave answers #3, #5, and #7 believe that recreation is a very high priority, although here again, not the highest. The person who gave answer #11 presumably believes *pain* seems absurd as an explanation. Similarly, *John believes that he must teach his children about behavior* seems silly too, but in that case we can imagine that there might be people who believe that all matters of children's upbringing ought best to be left to servants. Issues such as whether hitting children is a good idea, that is, issues that matter in our culture, usually also seem silly as explanations. The reason there is different, however. There we want a deeper explanation. We know that John must believe that. We can figure that out for ourselves. We want to know why he believes that, what his evidence is, and so on.

Understanding revolves, in principle, around filling in inferences in the belief-goal-plan-action chain. When we try to understand something that confuses us, we focus on inventing beliefs that would make a set of behaviors coherent. It is only after we have identified such a belief or set of beliefs that we can begin to determine how the actions we have seen might be steps in a plan that was intended to satisfy a goal that was generated by a given belief.

Beliefs generate goals. If John believes that drinking wine will make him happy, he is likely to generate the goal to drink wine. He may not be able to create a plan that will enable him to drink wine. Or he might be able to create the plan but not execute it. Further, he may be able to do all this, but he may have some conflicting belief that prevents him from actually generating the goal in the first place. For example, he may believe that drinking wine causes alcoholism and thus he would have to determine how to resolve the conflict between the goal to be happy and the goal to be healthy.

We must determine: first, if we understand the choices that are being made; second, if we understand the beliefs that underlie those choices; and last, what our own beliefs are about the actions that we are trying to understand.

This is what I was having trouble doing in Champagne. When someone does something that we cannot understand, we demand that he explain himself, or, if that is not possible, we create an explanation of his behavior on our own. Not to be able to understand, in this context, means that we cannot imagine what belief might be held, or if we can, we cannot imagine why he would hold such a belief. Explanation, then, in this context, means finding a belief, or a belief that is behind a belief.

Usually there is no right explanation in these cases. What we are really saying to ourselves is that we would not have acted that being with your own people is the highest priority, but not at the price of the loss of one's freedom.

How do we determine that these beliefs are the ones that these people hold? To construct explanations of this sort, a relatively simple technique is used. Normally, we make inferences during the course of understanding. In belief inference we combine assumptions and actions into a format that formulates a belief that determines what the subject must believe regarding which actions and which goals take priority over one another.

Belief inference requires that one match goals with actions. If someone claims to have goal A, but performs an action that is normally in service of goal B, then this person believes that goal B is more important than goal A, more noble than goal A, more attainable than goal A, or something of that sort. For example, the woman who would rather be in Colorado is saying that being in Connecticut is more something than being in Colorado. The task in belief inference is to figure out what the something is. We have some hints, of course. We know that goal A is driven by the belief that a woman should live with the man she loves. We must determine what would impede her from moving to Colorado. Perhaps her job is in Connecticut. In that case, she must believe that a career takes precedence over love in important life decisions. Perhaps her parents have forbidden her to go. In that case, she must believe that loyalty to her parents is more important than loyalty to her boyfriend.

Belief inference is possible if one knows what the goals are exactly. After the initial work on scripts in our laboratory, it became clear that people knew more than just scripts and would utilize that knowledge in understanding. We built two programs that tracked the goals that people used, and the plans that derived from those goals. The first was PAM (written by Bob Wilensky). The goal of PAM was to understand stories where there was no script, but where tracking goals and plans would make the text understandable:

Input Text:
John wants money.
He got a gun and walked into a liquor store.
He told the owner he wanted some money.
The owner gave John the money and John left.

Input: Why did John get a gun?
Output: Because John wanted to rob the liquor store.

Input: Why did the shopkeeper give John the money?
Output: Because John needed to get some money.

Input: Why did John leave?
Output: Because John didn't want to get caught.

Output:
Story from John's Point of View:
I needed to get some dough. So I got myself this gun, and I walked down to the liquor store. I told the shopkeeper that if he didn't let me have the money, then I would shoot him. So he handed it over. Then I left.

Output:
Story from the Owner's Point of View:
I was minding the store when a man entered. He threatened me with a gun and demanded all the cash receipts. Well, I didn't want to get hurt, so I gave him the money. Then he escaped.

Input Text:
John wanted to win the stockcar race.
Bill also wanted to win the stockcar race.
Before the race John cut Bill's ignition wire.

Input: Why did John break an ignition wire?
Output: Because he was trying to prevent Bill from racing.

Input:
    John wanted Bill's bicycle.
    He went over to Bill and asked him if he would give it to him.
    Bill refused.
    John told Bill he would give him five dollars for it.
    But Bill would not agree.
    Then John told Bill he would break his arm if he didn't let him have it.
    Bill gave him the bicycle.

Question: Q1
Why did John walk over to Bill?
Because he wanted to get his bicycle.

Question: Q2
Why did Bill give his bicycle to John?
Because he didn't want to get hurt.

Question: Q3
What were the consequences of John's walking over to Bill?
This enabled John to ask Bill to give him Bill's bicycle.

Question: Q4
What were the consequences of John's asking Bill to give him Bill's bicycle?
Bill told John that Bill wouldn't give him Bill's bicycle.

PAM tracked goals in order to infer the reasons for actions. POL-ITICS, written by Jaime Carbonell, was an attempt to track beliefs as well. POLITICS was supposed to act like a U.S. senator. It answered questions according to its beliefs. It reflected the reasoning processes that a senator might use in answering questions that were asked of him, by relying upon a set of beliefs through which to interpret information:

input:
The U.S. Congress is expected to approve the Panama Canal Treaty.

Conservative Mode:
Interpretation completed, ready to accept questions.

Q1: Should the U.S. approve the treaty?
A1: No, the treaty is bad for the United States.

Q2: Why is the treaty bad for the U.S.?
A2: The United States would lose the Canal to Panama and the United States will be weaker.

Q3: What might happen if the United States loses the Canal?
A3: Russia will try to control the Canal.

Q4: Why would Russia try to take over the Canal?
A4: Russia wants to expand its military control. The Panama Canal has high military value.

Q5: How might this happen?
A5: The United States may not be able to stop anyone taking over the Panama Canal. Torrijos is a Communist. Torrijos will let Russia control Panama.

Q6: Why should the U.S. worry about Russia taking over the Canal?
A6: Because Russia wants to control the world.

Q7: What should the U.S. do to stop Russia from taking over the Canal?
A7: Congress should vote against the Panama Canal Treaty.

Liberal Mode:
Interpretation completed, ready to accept questions.

Q1: Should the U.S. approve the treaty?

A1: Yes, the Panama Canal Treaty is good for the United States.

Q2: Why is the treaty good?
A2: The Panama Canal Treaty improves relations with Latin American countries.

Q3: What happens if the U.S. keeps the Canal?
A3: This will cause discontent and conflict in Panama and Latin America.

Q4: Why would this lead to conflict?
A4: The Canal Zone is a United States colony. Latin America does not like colonialism. The United States would maintain colonialism.

Q5: What if Russia tries to take over the Canal?
A5: Russia does not want conflict with the U.S. Russia will stay out of the Canal if the United States defends it. The United States defending the Canal is part of the treaty.

input:
Russia is massing troops on the Czech border.

Conservative Mode:
Interpretation completed, ready to accept questions.

Q1: Why did Russia do this?
A1: Because Russia thought that it could take political control of Czechoslovakia by sending troops.

Q2: What will Russia do next?
A3: Russia may tell its troops to start the invasion.

Q3: What else can Russia do?
A3: Russia may wait for Czechoslovakia to give in to Russian demands.

Q4: What happens if Czechoslovakia does not give in?
A4: Russia may decide to start the invasion.

Q5: What should the United States do?
A5: The United States should intervene militarily.

Q6: What else can the United States do?
A6: The United States can do nothing, or it can intervene diplomatically by conferring with Russia about Czechoslovakia. These alternatives are bad for the United States.

The point here is that understanding means tracking goals. Since I was trying to understand the makers of champagne, I was, in essence, asking myself, "What are the goals in Champagne?" I would have thought that someone who was in business would want to make as much money as possible. The plans used in executing this goal would be to market the product properly, to find the maximum number of buyers, in other words to create a business. But, these are American beliefs. They are not the beliefs of Frenchmen, at least not those I met in Champagne, not according to Laurance.

So my problem became trying to determine what goals these makers of champagne had, and what beliefs might have generated those goals. The first task was easy. Their goal seemed to be to drink champagne and not to sell it. The beliefs behind this goal were more difficult to figure out.

In fact, I did not really understand the underlying beliefs until a few years later when my French was better and I found myself traveling in Armagnac.

Armagnac, for those who are not familiar with it, is a liquor that is distilled from grapes. It is quite a bit like cognac, except, in general, and I suppose this is just a matter of opinion, Armagnac is better. People who like wine, especially French people who like wine, also like to have Armagnac and cigars after dinner. Anyway, I like that, so a visit to Armagnac was in order.

Thanks to Laurance, I had a script. Scripts don't take more than one or two trials to learn ordinarily. We usually expect every new experience to be like the closest previous experience. The problem is simply to determine which past experience is the closest. Upon entering Armagnac country I noticed a sign saying "route d'Armagnac," and upon taking it found myself riding past farmhouses in open countryside. I was reminded of Champagne.

Reminding is for prediction, after all. What happened last time should happen again, so I turned into a friendly-looking farm and was greeted by a farmer who was fixing his truck. "Can we taste some Armagnac here?" said I. "Certainly," said he. We were in business.

Armagnac is a lot stronger stuff than champagne. As we tasted various Armagnacs around the kitchen table of the farmhouse, we had plenty of time and enthusiasm for conversation. Fortunately, I remembered my old concern about champagne. And, also, fortunately, this particular maker of Armagnac was quite happy to talk.

Really good Armagnac requires a great deal of aging in the cask. Armagnac doesn't age in the bottle, so it really doesn't tell you much to find out that an Armagnac is from 1945, for example.

If it was bottled last week and is from 1945, well, that's nice. Armagnac that old ought to taste very good. But, a very old bottle of 1945 Armagnac, bottled, say, forty years ago, would not be of any great interest. This is a very important fact to know about Armagnac, not only because you might like to buy some Armagnac, but also because it provides a very important piece of the puzzle of how the Armagnac business works.

When the grandfather of the man I was talking to was pressing the grapes, distilling the liquor, and putting it into casks for the 1923 vintage, he was doing it so that his grandson, who was thirty years away from being born, would have some Armagnac to sell to me in 1988. The grandfather's business worked because he had Armagnac to sell that his grandfather had made for him, of course. The job of the man I met was to make Armagnac for his grandchildren and to keep the farm that had the vats of Armagnac that his grandfather had made and to bottle some from time to time.

Occasionally this man sold some of his stock to the big Armagnac companies that blend different growers' Armagnacs, and occasionally he sold some to people who dropped by. But, this was not a businessman. This was a lover of Armagnac, a lover of tradition, and a man who had no intention of doing any more than living off his farm the way his family had for generations. He was quite happy with the whole affair.

Suddenly I understood Champagne. These people didn't have the aging problem that the Armagnac folk had, but the problem was the same nevertheless. Their beliefs about what is important in life were just not the same as your average American's. They were not in business to make money at all. They were simply trying to live in a certain way, as their families had always lived. It was very easy for them to generate the plans that were intended to help them achieve the goals generated by the beliefs they held. They simply copied the plans that their parents had used.

My problem had been one of plan recognition. It is very easy to recognize plans that you yourself normally use, but rather difficult to recognize plans that you have never seen before. To understand other people's actions you must be able to recognize the plan of which they are a part. But recognition implies previously having seen what you are supposed to recognize, or better yet, previously having executed the plan you are supposed to recognize. I couldn't do this since it was all new to me.

How do we learn to plan, and hence to recognize plans? This is a question that lies at the root of Artificial Intelligence. Ever since people first thought about making machines intelligent, they thought about getting them to make plans. Most attempts to consider the nature of intelligence and research into the mechanisms of intelligence tend to dwell on the techniques of puzzle solving and planning, and on the understanding of complex, even bizarre situations. Traditionally, intelligence tests are problem-solving tests, and the most difficult questions on College Board exams and other standardized tests involve solving a problem one has never encountered before or attempting one that appears commonplace but may have an unusual twist.

Artificial Intelligence matured as a field with the invention of the General Problem Solver (GPS), a program whose goal was to be able to solve any problem by the use of first principles of problem solving. Newell and Simon provided GPS with heuristics, or rules of thumb, for good problem solving. These rules of thumb were outside of any particular domain; they were rules that were intended to work as well to help you fix your car as to help you solve a puzzle. The inherent appeal of a machine that would operate from first principles, and thus is able to solve any problem by reasoning from those principles, is obvious to any mathematically inclined scientist, that is, virtually any computer scientist.

The premise is that we reason the same way no matter what we are reasoning about and that a computer can be taught to reason by giving it those general principles and giving it ways of applying those principles to any domain. Scientists appreciate this kind of rigor and crave such systemization. No wonder the work of Newell and Simon attracted so much attention in both AI and psychology.

The best way to give a feel for the intention and tone of GPS is to use Newell and Simon's own words (taken from Newell and Simon, 1972):

GPS, the General Problem Solver

GPS is a problem solving program developed initially by the authors and J. C. Shaw in 1957. It grew out of the work on [the Logic Theorist]. . . . GPS's first task environment was the Moore-Anderson logic task, just as we have described it. GPS obtained its name of "general problem solver" because it was the first problem solving program to separate in a clean way a task-independent part of the system containing general problem solving mechanisms from a part of the number of different tasks (Ernst and Newell, 1969), and other programs essentially similar in structure have worked on yet other problems (Quinlan and Hunt, 1968). However, our concern in this chapter is with logic. We will describe GPS in a task-independent way (indeed that is the natural way to describe it), but we will not assess its suitability to other task environments.

GPS operates on problems that can be formulated in terms of objects and operators. An operator is something that can be applied to certain objects to produce different objects (as a saw applied to logs produces boards). The objects can be characterized by the features they possess, and by the differences that can be observed between pairs of objects. Operators for a given task may be restricted to apply only to certain kinds of objects; and there may exist operators that apply to several objects as inputs, producing one or more objects as outputs (as the operation of adding two numbers produces a third number, their sum).

Various kinds of problems can be formulated in a task environment containing objects and operators: to transform a given object into another; to find an object possessing a given feature; to modify an object so that a given operator may be applied to it; and so on.

To specify problems and subproblems, GPS has a discrete set of goal types. We shall introduce two of these initially:

Transform Goal Type: *Find a way to* transform *object.1 into object.2. (The objects, 1 and 2, may be any objects defined in specifying the task environment. The phrase "way to transform" implies "by applying a sequence of operators from the task environment.")*

Apply Goal Type: Apply *operator to object.1 (or to an object obtained from object.1 by admissible transformations).*

An example of a transform goal is: Find an expression (LO) from an initial expression (LI). An example of an apply goal is: Apply a rule (R7) to an expression (L1).

With each goal type is associated a set of methods related to achieving goals of that type. The principal heuristics of GPS are embedded in the methods, so that the executive organization is quite simple. When an attempt is made to achieve a goal, the goal is first evaluated to see whether it is worth achieving and whether achievement seems likely. If so, one of the methods is selected and executed. This leads either to success or to a repetition of the loop.

GPS executive program
achieve (goal):
1. *evaluate (goal), if reject stop and report fail;*
2. *select method for goal, if none stop and report fail;*

3. *apply method to goal, if succeed stop and report succeed, go to one.*

. . . *In general the methods attempt to achieve a goal by creating subgoals, whose achievement is to aid in achieving the main goal. The methods then invoke the executive [i.e., the program: achieve(goal)] in order to attempt the subgoal. Thus the methods are recursive, so that the attempt to achieve one goal leads to other goals, and these, in turn, to still others. In this way the methods form an organized, cooperating system of heuristics (though each method independently remains a rational approach to achieving goals of its goal type). This recursive structure makes GPS basically a depth-first problem solver, since each method attempts everything appropriate to achieving a subgoal before returning control to the method of the subgoal that invoked it.*

The main methods of GPS jointly embody the heuristic of means-ends analysis (which we touched on briefly in the cryptarithmetic task). Means-ends analysis is typified by the following kind of common-sense argument:

I want to take my son to nursery school. What's the difference between what I have and what I want? One of distance. What changes distance? My automobile. My automobile won't work. What is needed to make it work? A new battery. What has new batteries? An auto repair shop. I want the repair shop to put in a new battery; but the shop doesn't know I need one. What is the difficulty? One of communication. What allows communication? A telephone . . . and so on.

This kind of analysis—classifying things in terms of the function they serve, and oscillating among ends, functions required, and means that perform them—forms the basic system of heuristic of GPS. More precisely, this means-ends system of heuristic assumes the following:

1. *If an object is given that is not the desired one, differences will be detectable between the available object and the desired object.*
2. *Operators affect some features of their operands and leave others unchanged. Hence operators can be characterized by the changes they produce and can be used to try to eliminate differences between the objects to which they are applied and desired objects.*
3. *If a desired operator is not applicable, it may be profitable to modify its inputs so that it becomes applicable.*
4. *Some differences will prove more difficult to affect than others. It is profitable, therefore, to try to eliminate "difficult" differences, even at the cost of introducing new differences of lesser difficulty. This process can be repeated as long as progress is being made toward eliminating the more difficult differences.*

But the seeming right-headedness of a general purpose problem solver did not easily translate into a working program. Knowledge of specific domains was clearly also necessary. You cannot fix a car simply because you are good at crossword puzzles. The ideal of a general-purpose design for problem solving, plus the attention to specific knowledge relevant to only certain domains of inquiry, led to work that came to be known as expert systems, which attracted so much attention in the commercial world.

At the root of GPS is the view that we are all in possession of general-purpose planning knowledge, which we use when we want to create a plan to solve a new problem. But the evidence is that plans are really learned by imitation. The way people actually plan is considerably different from the kinds of plans to be found in the AI literature. It is unreasonable to assume that people construct new plans when faced with new problems. This is simply too difficult to do. Planning is very hard. Understanding others' plans that are new to you is also very hard.

It is more reasonable to assume that, just as we saw with using cases for reasoning help, people have a vast assortment of possible plans at their disposal, all stored in memory in terms of their appropriateness for various situations. That is, rather than having a set of abstract rules about what one should do in various situations, people know what they have done, and what others have done, and they copy past plans. Or, to put this another way, they get reminded of past plans. After a plan has been called to mind, it is highly likely that the plan, which was used in a different situation from the one now being considered, will have to be adapted in some way. So the basic planning algorithm is:

Get reminded of prior plan
Adapt plan from reminding to fit new situation

To see what I mean here, let's look at another "man in the street" radio interview done in Hartford:

What do you think of our increased assistance in El Salvador?
1. I'm against it. I don't want to see us get involved anymore. I think we have to start taking care of things at home first.
2. It makes me fairly nervous. I look at it as a sort of Vietnam. I think it's great for the U.S. when a country does indeed need help, but I also think we should be very careful about how we spend our money, the way the economy is here in the States ourselves.

3. What happened in Vietnam should have taught the American people a lesson.
4. I'm fearful that it might lead to a situation similar to what we faced in Vietnam fifteen years ago, and therefore I would examine carefully anything we did before we got ourselves stuck into a situation we can't get ourselves out of.

These people aren't planning exactly, what they are doing is attempting to recognize plans, yet it is rather striking that they are all reminded of Vietnam. Why does this reminding occur?

People find it very difficult to have to reason out everything in their lives from first principles. We find it much easier to adopt the plans of others that we know have worked. When someone close to us dies, for example, we don't then wonder what one should do in such a situation. There are experts who tell us what plans to use: relatives, religious leaders, funeral directors. We reason out very little for ourselves.

Oddly enough, when we have a great deal of time to reason things out for ourselves, we still find ourselves following the plans of others. I recall having to answer a question about why I was going to college when I first arrived at school. I was amazed by the question. I didn't recall making the choice. I was told what plan I was to follow and didn't think about it one way or the other. We are usually told plans by our parents, and we are often criticized for deviating from those plans. We are expected to recognize what plans are to be used at what time. We are rarely expected to derive our own from scratch.

One reason why we seek to understand the beliefs, goals, and plans that underlie people's actions is that we want to be able to copy them if we see that they have worked. The other side of that coin is that we want to avoid imitating bad plans of others when they have failed. We do not need a scientific explanation as to what caused the success or failure. We are happy to store away entire plans together with their results and the conditions under which one might use those plans. Then, when we must make a decision involving planning, whether we are choosing a plan for ourselves or evaluating the plans of others, we make these decisions by referring back to prior relevant plans.

It was, in a sense, impossible for an American to fail to be reminded of Vietnam in this instance. These people did not consider, in any great detail, how the situations in Vietnam and El Salvador might differ. They simply got reminded, evaluated the consequences that resulted from a similar plan last time, and made a decision.

And the same is true of the wine makers of Champagne and Armagnac. They did not decide to buy the farms they now occupy, nor did they determine that the best method for selling their wares was to hope that somebody came by who was interested in drinking some and then buying some. They didn't think about any of this one way or the other very much. They simply were born into some existing plans and learned to execute them.

One is tempted to say that this doesn't seem like a very smart way of acting, that case-based reasoning and case-based planning are a thoughtless way to act. And in some sense they are. But it is tremendously difficult to build a case-based planner. Perhaps not as difficult as a general-problem-solver-style, rule-based planner, but nevertheless quite difficult. Even more difficult is to build a plan recognizer. Knowing what plan others are following can be quite problematic unless you have seen that plan before and can pull it out of your plan library for comparison.

People in AI were right to emphasize planning as being at the core of human and hence artificial intelligence. But they missed the point when they tried to build planners that functioned on general principles. People don't plan unless they have to. They follow the plans they were told until they fail to function properly. When that happens, people look for other plans to copy. They ask for advice. They watch others. Sometimes while watching others they get confused. People need explanations of the behavior of others they cannot readily understand by recognition. Confusion and subsequent explanation can lead to new plans being added to the plan library. Now I know, and you know, the plans that are common in Champagne and Armagnac. They may not be using such a bad set of plans, after all. They just have a different point of view about what matters in life. We don't all share the same belief system.

CHAPTER 11

Happy Birthday to Me

was about to be forty. I was depressed. Only two things would cheer me up: food and friends. I thought about the parties that people throw; the food is always awful. I decided to invite my friends to a good restaurant. The good news was that I was in Paris—there are lots of good restaurants. More good news: My American friends like to eat, and they would come for a good meal. The bad news: Americans still can't get reservations at three-star restaurants in Paris. The solution to this appeared in the form of Monsieur Spielman.

I met Monsieur Spielman at a Bar Mitzvah in Paris. It was October and I had until March to find a three-star restaurant that would allow me to bring in a bunch of perhaps raucous Americans to help me celebrate. M. Spielman said, "No problem, let's discuss it at Jamin next week." I asked how he felt so sure that he could get reservations at Jamin next week, and he said that he could get them anytime he wanted. My kind of guy.

Sure enough, the next week we were seated with M. Spielman at Jamin. M. Spielman could not only get reservations at Jamin anytime he wanted, he also got first-class service. Free champagne was brought over to the table, extra desserts we didn't order. You name it, we got it. And the meal? It was superb. We ate a lobster ravioli in a truffle sauce that was simply the best single thing I had ever eaten. Even the rolls were the best rolls I had ever eaten. And the crème brûlée: There is no finer dessert in the world. I don't even like crème brûlée. You would have thought they were making this stuff up with mirrors. Food just couldn't be this good. I asked M. Spielman if he could get a bunch of loud Americans a room for fourteen in a few months.

"Would M. Spielman be there?" the management asked.

"Of course," said M. Spielman.

"Done," said the maitre d'.

What had M. Spielman done to merit this kind of treatment? It seems that in the early seventies, when Bordeaux was selling at an all-time low, M. Spielman had stocked up on thousands of cases of 1970, which turned out to be one of the great years for Bordeaux. Restaurants had not gotten much of this wine for reasons you can make up yourself, but some years later they noticed that they didn't have it and he did. He sold it to places he liked and sent friends to those places as well. After a while, Jamin, being one of the places he liked, became quite popular, since M. Spielman seems to know everybody. So they attribute their success, at least in part, to him. This will get you good service.

I was psyched. I had been to too many parties that had chicken livers in the shape of a chicken and bands playing music that was too loud to allow anyone to talk and people being bored sitting next to others they didn't like; that wasn't the kind of party I wanted to throw for myself. For me, as you might imagine, food was the thing. I wanted a party with good food, no, great food. I wanted my closest friends to eat a great meal that they might never otherwise have, at my expense. Now my fantasy was going to become real. As the saying goes: *Be careful of what you want, because you just might get it.*

By arranging an academic meeting, I arranged an excuse to come to Paris for those friends of mine who were academics. This meant that my non-academic friends wouldn't get to come, but I hadn't realized that when I started. The next issue was selecting the menu.

When fourteen people dine together in France, they are expected to eat the same thing. This makes life easier for the chef. It is also supposed to be a shared experience. It is also the way it is done. I had no choice.

I did have a choice of what to eat, however. But even that was a problem. In general, I don't like main dishes. I mean, some are great, but there is usually too much of them, and I like to taste lots of stuff. And though Jamin claims to make the best lamb in the world, and they are probably right, I am not such a great fan of meat, that is, just a hunk of meat. So I selected only appetizers. M. Robuchon, the chef-owner of Jamin, was not amused.

Nevertheless, he agreed, March 12 arrived, along with my friends, and we all dined at a glorious banquet.

I am telling you all this because, although my birthday party was a magnificent affair, and although I loved having my friends around for my party, and although I loved every dish, basically my party was a disaster. Instead of my telling you what went wrong, I have recorded some of the other diners' recollections, which we will hear about later on (in Chapter 13).

You might be wondering what we ate at this party. I also recorded various diners' responses to the question, asked three and a half years after the party: *Do you remember my party? What did we eat?* Here are the answers I received:

Andrew: My recollection is that there were on the order of six or seven courses. I can't remember the order in which these courses were. There was at least the following, I think. I can't remember what its technical name is—it was thyroid gland of something or other. Sweetbreads? Anyway, there was thyroid gland, there was a delicious, lightly cooked, I think it was goose liver. There was an early course, it was something with truffles on it. At least three of the courses were on the nature of what we call offal. Spelled o-f-f-a-l. I don't know how offal is defined but generally, everything in that category includes inside organs of creatures. There were . . . dessert. I know why I'm having a hard time recalling what we ate, because there was a lot of food in total, but there was no course that I could identify as the central course of the meal, in the way in which more traditionally known gastronomes would consider it. There was no course that was the main course, at least not that I could recognize as the main course. It was a long time ago and I'm not doing very well at remembering it. I recall the thyroid gland, I recall the goose liver, there was this early thing with truffles but I can't remember what it was and am trying to recall what the dessert was. I remember chocolate oranges, crème de caramel . . . I'm having a hard time recalling it.

Anatole: We ate ravioli with lobster, we ate this wonderful dessert that was something like a spider web. I don't remember specific dishes, but if I think more . . . I have to imagine the progressions from ravioli to the dessert. Towards-the-middle needs to be reconstructed. There was something with fish, I remember most of the fish kinds of dishes. I think there may have been some sweetbreads of some sort, but I'm not sure.

Jerry: What did we eat? Okay, we went to this two-story restaurant in Paris and we had a bizarre dinner of huge selections, in which it was all appetizers and desserts. And it was something like four appetizers and three desserts and then there were cheeses and wines. The thing that comes to mind first was the best crème brûlée I ever had with some crumbled stuff on the bottom that was vanilla. Among the appetizers—I don't remember it very well. I basically would have to fake it. There were—I don't usually have visual memories—I think maybe the presentation was more remarkable than the taste. This is interesting . . . I think I'm not going to do very well.

Don: What we ate. No, I can remember a large number of the activities and I can remember many courses and that there was a lot of champagne. Can I remember what we ate? No. I suppose if you gave me an appropriate setting and let me relax a bit, I could recall things. For example, as I start thinking about it now, I can remember where I was sitting and I can remember various courses, and I can remember that I . . . What was the entrée? Oh, someone refused to eat it, so I ate his, it was so very good. So I'm sure I could recall it. But no, no particular names come to mind. Not even the entrée, which I now remember eating a second helping of.

Elliot: We had eight courses of wonderful things. The best part was that I sat next to two women who were on diets, so I had three of everything. I had these raviolis in something or other and I thought that was astounding, with sweetbreads, and we had this chocolate with pistachio swirls—I had three of those—astounding, absolutely astounding. And I had lots of champagne. That's what I remember. I remember the food was just astounding.

Maurice: Maybe not everything, but it was impressive. I remember the dessert, which was crème brûlée. I remember—there were too many things—something with truffles at the beginning. I don't remember the details. Was there something with the truffles? The crème I remember, because we had too much wine and the crème was so delicious and I ate the whole thing, although I didn't think I could finish it because I was so full. There were about five or six dishes; one thing, maybe the first one, was truffles. There was . . . did we have sweetbreads or something? There was fish, I believe. That's all I can remember.

Steve: I remember we were at Jamin and we had several courses, and enough wine to make me want to lie down, which I think I did, and I'm drawing a blank on the food.

What do we make of this? Why, if this meal was so fantastic, did everyone have such poor recollection? Earlier I mentioned the experiment by Bartlett in which he asked subjects to recall a rather confusing Eskimo folktale that they had heard years earlier. His conclusion from that experiment was that memory recall involved reconstructing past experience on the basis of memory structures that describe the prototypes of that experience. All the diners in this experiment had enough training in psychology to be aware of Bartlett's work and its implications. They were aware of what memory search techniques are helpful, but knowing such things really didn't help much. In fact, sometimes it hurt. Some subjects tried to reconstruct the meal by asking themselves about the main course. This didn't help because, as one of them remembered correctly, there was no main course.

   The question for us is: Can we come to understand why certain things were remembered and why other things were not? What can we better understand about the nature of human memory by looking at the results of this experiment? The answer is "quite a bit," actually, so let's get started. First, let's consider Andrew's response.

   We need to know a few basic facts about him. Andrew is British, but has lived much of his adult life in a town in America that barely has a decent restaurant. He has very rarely eaten in a really first-class restaurant, but he does like to eat. These facts account for some of what he was able to recall. He found the idea of eating organ meats to be quite unusual. He had very rarely eaten goose liver, sweetbreads, or truffles, so he remembered eating them. He wasn't sure of the name *sweetbreads*, but he was sure of their category. He recalled the type of food that he had, but not the way a gourmet would. He didn't recall these foods as dishes, but rather as the type of meat that was in them. In other words, he really didn't know enough about what he was eating in order to recall them as, say, M. Robuchon might have hoped. We cannot remember what we failed to pay attention to in the first place. And we cannot pay attention to details we would fail to notice due to our lack of knowledge of the subject matter. Memory is a knowledge-dependent affair.

By contrast, let's look at the recollections of someone more seriously concerned with food. Maurice is a Frenchman, and a Frenchman who loves to eat. Since he is an academic, he does not frequent three-star restaurants very often, but when he does, he comes to dine seriously. As we shall see later on, he was quietly annoyed by those diners who did not come to really partake of this special experience. However, even he, who noticed every detail about every course, could really remember only one course very well, the crème brûlée. He did recall the sweetbreads and the truffles, as did Andrew, but he really was no better than Andrew at describing them.

Why did he recall the crème brûlée? Crème brûlée is, after all, a very pedestrian dish. Many French restaurants serve it. I rarely order it because it is so ordinary. He remembered it because Jamin serves the best crème brûlée in the world. After you have eaten it, if you have ever had a previous crème brûlée to compare it to, you come away so impressed, it is difficult to forget it. Maurice remembered the crème brûlée because he had had it many times before, and this time was so far superior to the others that he could not forget it.

Not everyone's memory was terrible. Anatole, for example, recalled two dishes fairly well: *"ravioli with lobster"* and *"this wonderful dessert that was something like a spider web."* Anatole is a Russian by birth who has lived in the United States for a long time and who has eaten in many of the top restaurants in France. But even he recalled only two dishes, no more. Why not? Looking at the responses of the others, we see that they too recalled the lobster ravioli and the crème brûlée. The sweetbreads are mentioned a few times. In fact, had the collective group sat down together and discussed it, they could have reconstructed most of the menu.

Here, then, is the menu, exactly as it was printed and left in front of each diner on that day:

Dîner Anniversaire de Monsieur Roger Schank
Mercredi 12 Mars 1986

Ravioli de Langoustines au Chou
Galette de Truffes aux Oignons et Lard Fumé
Homard Meunière aux Épices
Foie Gras Chaud à la Crème de Lentilles
Ris de Veau Truffé aux Asperges

Fromages Frais et Affinés

Chaud-Froid de Pommes à la Pistache
Crème Froide Caramélisée à la Cassonade
Café Express et Mignardises
Chocolats Fins

Cocktail Maison
Château La Rose Pourret 1980 "St.-Emilion"
Château Bourgneuf Vayron 1979 "Pomerol"
Muscat de St. Jean de Minervois 1984

Translated, this menu indicates that we ate:
   shrimp ravioli
   truffle and onion pie
   lobster in a spicy sauce
   hot goose liver in a lentil cream sauce
   sweetbreads in a truffle sauce with asparagus
   cheese
   cold apples with a hot sauce of pistachio
   caramelized cream
   coffee
   little chocolates
No one remembered the lobster at all. And, while truffles were remembered, very little about them was remembered. One of the desserts was virtually lost. What is going on here?

One question is: Why should people be able to remember a meal three and a half years later? Maybe their memories should be considered fantastic; their remembering anything at all is perhaps suspect. On the other hand, as we shall see later on, they did remember quite a bit about the whole experience. The experience was so unique that they were each able to tell a story that described that experience. So what is going on here? I can tell you in one word: representation.

Artificial Intelligence is a field that seems more complex to the outside viewer than it really is. In order to get machines to be intelligent, it is necessary for them to know things. What things they need to know is of course a serious issue. What it means to know something is a serious issue. When the knowledge one has is used and how it is found are serious issues. But, number one in importance, more important than any of these issues, is representation. Unfortunately, the problem of representation is not all that simple to explain. This will not, however, keep me from trying.

Suppose you wanted a machine to know the fact: *George Washington chopped down a cherry tree.* How would you tell that information to the computer in such a way that it would remember it and be able to use it? There are many choices. You could put the words into a particular place in the computer's memory; let's say, memory location #452. Then, every time you wanted this sentence, you could look in #452. The problem is that, if someone asked you what kind of tree old George chopped down, your only recourse would be to have somehow anticipated that question in such a way that you could go and look in #452. But even if you got there, all you would find would be the sentence given above. You could print it out and everything would be fine, but you would have no way to select *cherry.* Further, if someone asked what the last name of that George guy who chopped down the cherry tree was, you would still be saying the entire sentence in response.

Obviously, what is needed is to put meanings, or ideas, in the computer's memory, not English sentences. This presents a number of problems. First, we need to worry about what the meaning of any word is. For example, what is the meaning of *chopped down*? Earlier we pointed out that meanings carried inferences along with them, so that whatever the meaning of *chopped down* might be, it would include the idea that the tree had been harmed in some way, that it would no longer grow, and that either George had some purpose for doing this that was going to make use of the tree, or he was just being annoying and malicious.

When we hear that a tree has been chopped down, do we remember anything different, say, a month later, than if we had been told that the tree had been *hacked down, knocked down by somebody with an ax, cut down,* or *destroyed with a sharp implement*? Basically, people do not remember words that they were told. They remember the ideas behind the words. So the first problem in representation is to determine how to represent the ideas behind the words. This would mean, in this case, deciding upon some language-neutral expression that meant *cut down with a sharp implement as tool*. The problem for AI is determining a set of such concepts that can be used as a representation. Then one must invent methods of translating English-language expressions into this more conceptual, language-independent format. Some of the issues in doing this were discussed earlier when we mentioned the idea of TRANS and of the actor-action-object format for representing events.

The problem for people, who need not be taught how to do any of this, is attempting to retrieve details they have long since discarded. There is, after all, a slight difference between *chopped down* and *hacked down*. People can detect this difference, but they really don't pay any attention to it, unless they need to. The idea of "needing to" is very important here. Without a need for these nuances, they are ignored. People determine, at the time of processing, how they will represent what has happened to them.

This aspect of representation, call it the interest factor, has some serious ramifications on the understanding process. The nuances of meaning that we "decide" to forget, by not paying attention to them when we are forming representations in our minds, will not reappear when we are asked about them a month later. People simply cannot recall the words in which an idea was expressed to them when they are asked a month later, unless they had some special reason to. And this is by no means the only problem in representation.

A month later, it would be fairly difficult to recall whether the tree had been *destroyed by lightning, knocked down by a car, vandalized by teenagers*, or *hauled away by tree surgeons after dying of old age*, unless the death of this tree were of some real interest. Now the concepts listed above are really quite different from one another, but the representation of the underlying event, for someone who really didn't care much about the tree, or young George, would be that the tree was now gone. Representation depends heavily on interest. So much so, in fact, that, were one paying attention to the George part of the story and not the tree, it would be easy to forget the tree entirely, not paying attention to anything except that George did something bad and that this might affect George and his future life. And, in fact, we are told this story because George admitted it. The lesson of this story is that young George was an honest lad, even when doing childishly impish things.

To put all this another way, the right way for a person or a machine to represent this story would be to represent concepts of morality and ignore entirely concepts about tree death. And, if we were told that, in fact, George never chopped down any cherry tree, that, in fact, he lived in an apartment house with no trees in sight, we would not worry much about it. The information to be recalled, and therefore the information to be represented, has to do with honesty and fitness for public office, not cherry trees.

Suppose a computer had been invited to my party. What would it remember? It cannot, and should not, attempt to pay attention to every detail of the experience. If it did, it would not know whether to note the color of the tablecloth, the name of the waiter, or the expression on Anatole's face at precisely 9:10 P.M. An intelligent entity pays attention to what it finds of interest. The end product of "paying attention" is a representation of events that have transpired to which one was attuned. In some sense, one immediately "forgets" what one has failed to take seriously in the first place. We represent only the aspects of a situation that matter. And "mattering" is a highly idiosyncratic affair.

What mattered to each of the diners at my birthday dinner? The answer to this question will help us understand what they represented and therefore what they remembered.

Andrew: My recollection is that there were on the order of six or seven courses.

Andrew represented the evening in a variety of ways that reflected his memory organization and relative interests and experience. He first noted that the meal was an exception to his restaurant script in that there were more courses than he was used to. A more experienced eater at three-star restaurants would have expected this; one reason is that "tasting menus" are common at three-star restaurants so that you can sample a little of what makes the restaurant exceptional. These restaurants know that you don't eat at their establishment every day and are interested in showing off what they do well. Anatole, Steve, and Maurice fail to mention this in a surprised way because it was something they would have expected and therefore barely noticed since they have eaten at this type of restaurant many times before. The others mentioned it as a prime feature of the experience:

Jerry: We had a bizarre dinner of huge selections, in which it was all appetizers and desserts. And it was something like four appetizers and three desserts and then there were cheeses and wines.

Don: I can remember a large number of the activities and I can remember many courses.

Elliot: We had eight courses of wonderful things.

Another thing that Andrew remembered was the strangeness of the type of food served. Here again, Andrew had really never eaten food like this. He represented, and therefore was able to recall years later, what he noticed as being out of the ordinary. In particular, this meant:

Andrew: There was at least the following, I think. I can't remember what its technical name is—it was thyroid gland of something or other. Sweetbreads? Anyway, there was thyroid gland, there was a delicious, lightly cooked, I think it was goose liver. There was an early course, it was something with truffles on it. At least three of the courses were on the nature of what we call offal. Spelled o-f-f-a-l. I don't know how offal is defined but generally, everything in that category includes inside organs of creatures.

There were, as we have seen, more ordinary foods as well. The main part of the meal included shrimp ravioli, truffle and onion pie, lobster in a spicy sauce, hot goose liver in a lentil cream sauce, and sweetbreads in a truffle sauce with asparagus. But Andrew failed to recall the lobster or the shrimp. The reason is, he didn't notice them. Now, obviously, he noticed them at the time, but the only things he noticed for representation and therefore memory purposes were the things he found worthy of thinking about. He needed to think about all the organ meats, and how he felt about eating them, and so on. In other words, he remembered what was interesting. Interest is, after all, an idiosyncratic affair. With this in mind, let's look at what interested the others and why:

Anatole: We ate ravioli with lobster, we ate this wonderful dessert that was something like a spider web. I don't remember specific dishes, but if I think more . . . I have to imagine the progressions from ravioli to the dessert. . . . There was something with fish, I remember most of the fish kinds of dishes. I think there may have been some sweetbreads of some sort, but I'm not sure.

Anatole remembered what was especially good. To him, the meal was a gastronomic experience. To Andrew, it was more of a sociological experience. Anatole was interested in tasting the food, Andrew was interested in wondering why this food was being eaten.

Jerry: The thing that comes to mind first was the best crème brûlée I ever had with some crumbled stuff on the bottom that was vanilla.

I have to agree with Jerry about this. Not remembering the crème brûlée is hard to do if you have ever had it before. Notice that Jerry had had it before, and thus had something to compare it to. He could remember it because he could note its unusualness for its category. Or, to put this another way, we remember things when they cause us to change something in our memories. This would include correcting an impression of what a particular food tastes like or could taste like.

Elliot: I had these raviolis in something or other and I thought that was astounding, with sweetbreads, and we had this chocolate with pistachio swirls.

The shrimp ravioli get my vote for best of the appetizers, too. Elliot, who really likes to eat, notices tastes, not surprisingly.

Maurice: I remember the dessert, which was crème brûlée. I remember—there were too many things—something with truffles at the beginning . . . Was there something with the truffles? The crème I remember, because we had too much wine and the crème was so delicious and I ate the whole thing, although I didn't think I could finish it because I was so full. . . . One thing, maybe the first one, was truffles. There was . . . did we have sweetbreads or something? There was fish, I believe. That's all I can remember.

Maurice didn't do a bad job of remembering but we could expect this to be a more difficult task for him because he lives in Paris and eats, well, not like this every day, but something that tries to be like this quite often. In some sense, it is surprising that he remembered as much as he did, a testament to the quality of the food and Maurice's appreciation of that quality. Memory reflects interests, as I have said.

In general, people also remembered things they thought were strange. People remember expectation violation because they have to explain what went wrong to themselves so they won't be fooled next time. With that in mind, let's look at what else people took note of:

Andrew: There was no course that I could identify as the central course of the meal, in the way in which more traditionally known gastronomes would consider it. There was no course that was the main course, at least not that I could recognize as the main course.

Don: What was the entrée? Oh, someone refused to eat it, so I ate his, it was so very good. So I'm sure I could recall it. But no, no particular names come to mind. Not even the entrée, which I now remember eating a second helping of.

Elliot: The best part was that I sat next to two women who were on diets, so I had three of everything . . . we had this chocolate with pistachio swirls—I had three of those—astounding, absolutely astounding. And I had lots of champagne. That's what I remember. I remember the food was just astounding.

Steve: . . . and enough wine to make me want to lie down, which I think I did, and I'm drawing a blank on the food.

There was no main course. Some people remembered this, others were confused by it and misremembered because of it. The food was outstanding. Some remembered this, and others were confused by it. People ate too much, or drank too much, and remembered the experience. Memory is a tricky affair. It depends heavily on what is noticed and represented, which in turn depends heavily on what is in memory in the first place.

As we shall see, it also depends upon the construction of stories. I asked these diners another question about this experience, one not focused on the food, which revealed yet another aspect of human memory. Memory depends upon both wanting to remember and having to remember. We remember what interests us because we want to, because our interests and our goals are identical. We remember what we have to remember because circumstances require it, because someone or some need of memory asks us to.

CHAPTER 12

Rustic Questions

s I mentioned earlier, my kids often visit their grandparents, who have retired to Florida. In this trek, they join thousands of other children on Christmas and Easter vacations who give their parents a break for a week and cause their grandparents to spend weeks planning for their arrival and weeks after their departure discussing the visit of these small princes and princesses. Ex–New Yorkers who have become Floridians in their old age follow a massive script of their own invention. This includes prescriptions about how to dress (in pastels mostly); how to wear their hair (blond and puffed up is de rigueur for grandmothers); how to furnish their apartments (yellow, mirrors, wicker furniture, and flowered stuff are big); and, most of all, how to eat.

The rules about eating are quite specific. Florida has something called the "early bird," which is a way of eating dinner cheaply if you arrive at the restaurant before 5:30. Now, while 5:30 might strike a serious eater as a horrifying time to eat, the white-haired, tennis-shoed set can no longer eat at any other time. They have trained themselves to eat at this hour and, in fact, they go to sleep earlier and get up earlier, thus shifting their entire schedules in order to "catch the early bird" regularly. The food at these places is not exactly haute cuisine, but as this is a community of people who by and large came from very humble beginnings, eating well has never been a priority, unless of course by "eating well" one means eating a lot.

One of the prescriptions and rituals about food for this retired set includes "avoid cooking," so when the grandchildren arrive, they go out to eat every night. During these vacation periods, these grandparents are faced with the realization that their eating scripts bear little relation to those of children, and so they begin to wonder about where to take the grandchildren. Florida has so many retired people and so few children by comparison that far more restaurants are set up with old people in mind than with kids, so the grandchildren get taken out to Chinese restaurants or Burger King as a concession to their different eating habits. But if someplace else can be found especially of interest to children, of course, they go there.

My children returned home from one of their visits with excited discussion of a restaurant where you get to bang hammers on the table anytime you want to and are encouraged to whenever anyone is having a birthday, which, according to them, happened about every fifteen minutes. I never really understood what kind of restaurant this was, except I gathered that some kind of seafood was served there.

When I travel to Florida to visit my parents, they have to go through similar script alterations. I refuse the early bird and the restaurants that serve it, usually insisting on eating in whatever the best restaurants in their area happen to be. They go along, my mother happily, my father reluctantly, and we try out the best that Florida has to offer, but we cannot do this every night. So one night, as I was visiting after giving a lecture nearby, they suggested that we visit "a place that the kids like because they bang on the tables." I was interested enough to see what this was all about, but my mother, knowing my tastes, had suggested it for another reason: They serve crab.

When you travel, the best food to eat is the local food, both because it's probably fresh and because the locals have probably figured out the best way to cook it. So, when traveling, I try to keep up on what stuff is best where. In Florida, this means stone crab. So, of course, I was eager to go.

The place is called the Rustic Inn, which caused me to wonder immediately about why a place would call itself "rustic." Did rustic mean wooden chairs? Wooden tables with no tablecloths? Waitresses dressed in homey outfits? Food thrown at you? A beer list instead of a wine list? Would they be proud of these characteristics? The answer to all these questions was a loud "yes."

The racket as you enter the Rustic Inn is amazing. It is full of children, each with a wooden mallet in his hand. The mallets are theoretically for smashing the crabs, although I never saw anyone actually use them for that purpose. The tables are carefully covered in newspaper, not plastic-covered newspaper or something that looks like newspaper, just four or five pages of the local gazette. My mother pointed out that these were new newspapers, that is, unread ones, not ones collected from the trash. This was comforting in some vague way.

The menu had many different kinds of fish to choose from, but clearly the thing to order was a pile of crabs. Well, I shouldn't say that you know you are ordering a pile of crabs; rather, you order crabs and you receive a pile of crabs, virtually thrown onto the newspaper.

I ordered stone crabs, which, as I said, are the right thing to eat in Florida. I like them best cold, and as this was the only way you could get them here, I was encouraged. And they were delicious. Stone crabs ordinarily mean five or six stone crab claws. The more normal thing to order here, at least in terms of the sheer number of patrons who were ordering it, was a tremendous pile of what looked like Maryland crabs. As is often the case with Maryland crabs, they were served after having been rolled in a spicy dry sauce that rubs off on your fingers as you eat them. In Maryland, too, they are thrown on the table in a big heap, always more of them than you could possibly eat. Your hands get tired before your stomach does, since it's a lot of work to open each one and extract the little bit of meat in the body and the even smaller amount in the claws.

While I was wondering why Maryland crabs were the highlight of a Florida crab restaurant, my mother was wondering why the lights in the restaurant were all decorated with wooden baskets for lamp shades. My father was wondering why he was enjoying his beer so much and why, if he liked beer, he rarely drank it.

Also, he was curious about why he hadn't hated the place as much this time as he had the last time. This last question became easy to answer when my mother realized that we had had no birthday parties so far. Further, they had been to the Rustic Inn only during school vacation periods before, and the place was considerably less noisy with the kiddies safely ensconced up north.

Since I had not long returned from France, I began to think about how a Frenchman might view this restaurant. The French, after all, are some of the most highly scripted people in the world when it comes to eating. They have rules for everything, from where one should sit to who should order first, to what to drink when, and how much. Mostly, of course, they have rules for decorum in restaurants and one of the reasons they object to having Americans in their restaurants is that Americans are so incredibly loud. In fact, all cultures have very set ideas of how loud one should speak in ordinary conversation, how close one should stand to one's conversational partner, and so on. The French follow the "whisper and stand close" script while Americans believe in "stand far apart and yell." In restaurants, where everyone is the same distance apart regardless of cultural background, the decibel level fails to change in compensation. I always have difficulty hearing my French students when they ask a question in class. I am simply not used to hearing whispers.

Well, if the noise Americans make in restaurants bothers French people, just imagine their reaction to the Rustic Inn! Actually, I had a lot of fun imagining a Frenchman being told he was going to a restaurant, then entering a large roomful of mallet-banging children with piles of crabs on newspapers. It was so American, so incredibly un-French. So, when Jean-François showed up in New York one day, and we started to plan where we should eat, the Rustic Inn naturally came to mind. Of course, the Rustic Inn is in Florida, not New York.

Where do you take a French gourmet when he comes to visit you? To a French restaurant? When a Japanese comes to visit you, if a Japanese restaurant is handy, should you take him there? Actually, both of these cultures believe that the way they eat is really the only way to eat. They are willing to try other cuisines, but they won't really like them much. Americans, having no real cuisine of their own and being quite frequent travelers, like trying out the local food. But even Americans begin to crave hamburgers, never quite give up Cokes, and start to object to "all the raw fish" or "all the heavy sauces." People like what they are used to.

But, there is a difference between a French gourmet and your average Frenchman. A French gourmet doesn't want to eat French food in America because he can't believe it will be good French food. Further, as America has many cuisines not common in France, the right choice for a French gourmet in New York is Japanese or Chinese, not French.

So, as I am pondering where to take Jean-François, I think that showing him a brand of American culture he probably hasn't seen before would be a good experience, and I am reminded that New York has its own version of the Rustic Inn, called Sidewalkers. Sidewalkers doesn't have as much noise, nor baskets for lamp shades, but it does have piles of Maryland crabs on newspapers. And, I might add, the crabs are just a bit tastier, probably because they are fresher than they are at the Rustic Inn.

So, I did take Jean-François there. He hated it. Oh, he thought the crabs were very good, and he thought the place was, well, different. But it wasn't dining now, was it? It was eating.

All of this led me to wonder about why the Rustic Inn (and Sidewalkers) puts newspapers on the table instead of tablecloths. Of course, the answer is obvious. They are piling crabs on the table, so throwing away newspapers is easier and cheaper than re-covering the table with fancy linen. Well, suppose they didn't throw the crabs on the table; suppose they put them on a plate very neatly and artistically. Would they use tablecloths in that case? Probably they would. Would they have baskets for lamp shades? Probably not. So, one hypothesis is that once they decide to throw the crabs on the table in a heap, all the other rustic stuff follows. If you are going to eat messy, then the ambiance of the place should not be pretentious; maybe it should even be kind of crass.

Actually, this doesn't follow all that well or explain why eating crabs has to be messy. They do have to be eaten with the fingers. Further, with all the dry brown spicy sauce on your fingers and all the heaped eaten crab bodies on the table, the place is going to be a mess no matter how it started out. Dirty napkins and random crab legs everywhere means you may as well not even try to be civilized about it all. Give the kids mallets. What the hell.

Okay then. It is all quite reasonable to have the restaurant look and act this way if what they are serving is inherently sloppy, but why, then, didn't Jean-François like it? The food was good after all.

Here is a better question to ask that may help you figure out the answer to the first question. Let us suppose that Jean-François wanted to ask a young lady to marry him on a particular evening. He decides to do this over dinner. Does he choose the Rustic Inn? This question is easy to answer. It is a laughable question. Why? Because asking a young lady to marry you means romance, and the Rustic Inn is not romantic. Does it matter if a restaurant is romantic? It does to the French. And to me too. Even if it's a business dinner. Why? Because eating and dining are two different experiences.

What is the difference between eating and dining, you ask? Well, I'm not going to tell you. Questions are the important thing, answers are less important. Learning to ask a good question is the heart of intelligence. Learning the answer—well, answers are for students. Questions are for thinkers.

Questions occur to us constantly as we read or see, and most of these questions remain unanswered. Adults tend to inhibit their questions all the time, which may make them "adult" but probably doesn't make them any smarter. On the other hand, children have no self-editing mechanism to stop them from asking the questions that occur to them.

The reasons that questions get inhibited are manifold. Often, we just don't have the time. While watching the news on TV, we can start to think about the ramifications of something we have just seen, while some new piece of news is reported upon, causing us to forget our current questions or to miss the next news item. In dealing with other people directly, we don't always have someone to ask, or it is impolite to interrupt them, and so on. Even while reading a newspaper, which we can do at our own pace, we have difficulty asking questions because we have no one to ask.

Questions start the process of thinking. Questions come in when expectation failures occur. An anomaly is, in essence, a kind of question that causes us to seek an explanation. We fail to understand because our expectations have been violated; we attempt to understand by formulating a question, the answer to which will result in a new expectation. The next time, we won't fail to understand if we can ask the right question. In order to discover what might be anomalous about an event or an action, we have to have been asking ourselves a set of questions about the nature of that action. Anomalies appear when the answers to one or more of those questions are unknown. Then, we seek to explain what was going on; then, we can begin to create an explanation.

People have powerful models of the world. Through these

models, which are based on the accumulated set of our experiences, new experiences are interpreted. When the new experiences that a person perceives fit nicely into the framework of expectations that have been derived from experience, an understander has little problem understanding.

But new experiences often do not correspond to what we expect. In that case, we must reevaluate what is going on. We must attempt to explain why we were wrong in our expectations. We must do this, or we will fail to grow as a result of our experiences. Learning requires expectation failure—the recognition that we are confronted with an anomaly—followed by the explanation of that expectation failure.

As we observe the actions of various entities in the world around us, we ask questions: What is our neighbor doing? Why is the bank teller I see every day suddenly asking for an ID? Is this a new policy? What is the Libyan army doing in Chad? Why? The questions that are required for the normal understanding of other people's behavior can indeed be broken down into a few main groups.

We don't really have many different kinds of questions to ask. If this assertion seems odd, consider that most of our questions about the world fall into three basic categories of things that we try to explain:

Reasons: What goals does a relevant actor have?

Event Causation: What chain of events caused an event to take place?

Outcomes: What will happen next?

So, with these three questions in mind, let's revisit the Rustic Inn. My initial concerns were about the goals of the relevant actors, in this case, my parents, the workers at the restaurant, and the management of the restaurant. The chain of events is defined by the script, in this case, the not-so-fancy-restaurant script. The prediction of outcomes is relevant to the quality of the food, which translates here into deciding what to order.

I am armed with these basic questions upon arrival at the Rustic Inn. I am thinking about all of them. Why did my parents choose this place? *They know I like seafood. They wanted to show me a place that my kids liked. They didn't want to pay a lot of money. My mother likes seafood. My father likes filet of sole. They have it.*

The value of scripts is to take away questions, to save us for something else. I don't have to wonder whether the lady who is asking what I want is really willing to bring it to me or to figure out what she wants for performing this service. I don't have to think about causation questions. I found an appropriate script, and until it fails, I can ignore these issues.

I do have to worry about predicting outcomes, however. I want to know what to order. Ordering is predicting the future, just as voting and betting are a form of prognostication. I am about to predict that I will like what I order. This problem immediately starts me worrying about the goals of the management.

We know that they are in business to make money, but if that were their sole goal, I would be concerned. Usually people have multiple goals. Here, for example, their goal was also to create a fun atmosphere, especially for kids. Now, of course, achieving this goal can also be a way to make money. "Get those grandparents in with their darlings" is a pretty good strategy for Florida. So, I begin to get concerned. If money is the number one goal and fun for the customers is number two, then quality food might not even be number three. I start to think about this.

But what does it mean to think? In this case, thinking means asking more questions and trying to answer the interesting ones. We have seen where the questions come from initially. They come from the three available old standards that we are always asking ourselves, although not always consciously. But where do answers come from? Answers come from remindings. This is one reason that your mind wanders. Every time you get reminded, you get an answer of sorts, but, more important, you get a new question.

When I wonder whether the goal of management is to make money by providing a restaurant that is fun, I ask myself, not quite consciously, whether I know any restaurants where this is the case. I ask this question because I want to check on the quality of the food there. My mind readily supplies some answers in the form of reminding. I am reminded of Burger King again. I am reminded of a place called the Auto Pub in New York, where my parents used to take my kids. They got to sit in vintage cars while they ate. Imagine the quality of food there. Food was not the selling point.

These remindings cause me to ask myself whether the prediction they make is relevant here. Is the food not the primary concern here? Is atmosphere the main goal? I am reminded of Taillevent.

Atmosphere is everything at Taillevent, but the food is excellent as well. I am wondering whether the Rustic Inn can pull off both. One vote for, one vote against.

Suddenly, a new question occurs to me. Having been reminded of France, I am reminded of the fact that Taillevent is a very French place. In a sense, it typifies French restaurants. It would be out of place in Ft. Lauderdale, just as the Rustic Inn would be out of place in Paris. Where do these rather weird thoughts come from? They come from the questioning-reminding-questioning cycle. I am still trying to find out what to order. I cannot do so until I know the goals of the management. Are they good guys (people who care about food as a way to earn their money) or bad guys (people who take advantage of the fact that people have to eat to earn their money)? I need to know because I am attempting to predict what they will do with the food that I order. So my mind speculates on how the Rustic Inn might typify America, and this speculation leads to questions about where to take Jean-François and so forth, but I still have to order.

I have now generated the hypothesis that this place does not have food as its top priority, but that does not necessarily mean that the food is bad. It means that it isn't great. It means that they haven't got a $200,000-a-year chef on the payroll, but the food might be good, in spite of the management's goals. I begin to wonder about the other questions that I have left hanging, the ones about my parents' goals and the event chains that will take place.

We established that my parents' collective goal was to make me happy, etc., and they know that I like good food. Now possibly they might not know good food if it hit them in the mouth. I speculate on this thought. It is not true. My father is a filet of sole expert, after all. More important, my mother likes good food. She especially likes good seafood, the effects of being raised in a kosher home with no kitchen, no doubt. She wouldn't have brought me here if the food weren't good. One more vote in favor.

Finally, we can examine the cooking script. What cooking script might they be using? We know they aren't using the *great-chef-invents-while-coordinating-his-underchefs* script. But do we have reason to suspect they are using the *take-it-out-of-the-freezer-and-put-it-on-the-steam-table* script?

I think about this awhile and realize that this is a busy place. The food is likely to be fresh. Freezing would be unlikely here. Further, the cooking process for crabs is really no more than simple steaming or boiling and the production of a fairly simple sauce.

Finally, I have answered all my questions. I can order crabs and expect them to turn out okay. The management's rustic schtick is nice for attracting kids, and Americans probably like it. I store away a question for future inquiry about Jean-François which, as we saw, led to more questions. My mother's taste is to be trusted, and this trust is verified.

The role of all these questions is to generate new questions. The hypothetical explanation is used to match against the current situation. To the extent that it matches, that match generates questions about whether the match is appropriate, whether the circumstances are very different, or whether some other explanation should be sought.

Understanding is question-driven. To understand we must be able to ask questions, to wonder about the things we are reading or hearing about. We must be able to take phenomena that are out of the domain of our prior experiences and find remindings of two types. We must be able to find remindings from our own experiences that are quite close in spirit to the experience that we are currently processing. Or, when no personal remindings are available, we can access the explanations of others in the form of proverbs or general words of wisdom and try to make them fit.

In a sense, the first kind of reminding is a shortcut, an easy method of processing a new situation by finding a very closely related old experience to contrast with the current one. When that path is not open to us, usually because such a memory simply fails to come to mind, then we must take a more active role. We must find related explanation patterns that we have gleaned by listening to others and allow those explanation patterns to drive the questioning process. To put this another way, we must *try* to get reminded.

In order to understand or create, one has to have the desire to know the answers to questions that are generated during the process of understanding. If, for example, you are going to read a terrorism story, you must have some questions that are driving the process. In other words, you must have some reason for why you have begun to read this story in the first place, namely, to answer the background questions that you have about a subject, the answer to which you know will interest you.

Why *do* you read a story in the newspaper? When you read a story about a plane crash, for example, you are not just reading it to find out what happened but for some set of personal concerns about the world. Otherwise, you really have no reason to read the story.

When a story about a plane crash comes by, the ordinary reader has in mind questions such as:

I wonder why there's so much terrorism today.
or
Am I safe when I fly?
or
Why is it so easy to push America around? What should we do?
or
How can I better come to understand the world situation by seeing what is going on with terrorism?
or even
I feel the need to know about blood and gore, so give me all the details. How else will I know how to act if it happens to me?

It might seem, at first glance, that you can pick up a newspaper and just read the articles to kill the time or amuse yourself or whatever. What happens then? Actually, you are letting your background questions take over. You are always curious about hundreds, maybe thousands of things. You don't have to be thinking of them explicitly when you pick up the newspaper. The questions are there all the time, ready to be answered. Questions arise from the fundamental desire to know, and wanting to know implies having an active knowledge-seeking mechanism that can get frustrated when it is not fed frequently enough. In other words, you also wish to eliminate boredom.

Boredom is a paucity of questions, or, if questions are present, a paucity of information from which one can derive answers. One advantage of boredom is that it may begin the process of generating more questions simply because one is bored, without any outside stimulus. In any case, the capacity to be bored and the capacity to ask creative questions are very much related. When we see a news story for the second time, we need to get its earlier occurrence from memory, so we can use the original experience for comparison. If the new story is identical to the old or if the new information it provides is rather paltry or uninteresting, we get bored. Why? Because no new questions are raised and because we seem to have nothing to learn, nothing to think about as a result of the new experience.

This problem of boredom hit me one day when I was talking about FRUMP, our story-understanding program that read the UPI wire. Whenever an important visitor came to our lab, we would show him FRUMP. The program was pretty impressive as it zipped along, spitting out summaries as fast as it could get the stories to read.

To save the possible embarrassment of having it find nothing that it knew enough to read about, or, worse, finding a story to read that it might get wrong in some way, we had a set of stories stored that we knew it would read properly. This wasn't as deceitful as it might seem, since we were happy to talk about FRUMP's error rate. What we were trying to avoid was having everybody standing around watching, waiting for a story to come across the wire that was in FRUMP's domain of expertise, which was limited to earthquakes, oil spills, diplomatic visits, invasions, nationalizations, airplane accidents, and other such basically physical or political events. So, we stored fifty or so all-time favorites for FRUMP to read.

After maybe the tenth time of watching FRUMP read about an earthquake in Iran, the same earthquake in Iran, I began to wonder why FRUMP never got bored. Why didn't it say, *thank you very much but I've already heard about that ad nauseam*, or, at least, *gee, there have been a lot of earthquakes in Iran lately*. Well, it never said any of these things, to no one's great surprise, since it had in no way been programmed to be able to say these things.

I began to wonder what it was that triggered people to recognize past events as being the same as current ones.

There seemed to be two quite different types of answers to this question. The first was addressed by the idea of case-based reasoning and dynamic memory. People recognize B as an instance of A because the basic processing mechanism causes us, when processing B, to ask memory if anything like B has occurred before. FRUMP didn't do this, but CHEF did, as we learned to improve our programs by having them rely less on scripts and more on prior cases.

The second answer is that FRUMP was not especially curious. FRUMP was interested in how many people died and what the dollar value of the damage was, but it never had more profound questions. Had it had more profound questions, what would these questions have looked like?

For one thing, it might have wondered about the root cause

of earthquakes, why they occurred when they occurred and so on. It might have wondered about why so many people died in Armenia but not in San Francisco during earthquakes of similar magnitudes. But, in order to wonder about such things, it would have had to have been thinking about such things in the first place. It would have had to have had a need to know about such things for something it was trying to accomplish. Wonderment comes from a need to know. The need to know is based, at least in part, on the ability to use in some way what is found out. So, with this all in mind, we began to build AQUA.

AQUA was a question-based understanding program. Our motto in building it was *questions in, questions out*. The idea was that expectations are really questions anyway. When a reader begins to peruse a newspaper story, he comes prepared to read that story with a set of questions. Now, these questions are not necessarily conscious; he could not tell you which questions he wants to know.

When I entered the Rustic Inn, I had a set of questions about that experience that came to mind during the experience. These were questions that were really not all that new. They were questions that I think about all the time, or else questions that I have been recently thinking about. Recall that I had been living in France and thinking about French restaurants a great deal when I entered the Rustic Inn. My parents informed me that I had been to the Rustic Inn with them a few years earlier, but I had totally forgotten that experience. In any case, one can be sure that the questions that came to mind this time did not come to mind the last time. Some questions stay forever, I suppose, but most depend upon one's interests at the time.

So I was thinking about a set of things, I had a set of unanswered questions that I was ready to answer if any information came up that was relevant. A newspaper reader behaves the same way. He is wondering about certain things he has been following in previous days. He is looking for updates. He is full of questions about what various players in various plays have done now and why.

We decided to build AQUA to reflect this mode of operation. In other words, AQUA, like me in the Rustic Inn, never processed the same story in the same way. Its interests changed according to its most recent experiences. Here is an example of AQUA (written by Ashwin Ram) in action. First we see a newspaper story that AQUA is to read:

Terrorists recruit boy as car bomber

A 16-year-old Lebanese got into an explosive-laden car and went on a suicide bombing mission to blow up the Israeli army headquarters in Lebanon. The teenager was a Shiite Moslem but not a religious fanatic. He was recruited for the mission through another means: blackmail.

AQUA was a program that asked questions when it got interested in something. AQUA started with a set of questions about why anybody does anything and, if it could answer them itself, by referring to what was in its memory, it did. If it could not, it tried to find the answer to these questions in the story it was reading. If it could not find those answers there, it waited patiently until the next story it read. As a result, AQUA started with questions, and ended with questions, but they were usually not the same questions.

In the above story, AQUA first tries to find out why this actor did what he did. It detects an anomaly in what it assumes to be true about the behavior of most people (in other words, it finds killing oneself to be odd). The following is computer-generated output:

Trying to explain why did the teenage Lebanese boy do the suicide bombing?

Was the suicide bombing instrumental to another action?

Does the teenage Lebanese boy typically do suicide bombings?

Characterizing the outcomes death-state and destroyed-state of the suicide bombing from the point of view of the teenage Lebanese boy (the actor)

Does the teenage Lebanese boy want to achieve the death of the teenage Lebanese boy?

Anomaly! The suicide bombing violates the goal of the boy to preserve the life state of the boy.

Does the teenage Lebanese boy want to achieve the destruction of the Israeli army headquarters in Lebanon?

No relevant goals found.

Did the teenage Lebanese boy want to avoid a negative outcome of not doing the suicide bombing?

No relevant outcomes found.

Did the teenage Lebanese boy enjoy doing the suicide bombing?

No relevant goals found.

Did the teenage Lebanese boy habitually do suicide bombings?

No relevant activities found.
Characterized outcome as a bad outcome for the actor.

In addition to the above questions, which focus on the actor's reasons for performing an action, AQUA also considered the planner's reasons for planning that action, if the actor and the planner were different. AQUA would ask whether the planner wanted an outcome of the action, whether he knew the outcome of the action, etc. Thus, for the above story, AQUA also asks the following questions:

Trying to explain why did the terrorist group plan the suicide bombing?
    Did the terrorist group want the outcome of the car bombing?
    Characterizing the outcomes: death-state and damaged-state of MOP: the suicide bombing from the point of view of: the terrorist group (the planner)
    Does the terrorist group want to achieve the death of the teenage Lebanese boy?
    No relevant goals found.
    · Does the terrorist group want to achieve the destruction of the Israeli army headquarters in Lebanon?
    Matches typical goals
    Did the terrorist group typically do suicide bombings?
    Matches typical activities
    No anomaly detected.
    Anomaly! The suicide bombing violates the goal of the boy to preserve the life-state of the boy
    Searching for abstract explanation patterns
    Did the suicide bombing result in a state? and was the goal of the boy to achieve the state more important than the goal of the boy to preserve the life-state of the boy?
    No other results of the suicide bombing known.
    Suspending explanation
    Did the boy believe that the suicide bombing would result in the death-state of the boy?
    No relevant beliefs found.
    Suspending explanation
    Answering question: Did the boy believe that the suicide bombing would result in the death-state of the boy?
    with: The boy did not believe that the suicide bombing would result in the death-state of the boy.

Restarting suspended explanation

The boy decided to do the suicide bombing despite the violation of the goal of the boy to preserve the life-state of the boy.

The planner, the terrorist group, is not the same as the actor, the boy.

Anomaly! The planner, the terrorist group, planned an action with a bad outcome for the actor, the boy.

Searching for abstract explanation patterns

Did the terrorist group want to achieve the death-state of the boy?

Did the terrorist group want to destroy the Israeli army head-quarters?

and did the terrorist group want to avoid the death-state of the terrorist group?

Was the goal of the terrorist group to destroy the Israeli army headquarters more important than the goal of the terrorist group to preserve the life-state of the boy?

Searching for stereotypical explanation patterns

Asking: Is the boy a typical teenager?

Asking: Why would a teenager do a suicide bombing?

Situation index = suicide bombing

Stereotype index = teenager

No explanations found

Asking: Is the boy a typical Lebanese person?

Asking: Why would a Lebanese person do a suicide bombing?

Situation index = suicide bombing

Stereotype index = Lebanese person

Retrieved stereotypical explanations:

XP-religious-fanatic (category index = XP-sacrifice)

Is the goal of the teenage Lebanese boy to achieve the destruction of the Israeli army headquarters in Lebanon more important than the goal of the teenage Lebanese boy to preserve the life of the teenage Lebanese boy?

Not known

Applying XP-religious-fanatic to, why did the boy do the suicide bombing?

The boy did the suicide bombing

because the boy was a religious fanatic.

The boy is a religious fanatic

because the boy is a Shiite Moslem.

The boy wants to achieve the destruction of the Israeli army headquarters because the boy is a religious fanatic.

The goal of the boy to achieve the destruction of the Israeli army headquarters is more important than the goal of the boy to preserve the life-state of the boy.

The boy decided to do the suicide bombing
because XP-sacrifice.

Installing questions to verify explanation:
What is the religion of the Lebanese boy?
What is the religious zeal of the teenage Lebanese boy?

So, AQUA wound up, when all was said and done, with more questions. These questions were found by creating a series of hypotheses that in turn created a set of possible explanations, which in turn created more questions. Questions in, questions out.

The next sentence in the story happens to answer one of the questions that AQUA just decided it cared about, so, next, AQUA continues on in light of this new information:

S-16: The teenager was a Shiite Moslem but not a religious fanatic.
Answering question: What is the religion of the boy?
with: The boy is a Shiite Moslem.
Answering question: What is the religious zeal of the boy?
with: The boy is not very zealous about the Shiite Moslem religion.
Refuting hypothesis:
The boy did the suicide bombing
because the boy was a religious fanatic.
Processing word: mission
Instantiating concept: mission
Trying to attach bombing to the mission
Trying to attach suicide to the bombing mission
Asking basic questions for the suicide bombing mission
Who did the suicide bombing mission?
Searching for the actor of the suicide bombing mission
Using sentence subject: the teenage Lebanese boy
Filling actor slot of the suicide bombing mission
Trying to attach the car to the bombing
Initial list of candidates: (target instrumentation)
Building two hypotheses for car bombing:
The car is the target of the bombing.
The car is the instrument of the bombing.
Specializing the bombing to suicide bombing

Confirming hypothesis:
The car is the instrument of the bombing.
Attaching the car to the instrument slot of the bombing
What was the purpose of the recruit?
Transforming to: What terrorist act was planned by the terrorist group?
Processing word: car
Processing word: bomber
Trying to attach the car to the bombing
Answering question: What was the purpose of the recruit?
with: the car bombing
Satisfying prediction from as
filling Requested-MOP slot of the recruit
Searching of referent for the Lebanese teenager
Merging concepts:
the young boy
the Lebanese teenager
Filling to slot of get into with the car
Looking for possible specializations
Enter is a get into with to = container
Specializing get into with to = car to enter

Now AQUA has learned that the suicide bombing was not done because of religious zeal but because of blackmail. At this point, AQUA has determined that it has just created a new explanation pattern that may be useful in the future. In the next story, it attempts to use that pattern:

S-25: Jerusalem—A young girl drove an explosive-laden car into a group of Israeli guards in Lebanon. The suicide attack killed three guards and wounded two others. . . .

The driver was identified as a 16-year-old Lebanese girl. . . . Before the attack, she said that a terrorist organization had threatened to harm her family unless she carried out the bombing mission for them. She said that she was prepared to die in order to protect her family.

When this story is read, AQUA retrieves the new explanation blackmail-suicide-bombing and applies it to the story. The question that is pending from the last story, along with this explanation, is also instantiated:

Trying to explain why did the girl do the suicide bombing?
    Searching for stereotypical explanations
    Retrieved stereotypical explanations:
XP-blackmail-suicide-bombing
    Applying XP-blackmail-suicide-bombing to the girl did the suicide bombing.
    Instantiating pending questions:
    Did the girl want to prevent a state more than the girl wanted to preserve the life-state of the girl?

This new question is created while AQUA reads and is again answered when AQUA reads this story further:

Answering question: Did the girl want to prevent a state more than the girl wanted to preserve the life-state of the girl?
    with: The girl wanted to protect the family of the girl more than the girl wanted to preserve the life-state of the girl.
    Elaborating XP-blackmail-suicide-bombing:
    Answering question: Did the actor want to prevent a state more than the actor wanted to preserve the life-state of the actor?
    with: The actor wanted to protect the family of the actor more than the actor wanted to preserve the life-state of the actor.
    New questions for XP-blackmail-suicide-bombing:
    Why did the actor want to protect the family of the actor more than the actor wanted to preserve the life-state of the actor?

AQUA reads and wonders, creates questions and creates tentative explanations that are themselves questions. To put this another way, we look for new information when we read, or see, or experience anything. That is, we do if we are actively thinking. A thinking machine would be a questioning machine. This is as true of people as it is of computers, of course.

So, I wondered about the Rustic Inn because I was thinking about various matters that had caused questions to come to mind whose explanations might be found by observing the Rustic Inn. I wondered about certain questions, such as why France wouldn't have a similar restaurant, and whether that would be a reason to take Jean-François there or a reason *not* to take Jean-François there. I attempted to predict correctly; I failed. When Jean-François didn't like Sidewalkers, I had to find a reason. I decided that liking to eat and liking to dine are separate considerations, and that Jean-François likes to dine. This remains a hypothesis, an expectation that can get tested soon enough in our next encounter, if I choose to do so. But not every question is worth pursuing. Next time, I will take him to Le Cirque.

CHAPTER 13

It's a Long Story

not very long ago, I got an apartment in New York City and began to check out the restaurants within a few blocks of my place. Wherever you live in New York, you will probably find some nice restaurants nearby, but as I was living in midtown Manhattan, the choices were myriad.

I stopped in one day at a place called Biarritz, an unpretentious French restaurant, something quite difficult to imagine in this country. For some reason, in the United States, French food always comes with a heavy dose of pretension, supercilious waiters, tuxedoed maitre d's, and heavy prices. This seems to be true no matter what city you are in and how good the food is. But New York has everything, and this includes non-pretentious French. After all, not every restaurant in France is pretentious—some are downright grungy—so why must French mean stuffy? Biarritz is a bistro. It actually has French people running it and working in it; the food is the kind you would find in any nice bistro in France.

They have a choice of a variety of complete dinners for a reasonable price, and, as usual, after I finished with the menu, my attention turned to the wine list. Actually, my attention may have turned there immediately, as is common enough for me. The wine list at Biarritz is an atrocity. One sees lists at your average everyday restaurant like this, and even there they offend me, but this was a French restaurant, and they should know better. The list had items on it listed like this:

St.-Emilion 14.00
Pomerol 15.00
Beaujolais 12.00

Well, this list may include fabulous bargains or horrendous vinegars. Who would know? Does "St. Émilion" refer to 1961 Cheval Blanc, or does it refer to 1984 communal co-operative blend? My bets were with the latter, but how could I tell? I always figure that people who write wine lists that look like this know nothing about wine at all, and I began to suspect the food as well.

I called over the waitress and complained. She asked what I was looking for and I said "old wine"; she asked me to come over to the rack of wines that was in the corner and check out the years and châteaux for myself. Well, this was a reasonable offer, so off I went. The rack held all sorts of bottles from a variety of years and châteaux, and just as I was getting into the search, tearing the place apart, the man who served as the bartender came over and asked me what I was looking for. I said "old wine" again, and he told me to sit down, he would be back shortly.

He returned from what appeared to be a trip to the basement with an armful of wine. He showed me a bottle and said that this one was especially good. I looked at it. It was a Château Lafite-Rothschild 1973. Now Lafite-Rothschild is one of the world's great wines, and while 1973 was not the greatest year in Bordeaux, it was good enough. Any wine drinker who has not ever tasted a Lafite 1973 would, of course, want to do so, even if it might not be the greatest bottle of wine one could ever have.

I laughed. Of course, it was a great bottle, but how much did it cost? In the end, the issue is cost after all. Anyone can order the most expensive bottle on a wine list and stand a pretty good chance of getting one of the best bottles in the place. The game is to get the best bottle for the best price, to find the bottle that the management mispriced.

He said that it was thirty dollars. Well, that may have been expensive for this bistro; in fact, it probably was the most expensive bottle he had, but this bottle, if you could find it at all, which is unlikely, would certainly cost seventy-five dollars at least, and that would be in a store, not in a restaurant. Just for fun I asked about the price of the 1974 Beaune that he had in his arm as well, old Burgundy being usually wildly out of sight price-wise, and he said that was twenty-five dollars. I chose the Lafite and enjoyed every drop of it. It wasn't the greatest wine I had ever had, but I enjoyed it anyway.

I couldn't wait to tell this story to Arthur, who lives in New York. As you might imagine, he insisted that we go there as soon as possible, so the next week, off we went. The waitress—not the same waitress as before—came up to us and asked whether we would like a drink to start. I said that we would get right to the wine, and she responded, *the same one as last time?* I was floored. Had this event caused such a stir? Did they have cases of this stuff down there?

I said *sure*, and up came the '73 Lafite. We had a fine time with it and were soon in need of a new bottle. She offered another of the same, but I said, *no, I'd like to try one of the others that I had seen last time*, and she replied, *you mean the '74 Beaune?* Now completely blown away, I said *yes* and up it came. It was better than the Lafite actually. I still haven't figured out what is going on there exactly, but I am sure that I will go back a few more times in order to find out.

Why did I tell you this story? I tell it to friends, usually when we are about to order wine in a restaurant and I am feeling grumpy about the wine list for some reason. Why the story comes to mind is obvious. I am always hopeful that something similar will happen again. I wonder whether every restaurant has a secret stash of wine that it serves to only a select few.

I have tried to understand better why Biarritz might have such a stash, and the best conclusion that I can come to is that Biarritz has been around for more than twenty years, and a restaurant that old is likely to have some wine around that has been around for a long time. So searching through wine lists reminds me of my story, and, if I feel I have a willing set of listeners, I happily retell it.

The question here is: *Why*? Why do I love to tell stories about things that have happened to me that I found interesting? Actually, I am not at all alone in this. When something interesting or important happens, most people usually feel compelled to tell someone else about it. Even people who are reticent to talk about themselves can't help telling others about events that make up a good story.

Why do we tell stories? We often talk in order to tell about, comment upon, and analyze our own personal experiences. Imagine, for example, that you have just returned from a vacation or that you meet someone who knows that you have recently been on a date that you were especially looking forward to. In either of these situations, when you are asked how it went, you can respond with a pithy sentence or two, or you can begin to tell a story that captures the essential parts of the experience. Now imagine that another person asks you substantially the same question. How different is your second story likely to be from the initial story? Of course, the time you have to tell the story or differences in intimacy with the person you tell it to may affect the telling, but the likelihood is that the subsequent stories you tell will leave out and emphasize the same things. While telling about a trip to a great restaurant, if you don't mention the lovely park where you ate lunch, it will eventually cease to be part of the story.

The process of story creation, of condensing an experience into a story-size chunk that can be told in a reasonable amount of time, is a process that tends to converge. Subsequent iterations of the same story tend to get smaller rather than larger, and, after a while, all versions of the story are very similar. We leave out more details, more quickly get to the essence. In the end, we are left with exactly the details of the story that we have chosen to remember. In short, story creation is a memory process.

We need to tell someone else a story that describes our experience because the process of creating the story also creates the memory structure that will contain the gist of the story for the next telling. So in order to remember an experience, it is very helpful to tell it to someone. If we don't tell the story soon enough after the experience or often enough immediately after the experience, or if we don't tell the story at all, the experience cannot be coalesced into a gist. In other words, while parts of the experience may be remembered in terms of the memory structures that were activated—a restaurant may be recalled through cues having to do with food, a place, or the particular company—the story itself does not exist as an entity in memory. Any generalization that might pertain to the whole of the experience would get lost. We could remember the restaurant, but we might forget that the entire trip had been a bad idea. We might be able to reconstruct generalizations about the trip as a whole, but this process would require doing exactly what one would have had to do in the first place. That is, reconstruction with an eye towards generalizations creates gists which are then relayed as stories. In other words, we tell stories in order to remember them.

The opposite side of the coin is also true. We fail to create stories in order to forget them. When something unpleasant happens to us, we often say, "I'd rather not talk about it," because not talking makes it easier to forget. In some sense, telling a story makes it happen again. If the story is not created in the first place, it will exist only in its original form, i.e., distributed among the mental structures used in the initial processing. When the experience was a bad one, that sense of being in memory can have annoying psychological consequences. If we encounter a particular setting or prop, unhappy remindings may well occur when not expected.

When you begin to tell a story again that you have retold many times, what you retrieve from memory is the gist of the story itself. An old man's story that he has told hundreds of times shows little variation, and what variation exists becomes part of the story itself, regardless of its origin. People add details to their stories that may or may not have occurred. Why should they be able to remember? They are recalling gists and reconstructing details. If, at some point, they add a nice detail, not really certain of its validity, telling that story with the same detail a few more times will insure its permanent place in the story gist. In other words, the stories we tell time and again are identical to the memory we have of the events that the story relates. Stories change over time because of the process of telling, because of the embellishments added by the teller. The actual events that gave rise to the story in the first place have long since been forgotten.

But what about a story that is told for the first time? After it has been told once, what is remembered? The story or the events behind the story? Why is it very difficult to remember, for a long time, something that you haven't told someone else?

On the day I ate at Biarritz for the first time, I must have done some other things as well. I didn't just wake up, go to dinner, and then go back to sleep. But, while I remember the meal at Biarritz very well—I can recall all sorts of different details that I have not bothered to mention—I cannot recall a single other thing about that particular day unconnected to eating at Biarritz. Why not?

What makes an event memorable is both its uniqueness and its significance to us personally. For example, we easily remember the first time we do anything of significance. So, since good wine experiences are of interest to me, I am likely to remember this event. But, unique experiences are not sufficient to guarantee recall later on. What if I had never told this story to anyone?

Would I fail to recognize this restaurant if I saw it again the following week? Would I, upon entering this restaurant another time, be astounded that the wine list had no châteaux and no years? Would I forget how to get to the place? Of course not.

Obviously, we can remember events that we have not discussed with anyone. But how? How are events like eating in a particular restaurant remembered? Certainly many such events never become stories, so they are not maintained in memory by repeated telling. How are they maintained?

Psychologists have long noted that memory must be organized hierarchically because certain information seems to be stored around general concepts that help us understand more subordinate concepts. So, for example, if someone asks whether a flounder has gills, you can easily answer without ever having considered the question before, and, more important, without actually having that information explicitly in your memory at all. All you need to know is that a flounder is a fish and that fish have gills. Similarly, you know that a Buick has wheels because it is a car and that a female horse has teats because it is a mammal. The idea behind what some psychologists have called *semantic memory* is simply that this kind of information is shared hierarchically. We store the information that female mammals have teats and infer that, therefore, horses have teats because they are mammals. Clearly, people must have information organized at least to some extent in this way because they know a great deal more than they have ever actually experienced. Experiments by Collins and Quillian demonstrated this effect.

An episodic memory, proposed by Tulving, on the other hand, would be one in which we stored actual events that have occurred in our own lives. So visiting Grandma's house on Thanksgiving is an episode in memory. Such episodes don't seem to be organized hierarchically. Are *Grandma visits on Thanksgiving* stored under *visits to relatives, holiday get-togethers,* or *wild parties I have attended?* Or, has *Grandma visits on Thanksgiving* become a central category of its own? And, if so, what would the creation of such a category mean? Would it mean that the answer to what you ate that day was always turkey? It would if what you ate *were* always turkey, but the time that you ate duck instead might be remembered as well.

The distinction between semantic and episodic memory is a matter of some debate to psychologists largely because the issues are not at all well defined. A neatly organized hierarchy of semantic concepts is easy to imagine, but the world is full of oddities and idiosyncratic events that fail to fit neatly into a pre-established hierarchy. For example, we may "know" from semantic memory that female horses have teats, but we may more readily access this fact from an episodic store if we witnessed our pet horse giving birth and then suckling its young. Our first memories of playing ball may very well come to mind when the word *ball* comes up, and the properties we ascribe to *ball* may well be ones that a particular ball we remember actually had. In short, the nature and structure of memory remain at the frontiers of research.

Another distinction can be drawn between story-based memory on the one hand and a generalized event-based memory on the other. To understand this distinction, let's go back to the question of where the day that included a trip to Biarritz for the first time might be stored in memory. I experienced, after all, a complete day of which the meal at Biarritz was only a small part. Let us assume that on that day I worked on a book I was writing, went to the bank, and talked on the phone about an upcoming lecture. Let us also assume that none of these three events was in any way interesting enough to constitute a story that I would like to tell anyone.

I can safely assume that on that day I could have told my dinner companions about any of those other events. Let us also assume that, having nothing interesting to say about them, I did not do so. If, a week later, I needed to recall what I had done at the bank or what chapter of what book I had recently worked on or whether a given lecture had been properly arranged, most likely I would know the answer to all of these questions. I could certainly remember what I needed to about that day so that I wouldn't find myself going to the bank again or writing the same chapter again. How is this ability to recall different from my ability to tell the Biarritz story? I cannot tell the story of that day, but I can recall various important aspects of any day in terms of the items themselves as opposed to their being part of any given day. This difference reflects itself in a kind of abstract idea of "place" in memory.

To "recall" the bank visit means knowing that I have been there. Had something interesting happened there, especially something that taught me something new about the operation of banks, for example, I might have remembered it. But how can we make this assertion when I cannot recall this day, since I have never spoken about it to anyone? We seem to have a paradox here, but, in fact, we do not.

When people have experiences in a bank, they update their knowledge of banks. If this were not the case, people would never learn where the bank was or how to get money or how to get into the safe deposit boxes or whatever. When these things change, people change along with them. Sometimes it takes a few trials— they may still go to their old bank by mistake. But eventually changes in memory follow changes in reality. So, people learn from their experiences, but where does this learning take place in the mind?

People need a file of information about banks that includes specific information about where their bank is, what forms need to be filled out for what, how the cash machine works, and so on. This file must also include general information about banks apart from the one we use most often, however. When we enter a new bank, we want to be able to utilize expectations about our regular bank that will help us in the new one. For example, we want to predict how the cash machine works and where the safe deposit boxes are likely to be so that we can be more efficient in the new bank. In other words, we are constantly drawing upon our file of knowledge about banks and adding to that knowledge when new experiences teach us something worth retaining.

What we are decidedly not doing, however, is updating our memories on what we might call a daily unit basis. That is, we are not making note of the fact that on October 16 we got two hundred dollars and deposited three checks. We could try to do this, of course, but we would have to try very hard. We might make up a poem about what we did on that day and then memorize the poem, for example. But if we do not take some extreme measure like that, we will simply fail to remember the experience unless something rather strange or important occurred at the same time. Why can't we remember what we did in a bank on October 16, 1982?

Humans are intelligent rememberers. We remember an experience to add to a storehouse of knowledge that might be useful later on. We are looking for knowledge that tells us something about the nature of the world in general. This storehouse of knowledge is analogous to the psychologist's notions of semantic memory: that we must have a way to store knowledge so that it can be used again next time, knowledge that teaches us about the world in general, knowledge that is rather similar from human being to human being. Although this notion that a part of memory should be devoted to such general knowledge seems inherently correct, the notion seems equally wrong that such knowledge would not have at its core a seriously idiosyncratic component. We may all know that a flounder is a fish and that a fish has gills, but we do not all know that our father used to eat flounder every Tuesday and, therefore, so did we, and we refuse to eat it ever again. Yet, this latter fact is just as much a part of the definition of flounder for us as is the fact that a flounder has gills—maybe more, since one fact is far more real to us than the other.

Any general storehouse of knowledge, then, is likely to depend very strongly upon the expectations about various objects and situations that have been gathered over a lifetime of experience. Thus, when a new experience occurs that speaks to what we already know about something, perhaps updating it, perhaps overriding it, we add that experience to our memories. This is why I would be able to remember making the arrangements for my hypothetical lecture. We add the experience of making those arrangements to our general storehouse of similar experiences. That experience then becomes part of our general knowledge of trips to give lectures, which now includes this new one in particular. Similarly, when we read something, the facts we garner from our reading go to particular places in memory; information about restaurants updates what we know about restaurants; stories about travel to exotic places adds new information to existing knowledge in memory about those particular places, and to general information we may have about exotic places. Thus we build up generalizations about the world. Every time we use a particular body of knowledge in our interactions with the world, that knowledge gets altered by the experience. We cannot fill out a tax form without using the prior experiences we have in filling out tax forms as a guide to help us through the experience. But because that knowledge is being used as a guide, it changes. We add new information about tax forms, about the experience of filling them out, that overrides what we previously knew. When we are finished doing anything, therefore, our memories are altered by the experience. We don't know what we knew before.

But such a memory process has two important components. First, no general storehouse of information exists apart from actual experience; i.e., semantic memory cannot exist apart from real episodes. Naturally, we know that forms have lines and spaces just as we know that fish have gills, but this is knowledge that has been abstracted from experience and can be easily overridden by new experiences. One reason why the question about fish having gills is a good example for people who believe in semantic memory is that most people have very little experience with fish at that level. Therefore, little in the way of actual episodes might override knowledge that we were taught or abstracted for ourselves from limited experience. Believing that people have static encyclopedias of knowledge in their heads is a convenient fiction, but the reality is that everything we know is temporary. Our firmest beliefs today can be overridden by new evidence tomorrow. Oddly, we are not always conscious of how the updating process affects memory. We are, by and large, unaware that what we know now isn't what we knew before.

In Chapter 7 I discussed how this dynamic nature of memory must break up actual experiences into their component pieces in order for learning to take place. These pieces are being added to general event-memory bit by bit in different places, so no coherent whole remains. Breaking up our daily experiences into their component parts is terribly important. If we did not, we would never learn anything across contexts. Let me explain.

Earlier I mentioned, in passing, an experience in Sweden. I was at a conference that was held on an island in the large lake surrounding Stockholm. For a treat, the conferees were taken, by boat, to the king's palace to hear a concert. We were served dinner on the boat. I was seated next to Maurice, a French professor whom I met at the conference, and with whom I have since become quite friendly. Wine was served. It said on the label: "French wine" (in English).

I tasted some. It tasted the way one might have imagined a bottle with that label tasting. I chose to drink water.

I looked over at Maurice. He was happily drinking away. I knew him well enough, at this point, to know that he really appreciated good wine. I asked him how he could be drinking this garbage. He replied: *Why, are they serving some other wine?* His point was simply that he drank wine with dinner no matter what, and this was the only choice.

For years, I used this story as one to tell about Maurice, in front of Maurice, as a way of chiding him. And then, one day, I realized that I, too, having become used to drinking wine with every meal, was now likely to behave this way as well. I even find myself drinking New York State champagne at various relatives' Bar Mitzvahs. It is usually the best wine they serve.

Memory has to be constructed so that, at the very least, we update our store of knowledge with every new experience. The next time I visited Sweden I made sure to eat in a French restaurant where I suspected, quite rightly it turned out, good wine might be found. The next time I visited Maurice, I reminded him of this episode, which caused him to recall that I liked good wine and wanted to know more, so he took me to see his favorite personal wine distributor. The next time I get offered dinner on a boat, I am likely to refuse. Likewise I will also be skeptical about going into a Swedish restaurant in the United States, because this incident brought to mind the idea that the Swedish really don't drink wine. I also had to rethink, twice it turned out, my stereotypes about the French. This incident caused me to generalize from Maurice that Frenchmen must drink wine and thus, when I am to eat with someone French, I make sure good wine is available. This becomes a consideration in planning where to take a French visitor for lunch. But now I am like this too. If I come to lunch at your house, be prepared.

The lessons from this incident were myriad. Another way of putting this is that this incident had to be broken up into its component pieces. Each of these pieces must be connected to other similar pieces in order to gain from the generalizations. The whole, in this case, is much more than the sum of its parts. It is also the case that the whole really doesn't exist, as a coherent whole, at all.

Learning from experience, then, means learning a great many different kinds of things. Whole experiences must be broken up and analyzed in order to learn from them and to place the new information that has been learned where it can be found later when needed. For example, to make it through a visit to the doctor's office, we need to learn things about paying and about doctors, at both a specific and a general level. Therefore, in order to find these things when we need them, this visit to the doctor must be decomposed into its many component pieces and added to the storehouse of information associated with those pieces in memory.

We should not imagine that this acquisition and storage of new information is in any way conscious, of course. When a doctor asks for cash, we don't think, *how odd, I'll have to remember this incident as an example of an augmentation of expectations in the professional-office-visit script.* Rather, we consciously note the oddity, and our memory takes care of the rest, updating and altering expectations in a variety of places in memory that might need this new information. We would not be surprised a second time when a doctor asks for cash. In addition, that lack of surprise means our expectations have been altered in a variety of different places as well: expectations about credit cards, payments in general, doctors, professional office visits, and so on. Our memories unconsciously decide what expectations this new event relates to and update those expectations, searching for them in a variety of places in memory.

The process of updating our general knowledge base every time we have a new experience that relates to an aspect of that knowledge base has an odd side effect, however. The construction of a memory that organizes information around generalized events destroys the coherence between the particular instantiation of those events. The dynamic nature of the general knowledge base that makes up memory causes the experiences of walking to be placed with prior occurrences of walking, those of shopping to be placed together with others of shopping, and so on. Constant updating of a memory for events in general, one that houses expectations about what happens in various situations in general, causes a general storehouse about typical events to be built up by destroying the connectivity of one particular event to another particular event. A particular event of walking, therefore, becomes disconnected from its intended purpose of enabling one to go to a restaurant at one particular time, for example, thus rendering me useless when I am asked how I got to Biarritz. My only recourse is to make an educated guess: *I must have walked: It's not far, and I usually walk if it's a nice day, and it was June after all.*

Because of this need of memory to effect a constant disconnection of events from those that follow, we feel a need to undo this process when something of significance occurs. We can stop the dynamic disconnection from taking place and remember events in sequence by consciously giving our memories an event to remember that is a unit, specifically, a unit that we have rehearsed, sometimes frequently. In this process, the role of stories in memory comes into play, and hence the concept of *story-based memory* arises. Stories are a way of preserving the connectivity of events that would otherwise be disassociated over time. One reason we tell stories, therefore, is to help ourselves in remembering them.

For stories to be told without a great deal of effort, they must be stored away in a fashion that enables them to be accessed as a unit. If this were not the case, stories would have to be reconstructed each time they were told, a process that would become more and more difficult with time as particular events faded from memory. Telling a story would require a great deal of work, collecting all the events from memory and reconstructing their interrelation. Further, stories would be quite different each time they were told. Reconstruction would not be the same each time, and instead, different stories would result depending upon what parts of memory were looked at during the time of telling. This kind of storytelling does occur, of course, especially when stories are being told for the first time, but most storytelling requires so little work and is so repetitive, each version so much like the others, that many stories must be stored and retrieved as chunks.

A different type of memory process must be active here. Since I failed to tell any more than this one story from this particular day, all the other events of the day are lost forever as events capable of being isolated. Of course, I understand and remember what happened to me on that day, in the sense that I can make use of the facts that were updated on that day if need be. But those facts are available only when the various segments of that day are accessed for some reason, and I have no way of knowing that whatever else happened on that day that was retrievable by some other route happened to be on the same day as the Biarritz story, unless some real connection existed between them. When someone asks me about the arrangements for the trip that I made on that day, for example, I will be able to answer. What I have lost is the ability to tell a story about that particular day. The day has disappeared as a unit from memory. I can no longer access other events of the day by asking myself about what happened that day but can now find them only in the other parts of memory that will have subsumed them. What I will remember, then, is in terms of what I know about banks or that particular trip. The only story that remains, I have already told. Everything else is just part of my general store of knowledge, disassociated from the other events that made up the same day. The events of Biarritz are stored together as a unit, however, because a story has been composed that tied them together. To find that kind of story in memory, one must have put it there consciously in the first place, by telling it either to somebody or to oneself.

Story-based memory, then, is a different kind of memory from the memory that contains general world knowledge. Story-based knowledge expresses our points of view and philosophy of life and, as it comes from experiences, is closer in spirit to what psychologists have meant when they have spoken of episodic memory. Story-based memory, however, depends upon telling and gets built up by telling. The consequences of this process are interesting when one considers what we tell and why, since we are, quite unconsciously, making decisions about what to remember.

To see this, let's once again look at my birthday party. The people that went to my party told the story of that party to their wives, friends, colleagues, and so on. After all, it was not your everyday event. Three years later, long after they had stopped telling the story to others, I called them up and asked them to tell me the story they had told to others. Here are the stories of the people I called:

Andrew: Well, there were several things that stick out in my memory about it. In sequence, we were led up to this magnificent private room and the first thing that happened that I recall was a waiter serving champagne. And there were glasses of champagne on the tray. And I recall vividly that he spilled somehow a glass or two on the floor and managed to get it all over Jerry Feldman's wife. That struck me as humorous because it was so improbable in that context. One's expectation was that these people had done these things a thousand times and it was not very likely that they would spill the wine, spill the champagne, and even less likely that they would spill it over one of the clients—I remember that very vividly. And then we all sat down around this long table and I recall that I knew about three quarters of the people, and the people that I didn't know I had just met the day before. They were the French people mainly. And then we started this meal with multiple courses, with a different wine for most, if not all, of the courses.

I remember then that my wife isn't used to eating many of them, nor am I for that matter, nor were many of the people used to eating the kinds of food that we had, and also she found there to be a hell of a lot of this food. Also, she wasn't used to drinking as much wine as she was being provided. One's glass was constantly being filled up and the next thing I remember is that she would eat, on the average, about half of what was on her plate. She was sitting next to Elliot, who has an infinite capacity. So she would pass on to Elliot what she couldn't eat and he had no problem with eating it all, which is completely consistent with everything I know about him and the way he looks. Nor could she accommodate the amount of wine she was being served, so she passed that on to someone from Cognitive—Steve, I think, was his name. And only three courses of the way through the meal, she realized that this was a self-defeating proposition, because as soon as she emptied her glass—however she managed to give it to Steve, I don't know, pouring it into his glass—her glass was immediately refilled. So, the next vivid memory was that as this meal went on, Elliot became increasingly stuffed because he'd had fifty percent more than anyone else at the table. Steve became increasingly drunk because he'd had fifty percent more to drink than anyone at the table.

Then, at the completion of the meal, I recall that brandy and cigars were served, and I was dying for a cigar, but was banned from having a cigar by my wife, who doesn't want me to smoke. There ensued this very humorous parody written by Don Norman. It was all very jolly and great fun. That's basically my recollection of the evening.

Anatole: Well, it was in this wonderful French restaurant. We had a room on the second floor and it was very rowdy, everybody was reminiscing and paying very little attention to the food, and this old French professor was getting more and more sad. As time went by, Laurance was getting sadder and sadder because she couldn't believe that people weren't concentrating on this wonderful food. And I remember Jerry Feldman's wife kind of examining every little piece of food on her fork—you know, picking it up and examining it every time. And Laurance getting more and more vindictive and blowing cigarette smoke in their face. It was almost a riot. But everybody had a wonderful time.

Jerry: The thing about it that was most interesting to me was that there were three sets of people involved. There were some Americans, a couple of Brits, and the French. The Brits were loud and boisterous and fairly obnoxious. The French all sat in one corner and smoked constantly and refused to talk English to anybody, more or less, and looked very superior through the whole thing. Everyone else was, I think, mildly uncomfortable because it was kind of a funny situation. I guess I remember that there were some speeches at the end. I felt fairly embarrassed throughout the whole thing, I guess, what with the broken wineglasses, and the general feeling that somehow the thing wasn't quite working.

Don: Roger Schank turned forty and decided that this event required a formal announcement and a party either to celebrate or commiserate. And since he was in Paris at the time, what better thing to do than to have a party in Paris. He invited a number of his friends, a small number, but a reasonable crowd, to celebrate his birthday at perhaps best restaurant in Paris. In typical Roger Schank style, what he also did was to convince the French to run a conference on AI, which would help to pay for some of these expenses, and indeed pay for a small amount of the transportation fees for some people. I won't go into the conference, but it was an incredible waste of time. I don't recall any good that came out of it. I was in England at the time on my sabbatical and it was easy for me to hop on a plane and fly over to Paris, and I did.

At the Sorbonne where the conference was, I glanced up at the ceiling and saw this wonderful painting of a man desperately trying to read a book surrounded by naked women, a story that made it into my book, and, in fact, it was at the conference that I was convinced to write the book. On the evening of the dinner—actually I don't recall how we got there, whether we took taxis or walked or were driven—I recall being ushered upstairs into a private room. I recall that there was a vast array of champagne to start with—champagne that I thought was donated by Roger's publisher? Somebody. . . . We then sat down—it was a fairly formal setting, not that any of the guests were formal. We had menus—not menus but a list of what it is that we are going to receive.

Who do I remember? Elliot Soloway, Jerry Feldman, Yorick Wilks, and various spouses, Jerry's and Yorick's and, of course, Roger's. There must have been other people; I would estimate that I knew half the participants. I can't recall much of the dinner itself, that is, the eating, except that it was a wide variety of foods, relatively small in portion; I think Roger announced that that was the proper way to eat—rather than stuff yourself with a large amount of one thing, you should have a sampling of many such things. I also recall being in full agreement. The meal was typically high-cuisine French, that is, it was elegant with rich sauces, relatively textureless where the sauces dominated, and the texture of the food was sometimes deliberately invisible. I remember various speeches and goodwill. I had prepared myself several stories in the flavor of Roger Schank: several simple-minded stories with very simple elementary or even pre-school English in the style of the traditional computer story in which you read a simple story and then ask for a non-obvious conclusion. It's hard to remember what else there was except a good time was had by all, and if asked to attend another one I would. If asked whether I enjoyed the event, I would say I did, even though my memory for it seems to be so incredibly poor. And I guess that's how I would tell it to somebody.

I recall other aspects such as that I was sitting at the end of a table, I think to the left, but I was on the left end and Roger was in the center on the far right, so at this long narrow table I would have been as far away as possible on his left-hand side. And that Elliot was opposite me. All this may be wrong but that's my memory. I also remember that we were all dressed—that we were all wearing ties, which, in this particular crowd, is most unusual. I also remember . . . I seem to have a more vivid impression in my mind's eye of the details I recount, although as is typical with vivid impressions in the mind's eye, when I now try to describe them, I discover they're not quite so vivid after all. I guess this is consistent with the kind of recall I gave. It's the emotional affective side I recall most clearly, and when I try to recall a particular event, the details vanish.

Elliot: Well, the story is we had a birthday party with incredible individuals—the most interesting people in the field at the most incredible restaurant in Paris, France. And we had food that was just beyond belief and we had eight courses of it and it was just astounding. I sat next to two women who were on diets so I had three of everything, so I was in complete seventh heaven. It was an evening that you don't have very often—that's how I would describe it. Actually, I described it like that.

Maurice: It was a pity because very few people did appreciate the food. Maybe three or four of us. But the rest, some of these Americans didn't see that they were having the most fantastic food in the world. They were sort of bitching about the things being fat or salty. They couldn't perceive the odors—the perfumes of the stuff. I think that this was a waste. The invitation was partly wasted—not on friends maybe, but maybe on uneducated guests. We had a lot of champagne—a large amount, and nice wine.

Steve: We had a conference at the University of Paris where a half a dozen of us or a dozen gave presentations. I remember Tolya, I remember the guy from San Diego, what's his name? I can't remember his name. The guy from New Mexico, a well-known professor, I can't remember his name either, and whoever else was there. We each gave presentations. The conference was on Artificial Intelligence, which to the French was expert systems, and a lot of us were talking about natural language. Excuse me, I'm really drawing a blank on everything else. I'm remembering when we had gone to the restaurant, I remember we stood around in a private room or alcove and we were served various wines and champagnes, and we had a champagne toast. During the actual dinner I remember a couple of people read stories or something that was kind of amusing, but I don't remember exactly what they contained either. And the food I don't remember either.

I've referred before to Bartlett's well-known experiment involving an Eskimo folktale, which supports the notion of a reconstructive memory. People tend to recall coherence, rather than incoherence, so they add details that support coherence and forget details that were incoherent at the time. In other words, people remember what makes sense and tend to forget things that fail to make sense. Why would this be the case?

One reason is that, in order to remember something, we must have a place to put that something in memory. Where do we place an Eskimo folktale? One place to put it is with other Eskimo folktales. But if we have none, then we must store it in terms of other similar stories that we have heard before. This means, in effect, that we attempt to match what we have just heard to what we have previously heard. When parts of the story don't match, they are labeled incoherent. They fail to make sense in the context of stories that we know like this. So we forget the confusing parts. In a sense, we have no choice in this matter, since to remember them we must explain the confusing parts to ourselves, and as we pointed out earlier, such explanations are dependent on having available explanations that worked before. In other words, it is very difficult to understand something that is wildly out of the range of our experiences since we have no place to put it, and no way to explain it. When we hear, "Something black came out of his mouth; in the morning he was dead," it is too difficult to do anything but forget the black stuff.

The same is true when we experience anything. When what we experience is old hat, we will match that experience to other experiences like it, and then we will have trouble recalling that experience because of the difficulty we have in distinguishing the new experiences from the old ones that it was stored in terms of.

When we experience something wildly new, on the other hand, remembering every aspect of it is difficult, because we couldn't necessarily pay attention, that is, initially understand, all the new aspects. How can you note the greatness of the lightness and flavor of the lobster ravioli if you have never eaten anything at all like it? Do you just note that it doesn't taste much like Chef Boyardee and forget it? Actually you may have no other choice.

We remember what we are set up to remember, what our memories have prepared us to remember, because of what has been stored in them so far. With this in mind, let's look at the stories that each person told, this time not focusing on the representations of the food, but with an eye towards understanding how the story constructed about the experience might have turned out the way it did. Of course, much of what we do here will be speculative; we do not know what the memory of each individual was before the party or when I asked them to tell the story of the party. What we do know is that each individual had his own experience, that he understood what he chose to focus on, and thus that his story was idiosyncratic.

Let's look carefully at Andrew's story. Andrew is British by origin, but has spent most of his adult life in Champaign-Urbana, Illinois. His wife is British as well. Neither of them is inclined to eat in top restaurants at all, since there aren't any where they live, and although they travel in Europe a great deal, they would not consider spending their money in that way.

People's memories reflect their goals as well as their experiences. As Andrew is my friend, one goal he had was to enjoy my party, and certainly, in telling me the story of my party, he, as well as the others, had the goal of making it seem as if it was a good party. Andrew was not likely to have paid much attention to the food. He likes to eat, but he is by no means a fanatic on the subject. He had the goal to make his wife happy and so he noticed what was going on with her. His story reflects these goals as well as his lack of prior experience with restaurants of this type:

...we were led up to this magnificent private room and the first thing that happened that I recall was a waiter who was serving champagne. And there were glasses of champagne on the tray. And I recall vividly that he spilled somehow a glass or two on the floor and managed to get it all over Jerry Feldman's wife. That struck me as humorous because it was so improbable in that context. One's expectation was that these people had done these things a thousand times and it was not very likely that they would spill the wine, spill the champagne, and even less likely that they would spill it over one of the clients—I remember that very vividly.

Andrew's first memory is of an expectation failure. I had forgotten the entire episode. They are as likely to spill things at Jamin as anywhere else, I would imagine. But, someone unfamiliar with three-star restaurants is likely to imagine that they ought to be superhuman in some way. Thus he remembers the expectation failure.

And then we started this meal with multiple courses, with a different wine for most, if not all, of the courses.

Here again, we have a recalled expectation failure. He remembers that this meal was unlike other meals in that it had multiple courses. That it had multiple courses is not so bizarre that it simply cannot be recalled; rather, it is precisely what would be recalled by someone unfamiliar with meals of this kind. This is how it differed from the norm and hence this becomes an important part of the story that Andrew created as a result of this experience.

I remember then that my wife isn't used to eating many of them, nor am I for that matter, nor were many of the people used to eating the kinds of food that we had, and also she found there to be a hell of a lot of this food. Also, she wasn't used to drinking as much wine as she was being provided. . . . And only three courses of the way through the meal, she realized that this was a self-defeating proposition, because as soon as she emptied her glass . . . her glass was immediately refilled.

Here we see Andrew remembering his wife's discomfort. She was quite obviously unhappy throughout the meal. The meal contained a variety of foods I had chosen with regard for what I like, what my wife likes, and what I thought my friends might like. But I had not thought about their wives. For the most part, I had eaten many meals with these friends at various meetings around the world, but I had almost never eaten with their wives. People who are conservative eaters, and it turned out that all the wives except mine were quite conservative, would have been very upset by the meal I had selected. Andrew was painfully aware of this and it had to be a big part of what he remembered about the meal. We remember the feelings of the people we care about because memory is very goal-oriented and our friends' goals and our spouses' goals are usually rather important to us.

In the next part of the story we see Andrew probably reconstructing what happened as a result of his wife's behavior. If you know that someone ate or drank more as a result of your wife's behavior, you can reconstruct the rest.

So, the next vivid memory was that as this meal went on, Elliot became increasingly stuffed because he'd had fifty percent more than anyone else at the table. Steve became increasingly drunk because he'd had fifty percent more to drink than anyone at the table.

In what follows, Andrew tells about another goal of his that was violated.

Then, at the completion of the meal, I recall that brandy and cigars were served, and I was dying for a cigar, but was banned from having a cigar by my wife, who doesn't want me to smoke.

In this case, he remembers this meal as a special meal, which implies brandy and cigars, and thus tells of his frustration. I do not recall that there was brandy at all. We had a dessert wine and I am sure that I would not have served brandy too. Perhaps I don't remember well, but my guess is that he is confused. He simply reconstructed this from his fancy meal script. I probably offered cigars that I had brought, since I often do this, but I can't say that I remember that either. Andrew remembers it because he was probably embarrassed that he had to refuse my offer.

Anatole, by contrast, is very familiar with French food and fancy French restaurants. He had never eaten in Jamin before, but he had eaten in other three-star restaurants. He is a Russian by birth and has lived in America most of his adult life. He is certainly sensitive to what is deemed to be proper behavior in different cultures and would be aware of, and care about, how to act properly in this situation.

Well, it was in this wonderful French restaurant.

He feels no necessity to say more here because he has stored the experience away with others of its type. He merely notes that of its type, it was very good. He had no expectation failures there, so he didn't remember anything special. He did, on the other hand, attune to something that disturbed him:

... it was very rowdy, everybody was reminiscing and paying very little attention to the food, and this old French professor was getting more and more sad. As time went by, Laurance was getting sadder and sadder because she couldn't believe that people weren't concentrating on this wonderful food. And I remember Jerry Feldman's wife kind of examining every little piece of food on her fork—you know, picking it up and examining it every time.

He remembers this experience because it violated his expectations about how such things should be. He was particularly concerned with how the two French people there were reacting. He knew that they were very upset because one of their cherished cultural institutions was not only not being appreciated, but being absolutely violated. For Anatole, the story of my party was a story about how people in one culture failed to appreciate what was considered to be the epitome of another culture. Many other things went on at this party, but Anatole especially noted this and then the memory of the party got stored away with other memories of that type. One can imagine Anatole being reminded of my party when the question of cultural misunderstandings comes up, since that seems to be how he indexed the memory. His story is a story that illustrates that index.

What is happening here? Why are all these stories so different? They all describe the same event, don't they? Well, actually, they don't.

Memory is highly idiosyncratic. Understanding relies upon idiosyncratic memory in order to work. These storytellers did not experience the same situation; what similar experiences they did have were interpreted by different memories, full of different expectations, and possessing knowledge about different subjects. Further, their interests were different. They paid attention to different aspects of the evening's events, aspects that related to questions they were thinking about, and relied upon explanations that they had available to them. Viewed from the inside of the participants' memories, the experiences they had couldn't have been more different.

Their memory of the event was not really a memory of the event at all. Rather, they remembered the story they told at the time, more or less. The story they told at the time was not "the story of the event" at all. It was the teller's story that involved the event, which is quite a different thing. We can recall the stories we have told. The stories we tell reflect how we are thinking about events as they happen and indicate how we have fashioned those events and our involvement in them into a coherent whole. Our stories are *our* memories, and who says that one person's memory should look like another's? No wonder these stories are so different.

Since memory revolves around expectation, it follows that the primary thing each of these people remembered was the aspect of the evening that violated his expectations. Why did each of them remember different things? Because each of them had different expectations to begin with. The lesson of all this is that, if you want to remember something, you must tell it to someone. The more you tell it, the more you remember it. We remember significant events in our lives by telling them to others, which, in effect, is a way of telling them to ourselves. If you want someone to remember what you have said, say what you want to say in the form of a good story. If you want to remember what you have experienced, tell a story about that experience. But the stories will tell more than the facts. They also tell about the teller. The memory of the teller, and the events he tells about, interact in ways that make objective reality somewhat difficult to find.

Good stories are memorable. Our memories are set up to store and retrieve stories. As must be obvious, I have organized this book around stories. I want my readers to be able to remember what they have read. But, after all, they are only my stories.

CHAPTER 14

Teach Me to Fly, Cook, and Eat

Sometimes I get a call to go visit someplace, and it's a place I've been to without any great places to eat, and they aren't even paying me, yet I go anyway. What could be the answer to this riddle? The answer is that something strange must be going on.

One day I found myself in Denver at the helm of a DC-10. It took me two minutes to crash the plane. I survived. Why? Simulation.

United Airlines has its training facility in Denver. If you want to practice flying a plane without risk of injury, you get into a flight simulator, and off you go. Of course, United doesn't just take people off the street and put them into simulators. United and most other airlines use the United States Air Force as their major training facility. When you are through being a pilot for Uncle

Sam, United greets you with open wings. But, even if you have flown one hundred combat missions over Vietnam, you probably haven't flown a DC-10. The best way to learn anything is to do it, so the natural course of action would be to put you in a DC-10 and to send you up, up, and away. This course of action is rather impractical, however. Passengers probably would not appreciate it, for one thing. Well, send the planes up empty, then. But, this would be rather costly. United doesn't have extra aircraft lying around, nor would it like to pay for the fueling and such that would be required. Also, learning from failure would not occur if the failure were fatal. No, the best course is exactly what they have done—to build flight simulators.

Modern flight simulators are phenomenally real. Inside, they look like cockpits, down to the last detail. They bounce and rattle and jolt, and what you see out the window are pictures that accurately portray whatever airport you select from whatever perspective your airplane would be putting you in at the moment. It looks like the real thing. It feels like the real thing. And so you can take off and land at will, going in and out of your favorite airports. You can try things out and see what happens. You can crash and try to figure out what you did wrong. After enough time, you can teach yourself how to fly. Of course, it helps to have someone next to you whom you can ask for help, and it also helps a great deal if the person beside you is not in a panic about his own imminent demise because of your inadequacies as a pilot.

I speak from experience here, experience in both roles. I have flown a DC-10 and crashed it and lived to tell the tale without getting anyone angry, and I have sat with clenched fists about to pop a blood vessel as I taught my daughter to drive a car. Simulation is a far better alternative.

Why did United want to see me? One reason is that flight simulators are wildly expensive. In fact, they are so expensive that smaller airlines can't afford them. This means that United gets to run a lucrative training school for Air Nepal and other small airlines that own one 747. They rent out their simulators at something like six thousand dollars an hour. Consequently, when a United pilot wants to practice for an hour just because he is feeling the need, he has to wait a long time to find an empty simulator, and the time just might be three o'clock in the morning. Not surprisingly, United would just love to simulate the simulators, so I went to have a look.

But what do I know about flying? Nothing. All I know about

piloting comes from watching when the door is open between the cockpit and the cabin. But I do know about driving, so being a case-based reasoner, I drew upon my one and only relevant case. Having been recently tortured by my daughter, I was well prepared to think about this problem.

Here are some things to learn when you are learning to drive a car:

How to learn to drive a car:
 1. drive one
 2. learn the laws associated with driving
 3. learn the common-sense rules of the road
 4. learn well-known routes
 5. learn to read a map to find new routes
 6. learn to identify and deal with standard problems
 7. learn basic rules of how cars function so as to be able to deal with emergencies
 8. learn about ancillary parts of cars and how to detect whether they are working properly
 9. learn procedures for quick-thinking decision-making
10. learn to design a car so as to really understand it

Needless to say, I did not attempt to teach my daughter all of this. I was happy when she got her driver's license, and even though I didn't really believe that she knew how to drive, I let her go toddling down the road with her little brother in the car, despite my wife's panic-stricken face, soon after she passed her test.

I didn't teach my daughter to design a car, nor to understand how her car works in case it breaks down. I didn't teach her to read a map partially because I suppose I don't actually want her to go very far. Yet she drives. Of course, we wouldn't be happy if we knew that United pilots know about the same level of detail about their airplanes as my daughter knows about her car.

Actually, pilots know what they need to know in order to be effective pilots. My daughter doesn't know what she needs to know in order to be an effective driver. She just knows what she needs to know in order to get a license. But, in time, assuming she pays attention to what she is doing, she will learn to be a good driver. You can teach people all you think they need to know, but what they really need, you can't teach. They really need experience.

Suppose I decided to open a school that taught about food. We could teach how to order in a restaurant; how to select a wine;

how to understand what is likely to be good in a particular place; how to eat certain foods; and so on. But, it would indeed seem rather foolish without getting to eat. If you want to know what Korean barbecue, sushi, chestnut puree, or truffled egg tastes like, you've got to eat it. If you want to know whether the sushi you had was typical of what sushi should taste like, you have to have sushi a second time. If you want to know the extent to which freshness matters in sushi, you have to eat sushi that isn't fresh and then eat some that is especially fresh. To gain this experience in a restaurant means asking about when the sushi was made, when the fish was bought, when it was caught, and so on.

In short, learning about food means eating it, thinking about what you ate, eating things like what you have already eaten in order to contrast one experience with another, and asking questions to determine other information that may help you make sense of your experiences. This is how learning works. This is what education is all about.

Well . . . not really. This is what education should be about. It is actually about something else. Education, in today's world, is about training, usually training to pass some sort of achievement test that demonstrates competence in some area.

Would you like to become a police officer, a correction officer, or a teacher? How about a CPA? To become any of these things, you must pass a test. Because we have invested so much in the creation of standardized tests that officially certify people to do certain tasks, what the training for these tasks entails is obvious. One must learn to pass the tests. To put this another way, training takes place, in reality, by practicing test-taking. Once you know that a test is at the end of the road, the test becomes the medium of instruction. You learn what you need to know to pass the test, often simply by taking practice tests. Without necessarily realizing it, we have committed ourselves as an educational system to the philosophy that test-taking is the best possible mode of instruction. This view is odd to say the least.

Let's look at some of the questions on these tests. (The questions below are taken from books sold in bookstores that help one prepare for the test by presenting sample tests.)

In taking the following test, one is trying to be certified as a correction officer. Keep in mind that the way one learns to become a correction officer is by reading a book like this one, taking courses that contain what is in the exams, and then taking these practice tests.

Allowing inmates to read newspapers in their spare time is
(A) desirable since they should be kept informed of the news
(B) undesirable since they will read of crimes they can imitate after release
(C) desirable since the advertisements will make them more ambitious
(D) undesirable since they will read of prison escapes elsewhere

The first question is *what is the right answer here?* A great many of the questions on this test leave one wondering what answer is being requested and, more important, what the *correct* philosophy of life is for someone who works in a prison. Clearly, the tests presuppose that a *correct philosophy* does exist. As some of the following questions will show, that philosophy is at times at odds with reality.

Of course, we are not concerned here with becoming a correction officer *per se.* On the other hand, we must be concerned with the extent to which the question-and-correct-answer format utilized in standardized tests flies in the face of both reality and instruction. I will never forget my daughter complaining about her workbook answer being marked wrong in Language Arts when she listed school textbooks as appropriate for *skimming* and novels as *heavy reading* and newspapers as *light reading.* That was not the official answer, but it was her reality.

These tests impose their own reality and leave no room for argument. They attempt to make facts out of subjective issues. In the question above, the right answer is *A.* The implication here is that the correct philosophy for a correction officer is getting inmates to behave as normally as possible. This may even be true, but one would never really come to believe in such a philosophy unless one learned it by experience or by studying numerous cases or by other experiential-based methods. Here, trainees are being told to believe it, and they will, for at least as long as it takes to pass the test. But what will they have learned from this? They will have learned what every student learns, that one can learn to pass the test and then forget it all the next day. But if this is what education or training is about, we are all in trouble.

Let's look at some more questions:

The main reason for employing officers in correctional institutions is that they
(A) set the inmates a good example

(B) must operate the machinery in the shops
(C) usually have wide experience in social work
(D) are needed to maintain order and prevent escapes

The one of the following that is least desirable reading matter for a prison inmate is
(A) crime stories and local crime news
(B) sports news and stories
(C) poetry
(D) scientific articles

There would be no crime if there were no
(A) weapons
(B) criminals
(C) stupid laws
(D) private property

These are real questions, folks. Someone out there thinks that if you get these right, you are ready to work in a prison.

I suppose it's only a matter of time until we choose our chefs this way as well. Do you want to be a chef? Read a book. Answer some questions. And voilà, you are licensed. Fortunately, the munching electorate gets to vote for its chefs with its pocketbook. This is not true for correction officers, so we have exams, and the selection process—and hence the teaching process—is reduced to farce.

This wouldn't matter so much if it weren't the same model that we use in our schools. Just as you wouldn't expect to become a food expert by training to pass an exam like this on food, you won't learn anything if training consists merely of passing multiple-choice tests about the subject matter. United Airlines knows how to train pilots—it has built simulators. I knew how to teach driving to my daughter—I put her behind the wheel. If you want to know about food—eat. What are the implications of this for education? We must, as best we can, teach students to do things, rather than to answer questions about doing things.

In this book, we have talked about why learning is really the accumulation and indexing of cases and why thinking is really the finding and consideration of an old case to use for decision-making about a new case. Critical to all this is the process of expectation failure and explanation. To make thinking beings, we must encourage explanation, exploration, generalization, and case accumulation.

How do we do this? We probably cannot do this in classrooms with twenty-five children and one teacher all oriented towards the passing of a standardized test. Some other method must be found.

Recently, in a graduate class of mine, which has in it a few undergraduates, we were discussing learning. The students were making a variety of assertions about learning that caused me to wonder whether we were all talking about the same phenomenon. I asked various members of the class what they had learned recently. One told me that he had learned that a wok will rust if left overnight with the cooking residue in it. Another told me that she had learned that cheap paint doesn't work as well as expensive paint. Another told me that she had learned that she could buy cough medicine across the street and didn't have to walk as long a way for it as she had thought. Another told me that he had learned that I like to sit in a certain place in the classroom. Another said that he had learned how to handle himself better in certain social situations. These learners were all graduate students.

The undergraduates, on the other hand, noted that they had learned various facts such as certain events in history or certain methods of calculation in mathematics.

Why the difference? The graduate students were much older than the undergraduates. They had more daily concerns because their environment was not as sheltered as the undergraduates'. In addition, the undergraduates were engaged in the process of getting A's by learning what they were told. The graduate students were trying to find out about their new environment, living in new houses, cooking for themselves, trying to understand what was expected of them in graduate school. The graduate students were being forced, both in school and in life, to think for themselves.

What method were the undergraduates using for learning? Basically, they were copying what they were told. The graduate students, on the other hand, were experimenting, hoping to find out what was true by trying things out and attempting to make generalizations about what might hold true in the future.

What does all this tell us about learning? Learning is essentially a discovery process. We are all natural learners. As babies, we discover things by ourselves before we can be told. Even when we understand enough to be told, we still need to try things out for ourselves. The understanding cycle—expectation failure/explanation/reminding/generalization—is a natural one. No one teaches it to us. We are not taught to have goals, nor to attempt to develop plans to achieve those goals by adapting old plans from similar situations. We need not be taught this because the process is so basic to what constitutes intelligence. Learning is a natural act.

How do we enhance learning? Can we enhance learning? This is, after all, the real question for the schools. One way to enhance learning is by doing. If you want to learn about food and wine, you can read this book, but, really, you have to eat and drink. And, actually, you don't have to read this book at all. Many people know about food and wine who have not read this book or any other book on the subject. But nobody could really know about food and wine who has not eaten somewhat seriously, and drunk wine with interest and curiosity. Learning about something entails doing it much more than it entails reading about it.

Schooling should be a doing kind of affair. But, by and large, it isn't. Without much thinking about it, most people easily subscribe to the idea that the basic skills, the three Rs, are what need to be taught. But the world has changed since those ideas about what constitutes a basic education were first introduced. The schools are usually quite slow to change, so, in a changing world it is no surprise that the schools haven't quite kept up. The solution is not to go back to where we were.

To think about what kinds of things should be taught, let's consider some provocative questions, simply to challenge some basic assumptions:

Why teach math in the age of calculators?

Why teach reading in the age of television?

Why teach literature in the age of movies?

Why teach history in the age of computers?

Why teach writing in the age of the telephone?

Why teach programming in the age of Artificial Intelligence?

Learning, after all, is an expectation-based affair. To teach students, we need to teach about the cases that might violate their expectations. That is how learning naturally occurs. But, we hear instead about teaching the basics. However, the basic skills may not be so basic to modern life. There may be other subjects that are more basic. Or, perhaps different aspects of the basic skills ought to be emphasized. For example, it seems obvious that the ability to do square roots by hand is simply going to have to be a lost art. Reading may always be an important skill, but reading for pleasure is disappearing as a form of relaxation. That needn't mean that children shouldn't learn to read, but it might mean that the way they learn to read should relate to the things that they actually will have to read and the purposes they will have in reading.

Perhaps less obvious here is my question about history. Information of any kind is becoming more readily available via computer. The idea that it is the teacher's job, or, worse, the school board's job to sift the available information and determine what should be taught to children and what should be skipped is at best outdated, and, at worst, smacks of Orwell's world of 1984. Information is becoming easier to find if you have the tools to find it. History ought to be discovered, in response to current needs, not taught apropos of nothing. We need to hear wise advice when we are ready for it. We will ignore it if we get it before we need it.

This concept of teaching history is radical from the schools' point of view but is very important in light of the things we have been discussing here. If I want you to understand wine, I will first try to get you to enjoy wine. Start with a good wine, but not a great one, a 1982 L'Angélus perhaps. If you have never had a good wine before, you will like this wine. It is fruity, full of taste, and smooth. Next, I will give you a wine from a lesser year, perhaps from the same château, maybe a 1980 L'Angélus. It will taste lighter, less robust, less flavorful. Now, I give you a 1970 L'Angélus. You will like it a lot better than either of the two before. It will taste smooth, and flavorful, and not at all harsh.

At this point you might ask me what is going on. You might make an initial guess that, the older the wine the better it is, but then the 1980 wasn't as good as the 1982. Had I thrown in a 1984, you wouldn't have liked that as well as the 1982 but might have preferred it to the 1980. In any case, you might well have been reminded of the 1980. Now, if I added in a 1974, you probably would have disliked it more than the others. In an attempt to make the right generalizations, you might get curious. When I start throwing in other Bordeaux wines, and then proceed to Burgundies or Chilean wine, it gets harder and harder to make appropriate generalizations.

To learn, one needs at least two things: enough relevant experiences and some guidance through those experiences. You don't have to figure everything out for yourself. As your teacher I can suggest wines to try and, when you ask, when you really want to know, I can answer questions by explaining that 1980 was a particularly weak year and that 1970 was a particularly good one, and that, yes, in general, the older the wine the better for a good wine, but wines do get to be "over the hill." I could also explain what a good year is by discussing soil conditions and rainfall. This would give you the theory but would only make your job more difficult if you had to start learning about rainfall histories in order to know which wine to order in a restaurant.

The task of the teacher is to be an exposer of knowledge. We learn by doing, by trying things out, by formulating hypotheses and testing them. But we cannot do this in a vacuum. The teacher should be there to guide us to the right experiences, by giving us reasonable wines to taste in a reasonable order. The teacher should also be there to answer our questions, or at least to listen to our questions and perhaps suggest ways that we could discover the answers ourselves. I can tell you that 1970 was a great year, but some wines don't age that long. You could discover this for yourself, or I can warn you off spending a lot of money on a wine that is probably not good anymore. Both are good things. Curiosity comes from trying things out, from failing on occasion, from explaining why, and from trying again. This is what school should be like. Unfortunately, it isn't.

How do I know that you know all you need to know about wine? Well, I don't. And, I don't care that much either. As your teacher, I merely want to expose you to wine, enough so that you get curious on your own. Eventually, you will teach me things. A good teacher excites students. However, real teachers, in real schools, test students. It is the way of the world. At least right now.

The main idea behind teaching nowadays is to teach for the test. The more mass-oriented the society gets, the more we use standardized tests to determine who goes to college, who gets the job as postman, and who gets extra help in reading in the third grade. The concern that these tests may not test what they set out to test is serious enough. But, of even more concern is the possibility that our entire educational system has been ruined by the idea that one can measure and quantify how much has been learned. In order to make such measurements, one has to make sure that what is to be learned is quantifiable. We cannot be happy with the idea that a student has developed good mathematical intuitions, we must be able to measure the fact that he can now do something specific that we can test in a multiple-choice test. So, instead of teaching how to derive a theorem, or make a mathematical generalization, we teach how to apply a formula that gets a concrete answer. Instead of teaching how to see the beauty in literature, we teach concepts like the "main idea" and then test students to see if the main idea they got happened to be the one the examiner had in mind.

If we abandon the idea of easy measurement of achievement, then we can begin to talk about exciting learners with open-ended problems and can begin to create educational goals such as learning to think for oneself. Of course, such things are hard to measure, but one cannot help feeling that we'll know them when we see them.

Under this view, the problem of how we teach, how education is delivered, becomes far more important than one might initially imagine. Actual content may not be the issue at all, since we are really trying to impart the idea that one can deal with new arenas of knowledge if one knows how to learn, how to find out about what is known, and how to abandon old ideas when they are worn out. This means teaching ways of developing good questions rather than memorizing known answers, an idea that traditional school systems simply don't cotton to at all, and that traditional testing methods are unprepared to handle.

How would this work with teaching history, for example? We might pose a problem to a student, and have him suggest an answer. We might then talk about when such an answer has been tried before, and how things turned out. The student might then respond with a new idea, and the teacher with a new historical example.

This is case-based teaching. Its advantage is clear: Students hear about things that relate to ideas they themselves have had. They learn the cases of history and interpret them together with the teacher. The disadvantage is also clear: Each student would get his own individualized, not previously planned, curriculum. This would make standardized curricula and standardized testing impossible. Teaching would have to be one-on-one. This would make teaching very expensive.

This last objection might be met by building computers to do the teaching, a task we are currently engaged in doing. The other problems are not problems at all. As computer scientists say: *It is sometimes difficult to differentiate a bug from a feature.*

Let's go to wine school. Not a real wine school, but a wine school where the instruction is like that in the schools we send our children to.

We would start our instruction in wine by handing out four texts. One would be a geography text, teaching about where Burgundy is, where the wine-growing regions of the United States are, talking about Virginia and New York and Texas wineries, for example. The second would be an agricultural text. It would teach about the various grapes, where each is grown and why, discussing soil conditions, climate issues, optimal grape picking times, and so on. The third would be a text about the wine-making process: Fermentation, storage, blending, and such would be included, as well as a discussion of the wine business, including who owns which châteaux and so on. The fourth would be a history text, answering such questions as: What kind of wine did the Romans drink? Who invented the cork stopper? How were issues of proper storage discovered? Why do the British prefer to drink Bordeaux? Which wine-growing regions of France were there in Roman times?

After instruction in these various areas, we would begin testing. What was the best year for Bordeaux in the last thirty years and why? Who owns Château Margaux? When did Mouton-Rothschild achieve first-growth status? What grapes are grown in Oregon and why? What was the first French-American joint venture in wine-growing? Can you identify the Châteauneuf-du-Pape region of the Rhône valley on a map?

What is wrong with this picture? Nothing, I think. It is the way schools teach most subjects. Schools teach information that can be tested. How will they know if you have learned anything if they can't test you? So they must teach something testable. The tests drive the curriculum, and people lose sight of the original purpose.

How would I teach about wine? Well, the real question is, how *do* I teach about wine? I don't give lectures about wine. When I teach about wine it is always in the same situation. I am at dinner with someone who asks. The more I am asked about, the more I explain. I do not give long lectures because long lectures are dull and no one can absorb very much information at one time anyway. I do encourage drinking. Perhaps I open a few wines and encourage comparison. I always order a few different wines at a restaurant in a large crowd. I do this because I like to make the comparisons myself, because I am always trying to learn something new.

One night, for example, at a dinner at The Everest Room, in Chicago, I ordered three wines: a 1985 Alsatian Pinot Noir, a 1979 Vosne-Romanée, and a 1986 Oregon Pinot Noir. Pinot Noir is the grape that Burgundy wine is made from, and thus, as Vosne-Romanée is a Burgundy, we were sampling three wines made from the same grape in different styles. Unfortunately, the 1979 turned out to be a 1974, which is not as good a year, but it was still the best of the bunch, as one would have expected. The Oregon wine was second best, and that was expected too. The people at the table learned a little bit more about wine, but, more important, we enjoyed it.

Teaching about wine means drinking wine, not memorizing facts about wine. Drinking with some help from a friend is nice. When you are ready to learn more, it is nice to know whom to ask. What do people ask me? They ask about whether a certain year was good. They ask about what I would recommend buying in a certain price range. They ask about what words like *Pauillac* mean on the label. They ask about what wines I own.

Over time, a learner becomes curious about a wider range of issues. It took me a long time of wine drinking before I began to wonder about Rhône wines, or the British preference for Bordeaux. (They used to own it.) I know when Château Margaux changed hands because the quality has changed dramatically (down and then back up) and I really like Château Margaux and need to know which years to avoid. I visited Château Margaux a few years ago and appreciated the place and the wine I tasted there, but would not have if I hadn't liked the wine in the first place. A shrine isn't a shrine unless it means something to you. I know where Bordeaux is now because I had to find it on a map in order to get to Château Margaux. I drank Bordeaux for years without really knowing any more about the region of Bordeaux than that it was in the southwest of France somewhere.

However, I feel certain that if I had ever taken a course on wine, of the kind that I have described above, I would have hated it and found the whole experience silly and unbearable. I probably would have sworn off wine just to avoid thinking about the exam I failed because I thought 1972 was a uniformly bad year; in fact, it wasn't—I just didn't remember the St.-Emilions that were harvested early, thus avoiding the September rains that killed the cabernet grapes.

I really do know most of the stuff I mentioned in my fictitious course, but I know it because I followed my interests gradually. My interests grew as I drank more wine and became more curious. I found out what I wanted to know as I needed to know it. I learned about 1972, for example, because my daughter was born in 1972 and I was happy to hear there really was some Bordeaux wine of her birth year to celebrate with.

Teaching must occur naturally, in context, as the need arises.

The need should arise because of interest on the part of the student as a result of the actions the student has been taking. We learn by doing. We get curious as a result of doing.

Why can't school be like this? Because school is not easily individualized. Testing, established curricula, and group instruction kill off curiosity.

Learning is about failure and recovery from failure. Failure causes questions and questions cause old explanations to be brought to mind and adapted to current needs. To do this, one needs cases to be reminded of, so an important part of learning is the acquisition of cases. But, cases cannot be acquired without real live goals that drive their acquisition. People resist memorizing the experiences of others. People need to have experiences of their own in order to learn from the experiences of others. The goal of school must be the attempt to provide situations in which students want to know more cases and acquire more experiences by trying things out.

We have talked in this book about food and wine, but we really have been talking about thinking. Thinking is about learning, after all. No machine would be considered very intelligent if it failed to learn from its experiences. The same is true of people. People are intelligent to the extent that they can recover from failed expectations by creating explanations that enhance the creation of more finely honed expectations. Learning is, in essence, a creative process. Teaching, unfortunately, is often an anticreative process.

This was brought home to me one day in Germany.

There we were speeding along the highway, which had just changed from an autoroute to an autobahn. Jean-François had decided to meet me in yet another restaurant, but this time he had gone too far. Travel to Germany for dinner? I was in Brussels. He was in Paris. He could have eaten at Jamin. Surely you jest.

But Jean-François flew into Brussels, we met at the airport, and after a meal at the only three-star in town, about which you have already heard, off we went towards Grevenbroich. Now Grevenbroich is not exactly on the beaten track. It is near Düsseldorf, but it is not at all clear that even the people in Düsseldorf have discovered it yet. Anyway, Jean-François has, probably because Michelin gave it two stars and Frenchmen live by Michelin when they are outside of France (which is not entirely a bad strategy; in fact, it is life-saving in Germany.) Still, one has to be skeptical, since who knows why this restaurant was awarded anything at all. Does three stars in Germany equal three stars in France? My best guess would be that a three-star restaurant in Germany (one exists, by the way, but I haven't eaten there—I don't go out of my way to visit Germany ordinarily) would be better than its equivalent in France. They ought to get a fourth star just for resisting the tendency to schnitzel everything. And good wine in Germany is a kind of bizarre sacrilege, given that the beer is the best in the world, sort of like buying a Toblerone bar in Hershey, Pennsylvania—okay to do, but beside the point.

The situation demands an explanation. In fact, every situation demands an explanation. Sometimes we realize that we are demanding an explanation, and sometimes we unconsciously construct them, but we do need to have them all the time.

When Jean-François says that he is hungry, this demands an explanation. When he says that he wants to eat at a good restaurant, this demands an explanation. And, when he asks for the check, this too demands an explanation. The explanation needed differs, depending on the context. There are many possible contexts, but, for the sake of argument here, we will assume that there are only two: normal, and normal for Jean-François.

When we hear anything at all, we must explain it. We do not realize that we are doing this when things are normal. So, when Jean-François says that he is hungry, we can explain it simply by noting that he is a human and humans get hungry from time to time. This explanation, periodic hunger for humans, is one we use all the time without realizing it. When we can easily explain things, we don't think about them at all.

When Jean-François says that he wants to go to a good restaurant, we need to explain this as well. Again the explanation is simple under normal conditions. We need to know that one can eat in restaurants and that eating satisfies hunger. This is a simple explanation that we already are aware of, that applies to this situation. We access it and we are done explaining except for the "good" part. To explain wanting to eat in a good restaurant, we must know that good restaurants are expensive and provide food that is both tasty and innovative and that they are pleasant places to be. To explain Jean-François wanting to go there requires our knowing that Jean-François likes and can afford good restaurants. If we had heard that someone we knew who hated good food or was poor wanted to go to a good restaurant, the need to find an explanation would seem more pressing.

Finally, when we hear that Jean-François asked for the check, we simply assume that he finished eating at the restaurant and use the restaurant script itself to provide the explanation.

In short, we are full of standard explanations and we use them all the time to infer what is going on apart from what we were told explicitly. We seek to understand why people do what they do and we rely upon old favorite explanations to tell us. Usually these explanations are truisms about the world in general. But, we also have explanations that we develop for particular situations or individuals that we know about.

In the "normal for Jean-François" context, our explanations differ. When we hear that Jean-François is hungry, I might have trouble explaining this, because most of the time that I am with him we are either eating or finished eating. To explain his hunger I might have to assume that he didn't like a meal. When I hear that he wants to go to a good restaurant, I need to figure out why he is telling me this since I have never eaten with him at anything else. Does he think we have been eating at bad restaurants? Is he planning something extra special? These are the only standard explanations that might fit here. When he asks for the check, I have to ask myself where we are and what the conditions are. Jean-François often pays for me in France and I for him in the States. But, as we are in France more often, I pay in France as well sometimes. Does he think he invited me? Does he feel some obligation for some reason? Is it his turn? Did he just complete a good business deal and does he want to share his good fortune? These are all good explanations.

People are chock full of explanations. They use them to convince themselves that they understand what is going on. Understanding means explaining to yourself. When you can't explain what is going on to yourself, you are confused. Sometimes you ask for help.

Once, for example, I was trying to figure out why my wife couldn't make steak rare. As I have said, I really don't like meat all that much. The French liven things up a bit with nice sauces, which help, but at home, those sauces are hard to make. The only remedy I can see for this is ordering steak very rare, almost raw. You can do this in a good steak house, like Bern's in Tampa, but, by and large, it is very difficult to get Americans to cook steak rare. In France, one orders steak "blue" to get what I want. And, although the French do eat meat this way, they know that Americans don't eat it rare, so, hearing my accent, they often ignore me anyway. I have trouble getting steak done, or not done, the way I like it.

At home, one would think, it might be different. My wife is a very good cook and she should have no trouble with this simple task, one would think. But, the steak is always overcooked. My kids have taken to warning me, watching the broiler so we can snatch victory out of the oven of defeat. Even though my kids also like steak rare, medium is the best we can hope for.

One day I was complaining about this to Bob Abelson, a colleague of mine at Yale. He said that this reminded him of a time thirty years earlier, when he had tried to get his hair cut short while on a trip to England, as was the style in America at that time. No matter how much he insisted, the barber would not cut his hair as short as he wanted it.

We were both studying memory at this time and were bowled over by the weirdness of this reminding. How might it have been accomplished? Why did it occur? Could we get a machine to do something like this? Why would we want to?

These were, and are, important questions. The answer is bound up in the task of explanation. The task I had posed to Bob was to explain my wife's behavior. Many standard explanations might have applied. She might not care. She might be hostile. She might be incapable. For all of these there was evidence to suggest that they were wrong. Bob had tried to construct a new explanation. He came up with one that goes something like this: Sometimes people don't do what they are asked to do because their own standards for doing things right cause them to believe that what was requested of them was too extreme.

It seems likely that Bob constructed such an explanation because the story he told, the story he was reminded of, had precisely that explanation. Now think about what was going on here. Bob had something happen to him that he was confused about. He constructed an explanation to explain the expectation failure he had encountered that had confused him. But he didn't simply substitute the new explanation in place of the old expectation. Had he done so, he simply would have said: *Sometimes people don't do things that have been requested of them because they think they are too extreme.* But he didn't say that. He was reminded of a specific instance and told me about that.

He recalled this story because it was unique in his mind. He had yet to form the generalization that would lead him to adopt this explanation as one of his old standards. But he did remember the explanation he had constructed. He remembered it as an index. The explanation served as an index to a specific memory.

This tells us something very important about indexing and explanation. In an important sense, they are one and the same. We recall interesting things that happen to us by labeling those events with tentative explanations. When we construct that explanation again, we unconsciously recognize it and find the memory we have previously stored under that label.

What is the value of all this? Learning. We learn by comparing the two stories. Bob learned that his explanation was a good one and that he should modify his expectations in such situations. I learned that there was an explanation for my wife's behavior, I just hadn't been able to think of it. I asked my wife and she confirmed that that was probably why she did it, but she hadn't really thought about it. Since that time my wife has cooked steak the way I like it from time to time. But, she never fails to add: *You really are going to eat it that way? You'll get sick. That's disgusting.* Oh well.

Constructing new explanations is very difficult, but explanation is a very important part of understanding, of indexing, and therefore of learning. If it is so difficult, how do we do it? One answer is that we simply find old standard explanations, ones that have worked before, and adapt them to our needs. To see how easily we come up with old standard explanations, and how easily we adapt them, I asked some of my students why Jean-François, identified simply as a gourmet living in Paris whom I like to eat with, would take me to Germany especially for a meal. Here are some of their responses:

He is tired of French food.
Some French people live there and have created a French restaurant.
He was so surprised that it was good, that made it seem better.
It is a backwater and has developed its own special style.
It is a special holiday in France and all the restaurants are closed.
There are some special ingredients in Germany that they can't get in France.
Some industrial pollution is especially good for mushrooms.
He wants to spend more time with you so he wants to take a trip.
He wanted to shock you.

He is angry at the leading restaurateurs in Paris and he is doing
   this to snub them.

He decided that the world would be a better place if the French
   were the great engineers of the world and the Germans were
   the chefs.

He is trying to kill off the German economy by making them all
   into cooks.

He had to be in Germany and he wanted company, so he said a
   great restaurant existed there.

So I didn't know what to expect. Actually I did know one
thing: I knew Jean-François. If he said it was the second-best
restaurant in the world, then he was really talking about only one
food: caviar.

Maybe I was being unfair to Jean-François, I thought as we
were hurtling along trying to cover 120 miles in an hour and being
passed by bigger Mercedes than the one we had rented. He does
admire creativity, I realized. Nevertheless I was prepared for the
worst.

We arrived in what looked like any other German town and
entered what looked like any other German hotel in a small German town. The dining room was undistinguished and there were
waitresses instead of waiters, which lets you know that you are
outside of France for sure. Suddenly, I was excited. This was going
to be one great meal.

To understand why I was excited, you must understand something about the Michelin guide to restaurants. The Michelin raters
are clearly hooked on ambiance. By and large the raters don't eat
so well every day, so when they are doing their rating, they want
the works. They want people slobbering over them. The best example I know of this is, of course, Taillevent, an otherwise very
good restaurant, which probably would deserve its three stars anyway. These people are into the slobbering-over-you business in
spades, if you recall my story about my wife trying to taste the
pureed chestnuts.

What all this meant in Grevenbroich was that if they had
managed to get two stars with no class whatsoever, the food in
this place must be absolutely fantastic. I salivated. Pavlov would
have been proud. I had been trained by lack of ambiance to expect
a feast.

And a feast it was. Caviar too, I hadn't been wrong about that.

The only real problem was the menu, which, being in German, called every dish fleischwafen or something like that—which, in addition to being unpronounceable, also seemed very unappetizing. It all sounded like German food to me. But it wasn't. In fact, it wasn't any kind of food exactly.

Somewhere in the middle of the meal we called over the chef and asked him where he had learned to cook. Which great French chef had he trained with? He hadn't really trained with any, he said. In fact, he hadn't even been able to get a reservation at Jamin, and could we help him next time he was in Paris?

And there you have it, folks. That's all there is to say about creativity. Every dish at Zur Traube was inventive, novel, different, not like anything you'd ever had before. Why? Because the man didn't have anyone to teach him. No one would let him wash dishes or chop celery while he had the creativity knocked out of him. He couldn't learn to copy Bocuse's style, or Georges Blanc's pancakes. He had to invent it all himself. Few of us are so lucky.

This all sounds like the million-monkeys-typing-on-their-typewriters-allowing-one-of-them-to-write-Shakespeare theory. But it is hard to believe that Herr Kaufman was just randomly lucky. He had to have figured a few things out for himself. It is possible to be creative by reasoning from prior cases, but it is possible to be even more creative if you have no prior cases. It is also a whole lot more risky. Herr Kaufman took a chance with each dish he created. The chance was that people would think that he was very weird. After all, the diners at his restaurant reason from cases too. Suddenly their discriminations might be too far off from what was customary for them to be able to make a sensible judgment.

So what is learning? It surely isn't a process by which one sits in a group and is lectured to about the fundamental truths of subject X as found in the writings of Y. Learning, and creativity too, is a natural process, which starts with goals and revolves around the desire to achieve those goals.

But, probably, few of you are going to be great chefs. You might, on the other hand, desire to become great eaters and drinkers—inventive, creative eaters and drinkers. How does one learn about food and wine? One eats. And drinks. If you eat randomly, with no goals other than to be fed, with no plan of how to acquire new information about food, with the desire to have each experience be like the last, you will not learn much about food. But if you have goals about what you would like to learn about food, and make explanations to yourself that you later test out by trying certain kinds of foods or restaurants, then you will gradually acquire a set of cases about food that will begin to make you an expert. For example, if you have the goal to try weird things, then you would certainly eat at Prairie when you go to Chicago because it advertises itself as serving *Midwestern cuisine* and you would be dying to find out what that could possibly be. And, once there, you would have to order the *sweet potato praline cheesecake* because it sounds so improbable, and improbability is what new learning experiences are all about. And, boy, is this experimentation worth it sometimes. Try this cheesecake next time you are in Chicago and see what I mean.

The main role of the teacher is to help the student to acquire new goals. When a student has goals, the rest follows easily. I have just done my job.

You cannot be an expert if you fail to get reminded of similar events by a current event, and you cannot get reminded if you haven't had related experiences or haven't thought carefully enough about the experiences that you have had.

How do you learn about food and wine? Eat. And think.

Bibliography

Bartlett, F. C. (1932). *Remembering: A study in experimental and social psychology.* Cambridge: Cambridge University Press.

Bower, G. H., Black, J. B., and Turner, T. J. (1979). Scripts in memory for text. *Cognitive Psychology, 11,* 177–220.

Bransford, J. D., Barclay, J. R., and Franks, J. F. (1972). Sentence memory: A constructive versus interpretive approach. *Cognitive Psychology, 3,* 193–209.

Collins, A. M., and Quillian, M. R. (1969). Retrieval time from semantic memory. *Journal of Verbal Learning and Verbal Behavior, 8,* 240–47.

Graesser, A. C., Woll, S. B., Kowalski, D. J., and Smith, D. A. (1980). Memory for typical and atypical actions in scripted activities. *Journal of Experimental Psychology: Human Learning and Memory, 6,* 503–15.

Grice, H. P. (1975). Logic and conversation. In P. Cole and J. Morgan (eds.), *Syntax and semantics, volume 3: Speech acts.* New York: Academic Press.

Hammer, H. (ed.) (1983). *ARCO civil service test tutor: Correction officer.* New York: Prentice Hall.

Luria, A. R. (1968). *The mind of a mnemonist.* New York: Basic Books.

Minsky, M. A. (1975). A framework for representing knowledge. In P. Winston (ed.), *The psychology of computer vision.* New York: McGraw-Hill.

Nelson, K., and Gruendel, J. M. (1979). At morning it's lunchtime: A scriptal view of children's dialogues. *Discourse Processes, 2,* 73–94.

Neustadt, R. E., and May, E. R. (1986). *Thinking in time: The uses of history for decision makers.* New York: Free Press.

Newell, A., and Simon, H. (1972). *Human problem solving.* Englewood Cliffs, N.J.: Prentice Hall.

Norman, D. (1976). *Memory and attention.* New York: Wiley.

Schank, R. D., and Abelson, R. (1977). *Scripts, plans, goals and understanding.* Hillsdale, N.J.: Erlbaum.

Tulving, E. (1972). Episodic and semantic memory. In E. Tulving and W. Donaldson (eds.), *Organization of memory.* New York: Academic Press.

Tulving, E. (1983). *Elements of episodic memory.* New York: Oxford University Press.

Index

Allowing inmates to read newspapers in their spare time is
(A) desirable since they should be kept informed of the news
(B) undesirable since they will read of crimes they can imitate after
       release
(C) desirable since the advertisements will make them more am-
       bitious
(D) undesirable since they will read of prison escapes elsewhere

The first question is *what is the right answer here?* A great many of
the questions on this test leave one wondering what answer is
being requested and, more important, what the *correct* philosophy
of life is for someone who works in a prison. Clearly, the tests
presuppose that a *correct philosophy* does exist. As some of the
following questions will show, that philosophy is at times at odds
with reality.

Of course, we are not concerned here with becoming a correction officer *per se.* On the other hand, we must be concerned
with the extent to which the question-and-correct-answer format
utilized in standardized tests flies in the face of both reality and
instruction. I will never forget my daughter complaining about her
workbook answer being marked wrong in Language Arts when
she listed school textbooks as appropriate for *skimming* and novels
as *heavy reading* and newspapers as *light reading.* That was not the
official answer, but it was her reality.

These tests impose their own reality and leave no room for
argument. They attempt to make facts out of subjective issues. In
the question above, the right answer is *A.* The implication here is
that the correct philosophy for a correction officer is getting inmates
to behave as normally as possible. This may even be true, but one
would never really come to believe in such a philosophy unless
one learned it by experience or by studying numerous cases or by
other experiential-based methods. Here, trainees are being told to
believe it, and they will, for at least as long as it takes to pass the
test. But what will they have learned from this? They will have
learned what every student learns, that one can learn to pass the
test and then forget it all the next day. But if this is what education
or training is about, we are all in trouble.

Let's look at some more questions:

The main reason for employing officers in correctional institutions
is that they
(A) set the inmates a good example

(B) must operate the machinery in the shops
(C) usually have wide experience in social work
(D) are needed to maintain order and prevent escapes

The one of the following that is least desirable reading matter for a prison inmate is
(A) crime stories and local crime news
(B) sports news and stories
(C) poetry
(D) scientific articles

There would be no crime if there were no
(A) weapons
(B) criminals
(C) stupid laws
(D) private property

These are real questions, folks. Someone out there thinks that if you get these right, you are ready to work in a prison.

I suppose it's only a matter of time until we choose our chefs this way as well. Do you want to be a chef? Read a book. Answer some questions. And voilà, you are licensed. Fortunately, the munching electorate gets to vote for its chefs with its pocketbook. This is not true for correction officers, so we have exams, and the selection process—and hence the teaching process—is reduced to farce.

This wouldn't matter so much if it weren't the same model that we use in our schools. Just as you wouldn't expect to become a food expert by training to pass an exam like this on food, you won't learn anything if training consists merely of passing multiple-choice tests about the subject matter. United Airlines knows how to train pilots—it has built simulators. I knew how to teach driving to my daughter—I put her behind the wheel. If you want to know about food—eat. What are the implications of this for education? We must, as best we can, teach students to do things, rather than to answer questions about doing things.

In this book, we have talked about why learning is really the accumulation and indexing of cases and why thinking is really the finding and consideration of an old case to use for decision-making about a new case. Critical to all this is the process of expectation failure and explanation. To make thinking beings, we must encourage explanation, exploration, generalization, and case accumulation.

How do we do this? We probably cannot do this in classrooms with twenty-five children and one teacher all oriented towards the passing of a standardized test. Some other method must be found.

Recently, in a graduate class of mine, which has in it a few undergraduates, we were discussing learning. The students were making a variety of assertions about learning that caused me to wonder whether we were all talking about the same phenomenon. I asked various members of the class what they had learned recently. One told me that he had learned that a wok will rust if left overnight with the cooking residue in it. Another told me that she had learned that cheap paint doesn't work as well as expensive paint. Another told me that she had learned that she could buy cough medicine across the street and didn't have to walk as long a way for it as she had thought. Another told me that he had learned that I like to sit in a certain place in the classroom. Another said that he had learned how to handle himself better in certain social situations. These learners were all graduate students.

The undergraduates, on the other hand, noted that they had learned various facts such as certain events in history or certain methods of calculation in mathematics.

Why the difference? The graduate students were much older than the undergraduates. They had more daily concerns because their environment was not as sheltered as the undergraduates'. In addition, the undergraduates were engaged in the process of getting A's by learning what they were told. The graduate students were trying to find out about their new environment, living in new houses, cooking for themselves, trying to understand what was expected of them in graduate school. The graduate students were being forced, both in school and in life, to think for themselves.

What method were the undergraduates using for learning? Basically, they were copying what they were told. The graduate students, on the other hand, were experimenting, hoping to find out what was true by trying things out and attempting to make generalizations about what might hold true in the future.

What does all this tell us about learning? Learning is essentially a discovery process. We are all natural learners. As babies, we discover things by ourselves before we can be told. Even when we understand enough to be told, we still need to try things out for ourselves. The understanding cycle—expectation failure/explanation/reminding/generalization—is a natural one. No one teaches it to us. We are not taught to have goals, nor to attempt to develop plans to achieve those goals by adapting old plans from similar situations. We need not be taught this because the process is so basic to what constitutes intelligence. Learning is a natural act.

How do we enhance learning? Can we enhance learning? This is, after all, the real question for the schools. One way to enhance learning is by doing. If you want to learn about food and wine, you can read this book, but, really, you have to eat and drink. And, actually, you don't have to read this book at all. Many people know about food and wine who have not read this book or any other book on the subject. But nobody could really know about food and wine who has not eaten somewhat seriously, and drunk wine with interest and curiosity. Learning about something entails doing it much more than it entails reading about it.

Schooling should be a doing kind of affair. But, by and large, it isn't. Without much thinking about it, most people easily subscribe to the idea that the basic skills, the three Rs, are what need to be taught. But the world has changed since those ideas about what constitutes a basic education were first introduced. The schools are usually quite slow to change, so, in a changing world it is no surprise that the schools haven't quite kept up. The solution is not to go back to where we were.

To think about what kinds of things should be taught, let's consider some provocative questions, simply to challenge some basic assumptions:

Why teach math in the age of calculators?

Why teach reading in the age of television?

Why teach literature in the age of movies?

Why teach history in the age of computers?

Why teach writing in the age of the telephone?

Why teach programming in the age of Artificial Intelligence?

Learning, after all, is an expectation-based affair. To teach students, we need to teach about the cases that might violate their expectations. That is how learning naturally occurs. But, we hear instead about teaching the basics. However, the basic skills may not be so basic to modern life. There may be other subjects that are more basic. Or, perhaps different aspects of the basic skills ought to be emphasized. For example, it seems obvious that the ability to do square roots by hand is simply going to have to be a lost art. Reading may always be an important skill, but reading for pleasure is disappearing as a form of relaxation. That needn't mean that children shouldn't learn to read, but it might mean that the way they learn to read should relate to the things that they actually will have to read and the purposes they will have in reading.

INDEX

Roger Schank is the director of The Institute for Learning Sciences at Northwestern University in Evanston, Illinois. He is the John Evans Professor of Electrical Engineering and Computer Science, Professor of Psychology, and Professor of Education and Social Policy at Northwestern. The Institute was founded in 1989 with support from Andersen Consulting, a division of Arthur Andersen Worldwide, as a university center for the research and development of innovative software for education and training. The Institute's mission is to design computer programs that provide schoolchildren with independent learning opportunities.

Schank directed the Artificial Intelligence Project and was the Chairman of the Computer Science department at Yale. He was also an Assistant Professor of Linguistics and Computer Science at Stanford. He is the author of many books and dozens of articles on subjects related to his scholarship in creativity, learning, and artificial intelligence. He became familiar with three-star restaurants while living in France and Switzerland, and now he travels through Europe and Asia regularly, savoring food and wine.